MW01533945

1989 U.S.
FIRST DAY COVER
CATALOGUE
& CHECKLIST

Complete
Up-to-date Catalogue

Prepared by Scott Publishing Company
in conjunction with Michael A. Mellone

CONTENTS

ABOUT THE AUTHOR

Michael A. Mellone is a Computer Software Consultant by profession. He has written several computer performance programs, as well as a stamp and FDC inventory program for collectors.

Mike started collecting First Day Covers at age 15 and he soon became interested in the early cacheted covers.

He wrote the *Specialized Cachet Catalog of FDCs of the 1940s,* the *Specialized Cachet Catalog of the 1950's* the *Specialized Cachet Catalog of the 1960's,* and the two international award winning catalogs *The Cachet Identifier of U.S. Cacheted FDCs* and *Discovering the Fun in First Day Covers - 1st and 2nd Editions.* He also is the co-author of the *Planty Encyclopedia of Cacheted FDC's from 1923 to 1939.*

Mike is also a Director of the American First Day Cover Society.

ACKNOWLEDGMENTS

The author would like to thank the following people for contributing their expertise to this catalogue:

William Bayless, *Postal Stationery*
William Cummings, *Pricing*
Ed Densun, *First Day PNC's*
Lloyd A. de Vries, *New Issues*
Howard Grossman, *Patriotic Covers*
Allan Hagen, *First Day PNC's*
Lewis Kaufman, *Early Issues*
Arthur Kroos, *Kansas - Nebraska Issues*
Ken Lawrence, *First Day PNC's*
Steven Levine, *Postal Stationery*
Barry Newton, *First Cachets & Pricing*
Scott Pelegger, *F.D. Ceremony Programs*
Alan Piscina, *First Cachets & Pricing*
Howard Tiffner, *F.D. Ceremony Programs*
Al Zimmerman, *Early FDCs*

CATALOGUE PRICES

Prices for pre-1920 FDCs are for uncacheted FDCs with single stamps, based on retail and auction sales of FDCs. Many early FDCs or Earliest Known Use covers are unique. A dash in the price column means that FDCs are seldom, or never, found in these categories, or that no market value has been determined through recent sales of the covers.

Before 1920, stamps were not regularly released with an official First Day of Issue. In many of these cases, the First Day of Issue is determined by the earliest known postal use of the stamp.

Regular issues of 1922-26, Scott numbers 551-600, are priced as uncacheted FDCs with singles and blocks of four stamps or as singles and pairs of stamps.

During the issues of 1923-35, Scott numbers 610-771, cachets on FDCs first appeared. Prices are arranged in four columns, giving prices for singles and blocks both in uncacheted and cacheted FDCs. FDCs with plate blocks from this period sell for two to three times the prices for singles.

From 1935 to date, prices are given for average cacheted FDCs with singles, blocks and plate blocks. Coils are priced as average cacheted FDCs with singles, pairs (Pr) and line pairs (Lp). Uncacheted covers sell for about 25 percent of the catalogue value of average cacheted covers.

Cacheted FDCs, 1950 (Scott 987) to date prices, are for clean unaddressed FDCs. Addressed FDCs usually sell for about 75 percent of catalogue value. Uncacheted covers sell for about 10 percent of the catalogue value of cacheted covers.

Prices for Cacheted FDCs in this catalogue are for the average market value. FDCs with common mass produced commercial cachets usually sell for less than catalogue value. Some scarce cachets sell for several times catalogue value.

Prices for many various Cachets can be found in our Cachet Pricing Calculator section of this book. Specific prices for each cacheted FDC can be found in the *Planty Photo Encyclopedia of Cacheted FDCs 1923-1939, Mellone's Specialized Cachet Catalog of FDCs of the 1940s,* and *Mellone's Specialized Cachet Catalog of FDCs of the 1950's.* These books are available from FDC Publishing Co., Box 206-D, Stewartsville, NJ 08886, or from your local dealer.

An Introduction to Cachet Collecting, with eight FDC cachet makers illustrated and identified, is found in this book following the Introduction to FDC Collecting.

HOW TO USE THIS CATALOGUE

Sample Listing

Scott No.	Description	Uncacheted Sgl.	Blk.	Cacheted Sgl.	Blk.
1923	**Perf. 11**				
☐☐ 610	2¢ **Harding,** 9/1/23, DC	30.00	50.00	—	—
☐☐	Marion, OH (5,000)	15.00	30.00	—	—
☐☐	Brooklyn, NY; Mt. Rainier, MD; Caledonia, OH				
	(Unofficial)	50.00	—	—	—
☐☐	Pre-date, 8/31/23, DC (only 1 known)	250.00	—	—	—
☐☐	1st George W. Linn cachet (The 1st modern cachet)	—	—	700.00	—

The first number is the Scott catalogue number. This is followed by the denomination and identifier. Next is the official First Day (FD) date, 9/1/23, and the official FD City, Washington, D.C. In many cases this city is listed only as DC. This means Washington, D.C.

Marion, Ohio is another official FD City. Some issues have more than one official FD City. The number after Marion, Ohio, is the number of covers canceled there on the FD. There's no number after the Washington, D.C., listing, because it is not known.

Listed next is "Caledonia, Ohio, unofficial." This listing is for a first day cover postmarked in Caledonia, Ohio, which was not an official FD city. Often collectors have purchased stamps in the official FD city and taken them to other cities to create unofficial FDCs.

Unofficial cities which are related to the stamp are of more value than an unrelated city. Often a special slogan cancel, related to the new stamp, will be available on the FD. Even when these are from the official city, they are priced as unofficials on FDCs since 1940.

A Pre-dated FDC or Pre-FDC is a stamp or stamp on cover with a postmark before the official first day of issue.

A 1st Cachet is simply the first cachet that a particular cachet maker has produced.

EXPLANATION OF ABBREVIATIONS

Blk	Block of 4 stamps on FDC
DC	Washington, DC
eku	earliest known use
FD	First Day
FDC	First Day Cover
ln	line
lp	Line pair of coil stamps on FDC
Pl Blk	Plate block on FDC
Pr	Pair of coil stamps on FDC
Sgl	Single stamp on FDC
wmk	watermark

INTRODUCTION TO FDC COLLECTING

What is a First Day Cover?

When a new stamp is issued by the postal service, one day is designated as the "official" First Day of Issue. A special cancel is applied on that day in one special city related to the subject being honored. These cancellations can never again be duplicated.

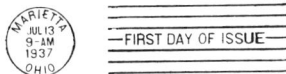

Figure 1
The first official First Day of Issue machine cancel, used for the Ordinance of 1787 commemorative issued July 13, 1937, in Marietta, Ohio, and New York, New York.

In the 1920's and 1930's FDCs were canceled with everyday working postmarks. The post office first used an official FD postmark with the words "First Day of Issue," in killer bars, for the 1937 Ordinance of 1787 Commemorative. An official "First Day of Issue" machine cancel has been supplied for almost every new issue since.

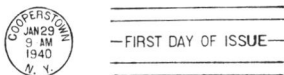

Figure 2
The first official First Day of Issue hand cancel used for the 1-cent and 2-cent Famous American Authors, issued in Cooperstown or Tarrytown, New York, on January 29, 1940.

An official "First Day of Issue" hand cancel was first used for the first stamps released in the Famous American Set, the 1-cent and 2-cent Authors, Irving and Cooper, both issued January 29, 1940.

Figure 3
The first official Pictorial First Day of Issue cancel, used for the Horticulture Commemorative issued on March 15, 1958, in Ithaca, New York.

A third official cancel has been available for many U.S. new issues. In the 1940's and 1950's this third cancel was a short bar hand cancel. Now it is a bull's eye, which is usually identical to the town machine cancel, without the killer bars or "First Day of Issue" slogan.

Usually the stamp with FD postmark can be found on some other object — be it an envelope, postcard, souvenir, a piece of wood, bark or cloth, or anything that will accept the stamp and postmark.

Most often a First Day Cover is found on an envelope. Some are just plain white envelopes. Some bear elaborate and attractive cachets.

What is a Cachet? (pronounced ka-SHAY)

A cachet is a design of words and/or pictures which refers specifically to the new stamp on the FDC. There designs are usually found on the front, left hand side of the envelope. They can be printed, rubber stamped, individually hand created or paste-on labels. The purpose of a cachet is to enhance the meaning and appearance of the cover.

Why collect Cacheted FDCs?

Until a few years ago, a First Day Cover was just a First Day Cover. Collectors wanted an example of every issue on a FDC, and they didn't really care if it was uncacheted or cacheted, or who made the cachet. If they could find one with an attractive cachet, all the better, but any FDC to fill the space in the collection would do.

Today, collectors don't want just any FDC. They are looking for cacheted FDCs. There are several reasons for this.

Information about cachet collecting has been published and promoted in many places and in many ways. The American First Day Cover Society has promoted FDCs through its magazine *First Days* for more than 25 years. In the past ten years, FDC cachet catalogues have been published by Earl Planty and the FDC Publishing Co. More recently, several more cover-oriented columns have appeared, helping to generate additional interest.

The real reason for the great increase in interest is the collector. Collectors have been becoming much more knowledgeable and sophisticated about FDC cachets. They have been captured by the quest for new cachets and information about them.

What to seek when buying FDCs

When you are buying a FDC, look at the whole cover. It should be in good condition, without tears, wrinkles, stains, or wear. The stamp should not be torn or damaged. The postmark should be legible and it should be the correct FD date.

Many collectors prefer unaddressed FDCs because they are neater and more attractive. Often the specialist will want to see an address on a cover because it can sometimes help identify the cachet or the servicer.

Just because this book emphasizes cacheted FDCs, that does not mean that uncacheted FDCs are not collectable. A number of the important early FDC servicers, like Adam Bert, C.E. Nickles and Edward Worden, made many uncacheted FDCs which are still considered valuable.

Only a small percentage of all pre-1930 FDCs that exist are cacheted, because most collectors and dealers of that period were happy to have an uncacheted FDC. Some collectors today prefer uncacheted FDCs because they look more like legitimate pieces of mail than elaborately cacheted covers.

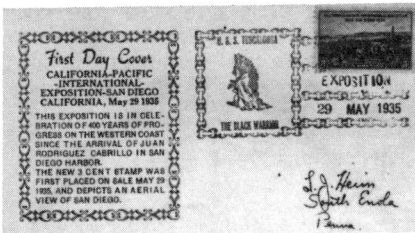

Figure 4
An unusual California Exposition First Day Cover, Scott 773. While this cachet is not as attractive as some mass produced commercial cachets of the period, such as Anderson or Ioor, it is much scarcer. What makes this First Day Cover even more interesting and valuable is the fancy postmark. This cover was canceled on the USS Tuscaloosa on the First Day of Issue. This is known as an unofficial FDC.

When buying cacheted FDCs, buy unusual looking cachets when you can. You will always be able to find the mass-produced commercial cachets for your collection. However, if you pass by an unusual cachet, you may not see the cachet offered for sale again in one year, five years, or maybe ever.

If you do collect one of the mass-produced commercial cachets, the same rule applies. Keep your eyes open for unusual color or text variety.

What the specialists are collecting

Specialists collect in many ways — by cachet maker, by issue, by set, by years or periods of years, and by topics. They collect First Cachets, combination FDCs, Unofficial FDCs, and handpainted cachets.

If you find a cachet maker that you particularly like, you can try to put together an entire run of FDCs. For example, Anderson, Artcraft and House of Farnam all started producing cachets before 1940. While you may not have too much trouble finding most of the cachets, it will be a challenge to fill in some of the early cachets of these three makers. It will be particularly hard to find some of the early cachet color varieties of Anderson and Artcraft.

Some specialists pick out a particular issue or set that they like and try to make a complete collection of cachet varieties. This can be a modern issue, such as a space issue, a Kennedy issue, or an older issue that is of special interest to you. Pick out a stamp issued in your home state, or issued for your profession, or one that is related to one of your other hobbies.

Check the new issue information in any one of the stamp newspapers. If there is a new stamp coming out near your home you might enjoy going to a First Day ceremony, collect-

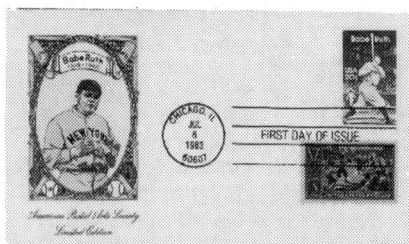

Figure 5
An interesting combination FDC, with the 1939 100th Anniversary Stamp and the 1983 Babe Ruth stamp. Both are tied to the envelope with the First Day cancellation. This cachet is a Post/Art cachet produced by the American Postal Arts Society.

ing all the cachets you can find on that issue, and perhaps printing a cachet for that stamp that you design yourself.

Collectors sometimes go after groups of stamps. Some try to collect all FDC cachets of the 3-cent Purples of the late 1930's. Others go after all cachets of the 28 stamps issued in 1948.

Cacheted FDCs are not the only possible specialties. Advanced specialists collect early uncacheted regular issues or commemoratives by set or for FD postmark varieties.

PEOPLE ALSO COLLECT BY TOPICS - Masonic, Military or Professional Topics, Women's History, National or Local History, Sesquicentennial or Bicentennial FDCs, or just about anything that you want to work on.

FIRST CACHETS collecting has become very popular with FDC specialists. A First Cachet is very simply the First Cachet that a particular cachet maker has produced. First Cachets have been researched, documented, and firmly established for many cachet makers.

For other cachet makers, the search for the first cachet is still going on. First Cachet collecting is just one of many areas in FDC collecting where the knowledgeable collector can find desirable cachets in dealers' shoeboxes. Very often they are priced the same as the more common mass produced commercial cachets.

Listings for many First Cachets appear under the appropriate Scott number.

A COMBINATION FDC is a FDC which has other stamps or labels along with the new stamp. Together the stamps help to tell a more complete story about the new issue.

The stamps or labels should be related thematically, usually by the history or topic of the stamp. For example, a stamp with a bird on it could be accompanied by other U.S. or foreign stamps with birds, or perhaps a wildlife conservation label.

A new stamp issued for an anniversary of statehood could be used in combination with older issues related to the state's history, or other stamps that had First Days in the state. The possibilities are almost limitless.

AN UNOFFICIAL FDC is a FDC canceled on the official First Day date, but not in the official First Day city. An unofficial FDC can be canceled in any city as long as it has a FD postmark. An unofficial FDC is more meaningful when the city is related to the new issue. These relationships can be historical relationships or relationships by name only.

In 1926, Edward Worden prepared a truly classic unofficial FDC on the 13-cent Harrison stamp. He took 500 stamps from Indianapolis, Indiana, one of the official FD cities, to North Bend, Ohio, Harrison's home town.

On the Fallen Timbers commemorative of 1929, unofficial FDCs are known postmarked in Fallen Timbers, Pennsylvania. The only connection here between the stamp and the unofficial FDC is the town name.

There are a number of issues from the 1920's and 1930's which have 50 or more unofficial FDCs known. While all of these unofficials are not related to the new issue, they are still eagerly collected.

A SEMI-OFFICIAL FDC is canceled in the official city, but with something other than the usual FDOI slogan or bull's eye cancels. Often these are pictorial cancels.

HAND-PAINTED cachets are collected because they often have attractive and colorful original artwork. Each FDC represents a lot of time, effort and talent on the part of the cachet maker. They are often difficult to find in dealers' shoe boxes, because they are usually produced in limited quantities. Some of the well known commercial cachet designers also make hand-painted cachets. Ralph Dyer, who designed cachets for Leo August, Artcraft, during the 1930's, produced hand-painted cachets for several decades after that.

How to learn more about FDCs

The best way to learn about FDCs is to get in touch with other FDC collectors. Visit them or write to them to exchange information and opinions on covers.

Join the American First Day Cover Society. It publishes the journal *First Days* eight times per year. The journal contains new issue information, free cover exchange ads, several columns on modern FDCs, and detailed research articles on the cachet makers discussed in this book, plus much more.

The AFDCS also has regular FDC auctions, annual conventions, periodic regional get-togethers, a FDC Expertising Committee and numerous slide shows on FDCs available on loan. For additional information write AFDCS, Box 234-D, Stewartsville, NJ 08886.

Also, FDC Publishing Co. offers a number of general and specialized FDC catalogues on various cachet makers. Each catalogue is profusely illustrated with photos and contains up-to-date market prices, descriptions, and spirited comments. A brochure describing all its publications is available for the asking. Write FDC Publishing Co., Box 206-D, Stewartsville, NJ 08886.

Which current FDCs will appreciate in value?

As previously stated, the prices in this catalogue are average market value. FDCs with mass-produced commercial cachets usually sell for less than catalogue value, while scarcer cachets can sell for many times catalogue value.

No one can accurately predict which FDCs will increase in value. However, by studying past performance of cacheted FDCs produced in the 1950's, 60's and 70's several parallels can be drawn as to why some FDCs outperform other FDCs.

1. Any new FDCs should be **unaddressed** or **light pencil** addressed.

When servicing your own FDCs write your address in light pencil or use peelable labels which are available from most stamp dealers. There are many arguments in favor of addressed covers. However, it is a clear fact of life that when you sell your collection, a dealer will pay very little or nothing for a common cacheted addressed FDC after 1955.

2. Make sure current FDCs that you collect contain a cachet. Cachets are art. They are miniature drawings, paintings produced, in some cased, in limited quantity. The cachet value, in some cases, can far exceed the value of the stamp on the envelope.

In summary, a current FDC has a better chance of increasing in value if it is cacheted and unaddressed. Choosing the right cachet is important. Currently there are over 200 cachet makers producing cachets for new FDCs. In many cases collectors collect several different cachets for each new issue.

When choosing a cachet to collect make sure that:

1. The cachet is produced in a relatively small number.

2. The cachet has a well-executed design.

3. That the FDC has a high overall quality, attractiveness and workmanship of the cachet and envelope.

The American First Day Cover Society, a membership organization devoted to the advancement of First Day Covers, has compiled a Directory of Current Cachet Makers.

The Director lists all current cachet makers, names and addresses.

How to acquire current FDCs

There are several ways that a collector can obtain current First Day Covers. The collector may service his own FDCs by sending envelopes to the First Day city postmaster as new stamps are released. Different unserviced cacheted envelopes can be purchased from local or mail order cover dealers. Or the collector might join a cover club or service offered by many cover dealers, and automatically receive each new FDC.

How to service your own FDCs

Many collectors feel that servicing their own FDCs is what First Day Cover collecting is all about. There is a tremendous feeling of involvement and accomplishment.

You may service your own FDCs by sending unserviced envelopes (preferably cacheted) to the postmaster of the city where the new stamp is to be initially placed on sale. You must include enough remittance to pay for the cost of postage to be affixed to your envelope.

Or a more convenient method of servicing your FDCs is to purchase the new stamp, when it is available, at your local post office. Affix the stamp to your envelope and forward the envelope for servicing to the First Day Post Office within 30 days of the issue date.

Your local post office has bulletins on upcoming stamps, their date of issue, and first day city, along with an illustration of the new stamp.

A detailed procedure for servicing your FDCs is outlined below:

Method 1: Post Office affixing stamp

1. Your cover must be addressed; use light pencil or peelable label (see "Which Current FDCs Will Appreciate in Value"), and bear an endorsement in the upper right-hand corner as to the number of stamps that are to be affixed.
2. Send your cover(s) to be serviced in an outer envelope addressed to the "Postmaster" of the proper First Day city. "First Day Cover" and the name of the new stamp should be written in the lower left corner of the outer envelope. Make sure you send your covers **before** the First Day Date.
3. Enclose a personal check or money order to cover the correct amount of postage to be affixed to your envelopes. Do not send cash or postage stamps as payment.

Method 2: You affixing your stamps

1. Purchase the new stamp at your local post office as soon as it becomes available. It usually will be available one or two days after the First Day Date. If not, try a USPS Philatelic Center.
2. Affix the stamps to your envelope in the upper right hand corner, ¼-inch from the top and ¼-inch from the right edge. Pencil address your cover or affix an addressed peelable label near the bottom of the envelope.
3. Send your cover(s) in an outer envelope to the First Day City within 30 days after the First Day of Issue. No payment is necessary.

Method 3: How to join an FDC service

A much more convenient method of obtaining current FDCs is joining a FDC Club or purchasing them separately. By belonging to a club there is no chance of missing upcoming issues due to oversight.

There are over 200 different cachet makers who sell their cacheted FDCs for current issues. Some cachet makers produce individually hand-painted cachets in very limited quantities. Also, there are "comic" cachets, "silks" and many others. Some collectors purchase current FDCs from several different cachet makers adding variety to their collections.

A Post/Art (American Postal Arts Society) cacheted FDC, individually hand-painted in watercolors.

A Jim Riggs "comic" cacheted FDC. Mr. Riggs, a retired cartoonist, has been producing such cachets since 1977.

Most cachet makers stock FDCs of past issues allowing you to add to your collection.

INTRODUCTION TO CACHET COLLECTING

As more and more FDC collectors turn to collecting FDCs by cachet varieties, the question is asked, "Who makes this cachet?" Included in this introduction to cachet collecting is a mini-identifier, with several popular cachet makers of the past 40 years.

Sixty cachet makers are identified and priced in *The Cachet Identifier,* available for $6.95 from FDC Publishing, Box 206D, Stewartsville, NJ 08886, or from your local dealer.

C. Stephen Anderson

C. Stephen Anderson produced cachets for every issue between 1933 and 1979. Anderson cachets are easy to identify. They usually are signed "C. Stephen Anderson" or "CSA" and contain an illustration and some historical information in the text. His cachets are usually one color, with the earliest ones printed in black. Later purple, and then other color varieties, were printed. Many cachets were printed in several different colors.

Figure AND-1
THE FIRST ANDERSON CACHET was prepared for the Oglethorpe Issue of 1933. Anderson cachets can usually be identified by the lettering style and use of scrolls. Most are signed "C. Stephen Anderson" or "CSA."

Artcraft Leo August - Washington Stamp Exchange

Leo August of Washington Stamp Exchange traces the history of Artcraft cachets back to the World's Fair Issue of 1939. The earliest Artcraft cachets were not signed, but can be identified by their usual high quality engraving. Some early Artcraft cachets exist both unsigned and signed with the familiar Artcraft pallet with brush trademark. Most Artcraft FDC cachets since 1940 are signed.

The first Artcraft cachet is not the first cachet produced by Leo August. August started to service FDCs in the late 1920's, and he started producing cachets in the early 1930's. Washington Stamp Exchange cachets of the 1930's were designed by J.W. Clifford, John Coulthard and Ralph Dyer. Many of these cachets are signed by the cachet artist, and occasionally with "WSE."

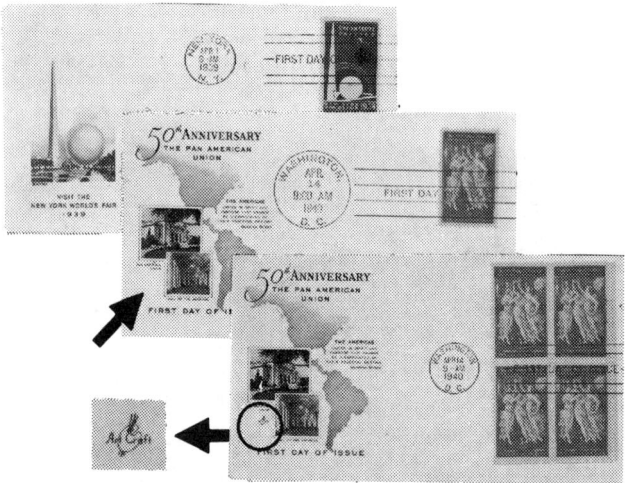

Figure ARC-1
THE FIRST ARTCRAFT CACHET was prepared for the New York World's Fair commemorative issue. This is an engraved cachet, printed in blue. Also shown are two Artcraft varieties for the 1940 Pan American Union commemorative. As with a number of early Artcraft FDCs, the cachet exists both with and without the Artcraft trademark.

Artmaster

Artmaster cachets have been created by Robert Schmidt of Louisville, Kentucky, since 1946. The firm is currently owned and operated by his nephew, Mike Zoeller. The first Artmaster cachet was prepared for the Honorable Discharge Emblem commemorative.

Artmaster cachets can be easily identified because they are high quality engravings signed "Artmaster."

Figure ARM-1
The first Artmaster cachet

W.G. Crosby

A typical Crosby cachet has a small photo pasted on the cover. Crosby thermographed the text and frames found around the photos, which resulted in an unmistakably heavy raised printing. Crosby often produced several cachets for each issue, and occasionally produced cachets without a photo. Crosby cachets without photos can be identified by a similarity in text and cachet design. Crosby cachet photos are not to be confused with Ioor's, since Crosby's are actual photos that have been pasted onto the envelopes after the cachet was printed, and Ioor's are printed on the envelopes.

A few of Crosby's covers are signed. The trick is to see his name, which he had printed in the upper right-hand corner, right where the stamp is affixed. To see his name, one must hold the cover up to a bright light.

Crosby made cachets for ship covers in the early 1930's. He died in 1947, but his wife continued to make the Crosby covers through the Annapolis Tercentenary issue of 1949.

Figure WC-1
Most Crosby covers contain a pasted-on photo, making them easy to identify.

It was not uncommon for Crosby to have more than one cachet for a stamp issue. There are some issues where he created as many as 20 different designs.

Notice that one of the cachets for this issue does not contain a photo. However, the cachet does contain the same familiar raised print.

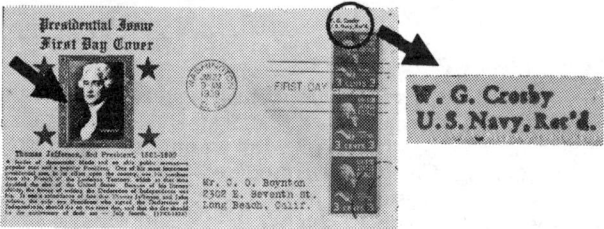

Figure WC-2
A few Crosby cachets are signed with a fine-line Crosby advertising imprint. This imprint is found in the upper right-hand corner of the envelope or, occasionally, on the back.

House of Farnam

House of Farnam cachets have been produced for nearly every issue since the TIPEX Souvenir sheet of 1936. Many Farnam cachets are signed 'HF' or "House of Farnam." The early unsigned Farnams are usually small, simple, one-color designs found in the upper left-hand corner of the envelope. They are printed from steel-die engravings with slightly raised printing.

Figure HF-1
THE FIRST FARNAM CACHET is an unsigned design pre-pared for the 1936 TIPEX Souvenir sheet. Also shown is a typical unsigned early Farnam and a signed Farnam from the 1980's.

Dr. Harry Ioor (pronounced EYE-or)

Dr. Ioor's cachet career spanned the period from 1929 to 1951. His cachet designs fall into three different patterns.

Figure OR-1
Two early Ioor's, including the first Ioor cachet prepared for the George Rogers Clark commemorative of 1929. Notice that both cachets contain fine line drawings.

Early Ioor cachets (1929-1933) followed no particular pattern except that many are fine line drawings. Several are printed in black and light pink ink. In some cases the covers are addressed to Ioor, which allows for easy identification.

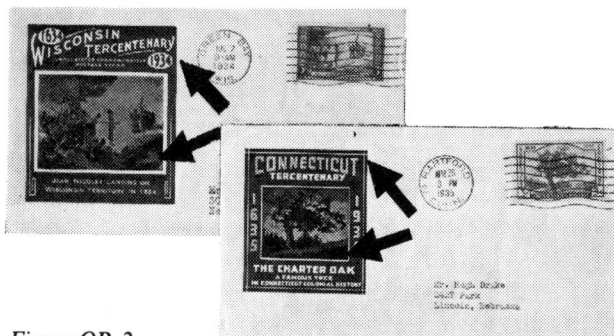

Figure OR-2
From 1934-1940 Ioor's covers followed a definite pattern. Almost all of them contained a printed photo as part of the cachet. These photos are printed on the envelopes and are not to be confused with Crosby's cachets, where the photos are pasted on the envelope. During this period, Ioor often produced several cachet varieties, using different black and white photos, with different colors around them.

Figure OR-3
Harry Ioor died before the completion of the Famous American series of 1940. His sister completed the series and then continued to produce cachets with a different design pattern. This particular period of Ioor is easy to identify since most of the covers are signed.

F.R. Rice

Rice cachets are undoubtedly one of the easiest cachets to identify. Most are signed and have a definite and consistent style. Rice's career spanned from 1932 to 1940.

Figure RI-1
Rice used different illustrations or text inside this common border for about 75 percent of his cachets.

U.S. CACHET PRICING CALCULATOR

As discussed under "Catalogue Prices," prices in this catalogue are for an **average** market FDC. Some FDCs, depending on the cachet, sell for many times the catalogue price, while others sell for less.

Below is a list of cachet makers, the dates they serviced FDCs and a market value multiplier. By taking the multiplier range listed below, and multiplying it by the Catalogue Price for a cacheted FDC, you will get the approximate catalogue value of various cacheted FDCs.

First Cachets of all makers are in great demand and usually sell for a substantial premium. Prices for the First Cachets of most of the cachet makers listed below can be found under the appropriate Scott number.

Cachet Maker Dates	Pricing Multiplier
C. Anderson	
1933-1934 . .	1½ to 2 times
1935 to date . .	½ to 1 time
Andrews	
1978	3 times
1979-1982	1½ times
Aristocrat	
1936-1940 . .	1 to 1½ times
1941 to date . .	½ to 1 time
Artcraft	
1939	2 times
1940 to 1945	1 to 1½ times
1946 to date . .	¼ to 1 time
Artmaster	
1946 to 1950	1 to 1½ times
1951 to date . .	½ to 1 time
R. Beazell	
1929-1934	3 times
1935-1937	15 times
Adam Bert	
1929-1933 . .	1½ to 2 times
Bazaar	
1971-1972	2 times
1973 to date	1 to 1½ times
Aubry	
1936-1938	2 times
Ira Bennett	
1948-1949	10 times
Beverly Hills	
1933-1937 . . .	2 to 3 times
Brookhaven	
1933-1938 . . .	3 to 4 times

Cachet Maker Dates	Pricing Multiplier
Cachet Craft	
Pre-1950	1 to 2 times
1950-1972	1 time
Calhoun	
Collectors Soc. - Gold	
1978	8 to 9 times
Chambers Gold Bond	
1935-1953	5 times
J. Clifford	
1936-1944 . . .	1 to 2 times
F. Collins	
1978 to date .	10-40 times
Colonial	
1974	2 times
1975 to 1983	1 to 1½ times
Colorano 'silks'	
1971-1973 .	10 to 14 times
1974-1976 . . .	2 to 3 times
1977 to date . . .	1½ times
Comic Cachets	
1977-1982 . .	1 to 1½ times
Cover Craft	
1964-1966	5 times
1967 to date . . .	1½ times
Covered Wagon	
1931-1934 . .	1½ to 2 times
W. Crosby	
Pre-1939	4 to 5 times
1940-1948 . . .	3 to 4 times
W. Czubay	
1936-1954 . . .	2 to 3 times

Cachet Maker Dates	Pricing Multiplier
DeRosset Handpainted	
1986 to date	30 times
Double A	
1981 to date	1½ times
R. Dyer	
1928-1938	1½ to 2 times
Eagle Cover Service	
1933-1936	1 to 2 times
Egolf	
1928-1931	1 to 2 times
Elliott	
1929-1931	1 to 2 times
Emeigh	
1929-1930	1 to 3 times
Emerson	
1925-1932	2 to 3 times
Espenshade	
1935-1942	2 times
Fairway	
1931-1940	1 to 1½ times
Fidelity Stamp Co.	
1937-1950	1 to 1½ times
Fleetwood	
1941-1947	3 to 5 times
1948-1960	2 to 3 times
1961 to date	1 to 3 times
I. Fluegel	
1945-1959	3 to 4 times
1960-1964	10 times
Fulton Stamp Co.	
1947-1949	1½ to 2 times
Gamm	
1977	5 to 6 times
1978 to date	1½ to 2 times
Geerlings	
1984 to date	15-25 times
Gill Craft	
1980	5 times
1981 to date	1½ to 2 times
Glen	
1974	3 times
1975 to date	1½ times
T. Gundel	
1929-1941	6 to 7 times
A. Gorham	
1932-1938	3 to 4 times

Cachet Maker Dates	Pricing Multiplier
W. Grandy	
1935 to date	2 to 3 times
H. H. Griffin	
1926-1933	1 to 2 times
H. Grimsland	
1932-1934	1½ to 2 times
1935-1952	1 to 2 times
C.W. George	
1927-1931	2 to 3 times
1931 to 1950	2 times
E. Hacker	
1931-1938	4 to 5 times
Hobby Life-WCO	
1945-1950	2 to 3 times
House of Farnam	
1936-1939	2 to 3 times
1940-1950	1 to 1½ times
1950 to 1973	1 time
1974 to date	1½ to 3 times
HAM Handpainted Cachets	
1977-1978	40 times
1979 to date	15-40 times
HUX	
1928-1950	1½ to 2 times
H. Ioor	
1929-1931	2 to 3 times
1932 & later	1 to 1½ times
Imperial	
1934-1940	2 to 3 times
Gladys Jackson	
1948 to date	1½ to 2 times
N. Joseph	
1929-1933	4 times
Justice Covers	
1979 to date	1½ times
Kapner	
1934-1937	1 to 1½ times
Ed Kee	
1933-1935	1 to 1½ times
Klotzbach	
1929-1935	1 to 2 times
Kolor Kover	
1948	5 times
1949-1960	3 to 4 times
1960-1973	2 times

Cachet Maker Dates	Pricing Multiplier
KMC Venture	
1978	4 times
1979 to date	1½ times
Laird	
1935-1937	1 to 2 times
Linprint	
1932-1941	1 time
Marg	
1962-1964	6 times
1965 to date	1½ times
Mauck	
1927-1930	1 to 2 times
J. Minkus	
1940 to date	1 time
C. E. Nickles	
1925-1929	1 time
Nix	
1934-1958	3 to 5 times
Overseas Mailers	
1953-1977	6 to 10 times
Pavois	
1937-1940	1 time
Pent Arts	
1943-1958	1 to 1½ times
Pilgrim	
1937-1941	6 to 8 times
Plimpton	
1936-1939	1 time
Post/Art Engraved	
1980-1981	5 times
1982 to date	2 times
Post/Art Handpainted	
1983 to date	10 times
Postmasters of America	
1976	3 times
1977 to date	1 time
Pugh Cachets	
1979 to date	6 to 7 times
Raley	
1932-1938	2 to 3 times
F. R. Rice	
1932-1941	1 to 2 times
Risko Art	
1935-1938	5 times

Cachet Maker Dates	Pricing Multiplier
A.C. Roessler	
1925-1931	1 to 1½ times
1932-1938	2 to 3 times
Rothblum	
1929-1934	2 to 3 times
J. A. Roy	
1934-1937	1 to 1½ times
J. Stoutzenburg	
1928	2 to 2½ times
1929-1934	1 to 2 times
L. W. Staehle	
1938-1943	1½ to 2½ times
1944-1953	1 to 2 times
Shockley	
1929-1930	1 time
Sidenius	
1932-1939	1½ to 2 times
Smartcraft	
1942-1952	1 to 1½ times
Softones	
1978-1980	2 to 3 times
Spartan	
1948-1950	2 to 3 times
Spectrum	
1977	3 times
1978-1983	1½ to 2 times
Sudduth	
1936-1937	1 to 1½ times
Top Notch	
1934-1937	1½ to 2 times
Truby	
1931-1934	5 to 6 times
Tudor House	
1977	3 times
1978 to date	1½ times
Velvatone	
1951-1970	3 to 5 times
Warneford	
1937-1940	1½ to 2 times
Western Silk Cachets	
1978	4 times
1979-1983	1½ times
Zaso	
1977	4 times
1978-1983	1½ to 2 times

COMMEMORATIVES AND REGULAR ISSUES

| 1 | 2 | 230 | 231 |

Scott Number	Description	Uncacheted Single

1847

☐ 1	**5¢ Franklin,** July 7, 1847, New York, NY	—
☐	July 12, 1847, Phila., PA	—
☐ 2	**10¢ Washington,** July 9, 1847, New York, NY	—
☐	July 2, 1847, Phila., PA	—

1851

☐ 5	**1¢ Franklin,** July 5, 1851, earliest known use	—
☐ 5A	**1¢ Franklin,** July 1, 1851, Boston, MA	18500.00
☐ 7	**1¢ Franklin,** July 1, 1851	13000.00
☐	on printed circular	2500.00
☐ 10	**3¢ Washington,** July 1, 1851	7000.00
☐ 17	**12¢ Washington,** August 4, 1851, Brattleboro, VT	9000.00

Earliest known use

1857

☐ 18	**1¢ Franklin,** Jan. 25, 1861	—
☐ 19	**1¢ Franklin,** July 26, 1857	—
☐ 20	**1¢ Franklin,** July 25, 1857	—
☐ 21	**1¢ Franklin,** July 26, 1857	—
☐ 22	**1¢ Franklin,** July 26, 1857	—
☐ 23	**1¢ Franklin,** July 25, 1857, Castleton, VT	—
☐ 24	**1¢ Franklin,** Nov. 17, 1857	—

Listed above are the earliest known postmarks for all 1¢ 1857 varieties. These different varieties are found on a number of plates, hence the different earliest known uses.

| ☐ 26a | **3¢ Washington,** July 11, 1857 | — |
| ☐ 32 | **10¢ Washington,** July 27, 1857, Lancaster, PA | — |

The four varieties of the 10¢ 1857, Scott 31-34, all came from one plate, but to date only Scott 32 is known postmarked July 27, 1857.

| ☐ 36 | **12¢ Washington,** July 30, 1857, New York, NY | 10000.00 |

1861-66

☐ 63	**1¢ Franklin,** August 17, 1861	10000.00
☐ 69	**12¢ Washington,** August 30, 1861	—
☐ 70c	**24¢ Washington,** August 20, 1861, Boston, MA	—
☐ 71	**30¢ Franklin,** August 20, 1861, New London, CT	—
☐ 77	**15¢ Lincoln,** April 14, 1866, Chicago, IL	—

Earliest known use

1867 Grilled Issue

| ☐ 79 | **3¢ Washington,** August 13, 1867 | 5000.00 |

Scott 79 is the first U.S. grilled stamp. August 13, 1867 covers are known from Richmond, VA and Cleveland, OH.

1869 Pictorial Issue

☐ 113	**2¢ Post Horse & Rider,** March 27, 1869	5000.00
☐ 114	**3¢ Locomotive,** March 27, 1869, New York	5000.00
☐ 115	**6¢ Washington,** April 26, 1869	6000.00
☐ 116	**10¢ Shield & Eagle,** April 1, 1869	6000.00
☐ 117	**12¢ S.S. "Adriatic",** April 5, 1869	6000.00

Scott Number	Description	Uncacheted Single
☐ 118	15¢ **Landing of Columbus,** April 2, 1869	6000.00
☐ 119	15¢ **Columbus,** May 23, 1869	—

Dates for Scott 113 thru 119 are earliest known use

1883

☐ 205	5¢ **Garfield,** Feb. 17, 1882	—

Earliest known use

☐ 210	2¢ **Washington,** Oct. 1, 1883, any city	1700.00
☐ 211	4¢ **Jackson,** Oct. 1, 1883, any city	8500.00
☐	210 & 211 on one cover	10000.00

1890

☐ 219D	2¢ **Washington,** Feb. 22, 1890, any city	14500.00
☐ 220	2¢ **Washington,** May 31, 1890	—

Earliest known use

1893   Columbian Exposition

☐ 230	1¢ **Columbian,** Jan. 1, 1893, Boston, MA	3000.00
☐	Dec. 31, 1892, Salem, MA, backstamped Lynn Dec. 31, 1892	—
☐ 231	2¢ **Columbian,** Jan. 1, 1893, New York, NY or Boston, MA	2400.00
☐	Dec. 31, 1892, Salem, MA, backstamped Lynn Dec. 31, 1892	—
☐ 231	2¢ **Columbian,** Jan. 2, 1893, Boston, MA	2400.00
☐ 232	3¢ **Columbian,** Jan. 1, 1893, Boston, MA	6000.00
☐ 233	4¢ **Columbian,** Jan. 1, 1893, Boston, MA	6000.00
☐ 234	5¢ **Columbian,** Jan. 1, 1893, Boston, MA	6250.00
☐ 235	6¢ **Columbian,** Jan. 1, 1893, Boston, MA	6750.00
☐ 237	10¢ **Columbian,** Jan. 1, 1893, Arlington Heights, MA	7500.00

There is a legitimate early use of the 10¢ Columbian dated Dec. 31, 1892, on a special delivery letter, backstamped East Lexington, Mass. Because Jan. 1, 1893 was a Sunday, few P.O.s were open. Jan. 1 and Jan. 2 covers are both collected as First Day Covers.

☐ 242	$2 **Columbian,** Jan. 2, 1893, any city	15000.00

1898   Regular Issue

☐ 279	1¢ **Franklin,** Jan. 25, 1898, New York, NY	—

Trans Mississippi

☐ 285	1¢ **Marquette,** June 17, 1898, DC	4500.00
☐ 286	2¢ **Farming,** June 17, 1898, DC	4000.00
☐	June 17, 1898, Pittsburgh, PA	5000.00
☐ 288	5¢ **Fremont,** June 17, 1898, DC	5000.00
☐ 289	8¢ **Troops,** June 17, 1898, DC	7500.00
☐	285-290 on one cover, June 17, 1898	13000.00
☐ 291	50¢ **Mining,** June 17, 1898, DC	9000.00
☐ 292	$2 **Cattle,** June 17, 1898, DC	10000.00

1901   Pan American Exposition

☐ 294	1¢ **Navigation,** 5/1/01	3500.00
☐ 295	2¢ **Express,** 5/1/01	3000.00
☐ 296	4¢ **Electric Auto,** 5/1/01	4250.00
☐ 297	5¢ **Bridge,** 5/1/01, New York, NY	4500.00
☐	296 and 298, 4¢ Automobile and 8¢ Canal Locks, on one cover, 5/1/01, Boston, MA	6000.00
☐	294-299 Complete Set of 6 on one cover	10000.00

No FDC of the 8¢ value alone on cover is known at this time. May 2, 1904, is now the earliest known use of the 10¢ Pan American on cover. The 10¢ value is known on a number of FDCs as part of a full set of stamps on one cover.

Scott Number	Description	Uncacheted Single
1902-03	**Regular Issues**	
☐ 300	1¢ Franklin, 2/3/03	3000.00
☐ 301	2¢ Washington, 1/17/03	2750.00
1904	**Louisiana Purchase Exposition**	
☐ 323	1¢ Livingston, 4/30/04	3000.00
☐ 324	2¢ Jefferson, 4/25/04, Moline, IL	2750.00
☐	4/29/04, St. Louis, MO	3250.00
☐	4/30/04	3250.00
☐ 325	3¢ Monroe, 4/30/04	3250.00
☐ 326	5¢ McKinley, 4/30/04	5500.00
☐ 327	10¢ Louisiana Purchase, 4/30/04	7500.00
☐	Set on one cover, 4/30/04	12500.00

Notice was sent to postmasters that this set was being shipped from Washington on April 21, but could not be sold to the public before April 30, 1904. Because of these instructions, any covers dated before 4/30/04 are considered a pre-dated FDC.

1907	**Jamestown Exposition**	
☐ 328	1¢ Capt. Smith, 4/26/07, Fortress Monroe, VA	3750.00
☐ 329	2¢ Jamestown, 4/26/07, Norfolk, VA	5500.00
☐ 330	5¢ Pocahontas, 5/10/07, Norfolk, VA	10000.00

Earliest known use

1909	**Lincoln Issue**	
☐ 367	2¢ Lincoln, 2/12/09	350.00
☐ 367	2¢ Lincoln, 2/10/09, or 2/11/09, pre-dated FDC	400.00
☐ 368	2¢ Lincoln *Imperf.*, 2/12/09, Canton, OH	1900.00
☐ 369	2¢ Lincoln, blue paper variety, 3/27/09	2500.00

Earliest known use

February 12, 1909 was designated as the official FD of the Lincoln Stamp by the P.O. Nine pre-dated FDCs are known on this issue postmarked on Feb. 10 from Boston, MA (five covers); Ovilet, KS; and Brooklyn, NY; and on Feb. 11 from Mechanicsburg, PA, and Superior, WI. 149 different cities are known on Lincoln, Scott 367 FDCs, with Boston, MA, and Canton, OH, being the most common cities.

Alaska-Yukon Issue

☐ 370	2¢ Seward, 6/1/09, Modesto, CA	1800.00
☐ 371	2¢ Seward *Imperf.*, 6/13/09, any city	—

Earliest known use

Hudson-Fulton Issue

☐ 372	2¢ Hudson-Fulton, 9/24/09, Boston, MA	850.00
☐	9/25/09	950.00
☐	9/25/09, Lancaster, PA, on 2-part Hudson-Fulton picture post card	1000.00
☐ 373	2¢ Hudson-Fulton *Imperf.*, 9/25/09	2000.00

May 25, 1909 was designated as the official First Day of Issue by the Post Office notice of this issue. The May 24, 1909, cover listed is a pre-dated FDC.

1910-13	**Regular Issues**	
☐ 394	3¢ Washington, coil, 11/22/11, Orangeburg, NY	2000.00

Earliest known use

1913	**Panama-Pacific, *Perf. 11***	
☐ 397	1¢ Balboa, 1/1/13	3250.00
☐ 398	2¢ Panama Canal, 1/18/13	4000.00
☐ 399	5¢ Golden Gate, 1/1/13	4000.00
☐ 400	10¢ San Francisco Bay, 1/1/13, San Francisco, CA	—
☐	397, 399 & 400 on one cover, 1/1/13, San Francisco, CA	5000.00

Scott Number	Description	Uncacheted Single

1912-14 Regular Issues

☐ 405	1¢ **Washington,** 2/12/12	1000.00
☐ 414	8¢ **Franklin,** 2/12/12	1000.00
☐ 416	10¢ **Franklin,** 1/11/12	1000.00
☐ 418	15¢ **Franklin,** 2/12/12	1000.00
☐ 424d	1¢ **Washington,** Single from booklet, 12/20/13	—

Earliest known use

☐ 425e	2¢ **Washington,** Single from booklet, 1/6/14	—

Earliest known use

1916-22 Regular Issues

☐ 497	10¢ **Franklin,** 1/31/22, DC	1750.00

Only H. Hammelman cover exists. He's the only one who serviced this cover.

1918-20 Regular Issues

☐ 523	$2 **Franklin,** 8/19/18	3000.00
☐ 526	2¢ **Washington,** 3/15/20	800.00

1919 Victory Issue

☐ 537	3¢ **Victory,** 3/3/19	700.00

1920 Issues

☐ 542	1¢ **Washington,** 5/26/20	700.00
☐ 548	1¢ **Pilgrim,** 12/21/20, DC	700.00
☐ 549	2¢ **Pilgrim,** 12/20/20, DC	625.00
☐	12/21/20, DC	625.00
☐	12/21/20, Philadelphia, PA	625.00
☐	12/21/20, Plymouth, MA	900.00
☐	Set on one cover, 12/21/20, DC	2500.00
☐	Philadelphia, PA	2000.00

1922-26 *Perf. 11*

		Uncacheted Sgl	Blk
☐☐ 551	½¢ **Hale,** 4/4/25, DC	—	22.50
☐☐	New Haven, CT	—	35.00
☐☐	Unofficial city	—	40.00
☐☐ 552	1¢ **Franklin,** 1/17/23, DC	32.50	50.00
☐☐	Philadelphia, PA	65.00	100.00
☐☐	Norristown, PA	75.00	—
☐☐	Unofficial city	65.00	—
☐☐ 553	1½¢ **Harding,** 3/19/25, DC	35.00	60.00
☐☐ 554	2¢ **Washington,** 1/15/23, DC	45.00	75.00
☐☐ 555	3¢ **Lincoln,** 2/12/23, DC	37.50	75.00
☐☐	Hodgenville, KY	225.00	400.00
☐☐ 556	4¢ **Martha Washington,** 1/15/23, DC	50.00	100.00
☐☐ 557	5¢ **Roosevelt,** 10/27/22, DC	125.00	200.00
☐☐	New York, NY	250.00	350.00
☐☐	Oyster Bay, NY	675.00	800.00
☐☐ 558	6¢ **Garfield,** 11/20/22, DC	200.00	300.00
☐☐ 559	7¢ **McKinley,** 5/1/23, DC	100.00	175.00
☐☐	Niles, OH	200.00	300.00
☐☐ 560	8¢ **Grant,** 5/1/23, DC	100.00	150.00
☐☐ 561	9¢ **Jefferson,** 1/15/23, DC	100.00	150.00
☐☐	554, 556, 560, 561 on one cover	1500.00	—
☐☐ 562	10¢ **Monroe,** 1/15/23, DC	100.00	175.00
☐☐ 563	11¢ **Hayes,** 10/4/22, DC	550.00	700.00
☐☐	Fremont, OH	1000.00	—

551

552, 581,
597, 604

553, 576, 582,
598, 605, 631

557

562

565

567

571

572

573

Scott Number	Description	Uncacheted Sgl	Blk
564	12¢ Cleveland, 3/20/23, DC	135.00	200.00
	Boston, MA (Philatelic Exhibition)	165.00	200.00
	Caldwell, NJ	200.00	250.00
565	14¢ Indian, 5/1/23, DC	300.00	450.00
	Muskogee, OK	850.00	—
	565 and 560 on one FDC, DC	1000.00	—
566	15¢ Statue of Liberty, 11/11/22, DC	350.00	—
567	20¢ Golden Gate, 5/1/23, DC	400.00	—
	San Francisco, CA	900.00	—
	5/1/23, Oakland, CA, Unofficial city	1200.00	—
568	25¢ Niagara Falls, 11/11/22, DC	600.00	900.00
569	30¢ Bison, 3/20/23, DC	725.00	1200.
	569 and 564 on one FDC, DC (1 exists)	1500.00	—
570	50¢ Arlington, 11/11/22, DC	1000.00	1500.
	566, 568, 570 multiple on one cover	3000.00	—
571	$1 Lincoln Memorial, 2/12/23, DC	4000.00	—
	Springfield, IL	5000.00	—
	571, 555 3¢ Lincoln, $1 Lincoln on 1 cover, DC	5500.00	—
1 exists - legal size			
572	$2 U.S. Capitol, 3/20/23, DC	10000.00	—
573	$5 America, 3/20/23, DC	11000.00	—

Imperf.

576	1½¢ Harding, 4/4/25, DC	45.00	60.00

Perf. 10

581	1¢ Franklin, 10/17/23, DC (1 exists)	2000.00	—
582	1½¢ Harding, 3/19/25, DC	47.50	75.00
583	2¢ Washington, 12/3/24, New York, NY, eku	—	—
583a	2¢ Washington, Booklet Pane, 8/27/26, DC	1200.00	—
584	3¢ Lincoln, 8/1/25, DC	55.00	100.00
585	4¢ M. Washington, 4/4/25, DC	55.00	100.00
586	5¢ Roosevelt, 4/4/25, DC	55.00	100.00
587	6¢ Garfield, 4/4/25, DC	70.00	135.00
588	7¢ McKinley, 5/29/26, DC	70.00	135.00
589	8¢ Grant, 5/29/26, DC	72.50	150.00
590	9¢ Jefferson, 5/29/26, DC	75.00	150.00
	588, 589, 590 on one cover	300.00	—
591	10¢ Monroe, 6/8/25, DC	100.00	175.00

Rotary Press Coil Stamps   *Perf. 10 Vertically*

		Pr.	L.Pr.
597	1¢ Franklin, 7/18/23, DC	450.00	550.00
598	1½¢ Harding, 3/19/25, DC	55.00	75.00

Scott Number	Description	Uncacheted Sgl	Blk
☐☐ 599	2¢ **Washington,** 1/10/23, Lancaster, PA (1 exists)	850.00	—
☐☐	1/11/23, South Bend, IN (1 exists)	1000.00	—
☐☐	1/13/23, St. Louis, MO (1 exists)	1000.00	—
☐☐	1/15/23, DC (37 exist)	600.00	—
☐☐ 599A	2¢ **Type II,** 4/20/29, Ithaca, NY, eku		
☐☐ 600	3¢ **Lincoln,** 5/10/24, DC	72.50	125.00
☐☐ 602	5¢ **Roosevelt,** 3/5/24, DC	75.00	125.00
☐☐ 603	10¢ **Monroe,** 12/1/24, DC	95.00	150.00

Note: 1/10/23 is the earliest known use of 599. Philip Ward prepared 37 covers on 1/15/23, the earliest known use in Washington, D.C.

Perf. 10 Horizontally

		Uncacheted Sgl	Blk
☐☐ 604	1¢ **Franklin,** 7/19/24, DC	85.00	—
☐☐ 605	1½¢ **Harding,** 5/9/25, DC	55.00	—
☐☐ 606	2¢ **Washington,** 12/31/23, DC	80.00	—

1923 **Perf. 11**		Uncacheted Sgl	Blk	Cacheted Sgl	Blk
☐☐ 610	2¢ **Harding,** 9/1/23, DC	40.00	50.00	—	—
☐☐	Marion, OH (5,000)	22.50	30.00	—	—
☐☐	Brooklyn, NY; Mt. Rainier, MD; Caledonia, OH (Unofficial cities)	50.00	—	—	—
☐☐	Pre-date, 8/31/23, DC. *Only 1 known*	250.00	—	—	—
☐☐	1st George W. Linn cachet (The 1st modern cachet)	—	—	700.00	—

Imperf.

☐☐ 611	2¢ **Harding,** 11/15/23, DC	100.00	175.00	—	—
☐☐	Pair	125.00	—	—	—
☐☐	Pair or Block with line	150.00	200.00	—	—
☐☐	Center line block	—	200.00	—	—
☐☐	Unofficial city	150.00	200.00	—	—

Perf. 10

☐☐ 612	2¢ **Harding,** 9/12/23, DC	110.00	175.00	—	—

1924

☐☐ 614	1¢ **Huguenot-Walloon,** 5/1/24, DC	27.50	50.00	—	—
☐☐	Albany, NY	27.50	50.00	—	—
☐☐	Allentown, PA	27.50	50.00	—	—
☐☐	Charleston, SC	27.50	50.00	—	—
☐☐	Jacksonville, FL	27.50	50.00	—	—
☐☐	Lancaster, PA	27.50	50.00	—	—
☐☐	Mayport, FL	27.50	50.00	—	—
☐☐	New Rochelle, NY	27.50	50.00	—	—
☐☐	New York, NY	27.50	50.00	—	—
☐☐	Philadelphia, PA	27.50	50.00	—	—
☐☐	Reading, PA	27.50	50.00	—	—
☐☐	Unofficial city	50.00	—	—	—
☐☐ 615	2¢ **Huguenot-Walloon,** 5/1/24, DC	35.00	60.00	—	—
☐☐	Albany, NY	35.00	60.00	—	—
☐☐	Allentown, PA	35.00	60.00	—	—
☐☐	Charleston, SC	35.00	60.00	—	—
☐☐	Jacksonville, FL	35.00	60.00	—	—
☐☐	Lancaster, PA	35.00	60.00	—	—
☐☐	Mayport, FL	35.00	60.00	—	—
☐☐	New Rochelle, NY	35.00	60.00	—	—
☐☐	New York, NY	35.00	60.00	—	—

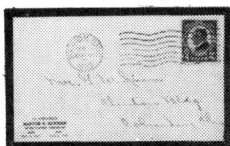
1st George W. Linn cachet

610, 611, 612

614

615

616

617

Scott Number	Description	Uncacheted Sgl	Blk	Cacheted Sgl	Blk
	Philadelphia, PA	35.00	60.00	—	—
	Reading, PA	35.00	60.00	—	—
	Unofficial city	70.00	—	—	—
616	5¢ **Huguenot-Walloon,** 5/1/24, DC	70.00	125.00	—	—
	Albany, NY	70.00	125.00	—	—
	Allentown, PA	70.00	125.00	—	—
	Charleston, SC	70.00	125.00	—	—
	Jacksonville, FL	70.00	125.00	—	—
	Lancaster, PA	70.00	125.00	—	—
	Mayport, FL	70.00	125.00	—	—
	New Rochelle, NY	70.00	125.00	—	—
	New York, NY	70.00	125.00	—	—
	Philadelphia, PA	70.00	125.00	—	—
	Reading, PA	70.00	125.00	—	—
	Unofficial City	150.00	—	—	—
	614 to 616, set of three on one cover, any Official city	140.00	375.00	—	—

1925

Scott Number	Description	Uncacheted Sgl	Blk	Cacheted Sgl	Blk
617	1¢ **Lexington-Concord,** 4/4/25, D.C.	27.50	50.00	—	—
	Boston, MA	27.50	50.00	100.00	—
	Cambridge, MA	27.50	50.00	100.00	—
	Concord, MA	27.50	50.00	100.00	—
	Concord Junction, MA	35.00	65.00	—	—
	Lexington, MA	35.00	65.00	100.00	—
	Unofficial city	60.00	—	—	—
	1st Guy Atwood Jackson cachet (on any value)	—	—	150.00	—
618	2¢ **Lexington-Concord,** 4/4/25, DC	35.00	65.00	—	—
	Boston, MA	35.00	65.00	100.00	—
	Cambridge, MA	35.00	65.00	100.00	—
	Concord, MA	35.00	65.00	100.00	—
	Concord Junction, MA	35.00	65.00	—	—
	Lexington, MA	50.00	65.00	100.00	—
	Unofficial city	70.00	—	—	—
619	5¢ **Lexington-Concord,** 4/4/25, DC	50.00	100.00	—	—
	Boston, MA	70.00	100.00	125.00	—
	Cambridge, MA	70.00	100.00	125.00	—
	Concord, MA	70.00	100.00	125.00	—
	Concord Junction, MA	70.00	100.00	—	—
	Lexington, MA	80.00	100.00	125.00	—
	Unofficial city	125.00	—	—	—
	617-19 Set on one cover, Concord Junc. or Lexington	175.00	450.00	—	—

1st Guy Atwood Jackson cachet

618

619

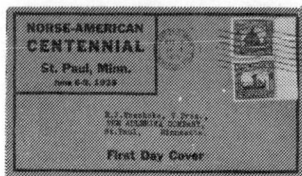

1st Ernest J. Weschcke cachet

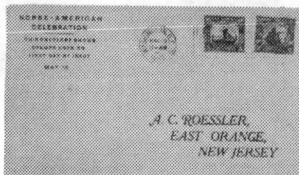

1st Albert C. Roessler cachet

620

621

622

623

Scott Number	Description	Uncacheted Sgl	Blk	Cacheted Sgl	Blk
	617-19 Set on one cover, any other Official city	130.00	325.00	—	—
	617-19 Set on one cover, Unofficial city	200.00	400.00	—	—
	551, 576, 585-7, 617-9 multiple on one cover	—	—	2000.	—
620	2¢ **Norse-American**, 5/18/25, DC	25.00	50.00	—	—
	Algona, IA	25.00	50.00	—	—
	Benson, MN	25.00	50.00	—	—
	Decorah, IA	25.00	50.00	—	—
	Minneapolis, MN	25.00	50.00	—	—
	Northfield, MN	25.00	50.00	—	—
	St. Paul, MN	25.00	50.00	—	—
	Unofficial city	50.00	—	—	—
621	5¢ **Norse-American**, 5/18/25, DC	45.00	65.00	—	—
	Algona, IA	45.00	65.00	—	—
	Benson, MN	45.00	65.00	—	—
	Decorah, IA	45.00	65.00	—	—
	Minneapolis, MN	45.00	65.00	—	—
	Northfield, MN	45.00	65.00	—	—
	St. Paul, MN	45.00	65.00	—	—
	Unofficial city	65.00	—	—	—
	620-21 Set on one cover, any city	70.00	125.00	200.00	—
	1st Ernest J. Weschcke cachet	—	—	275.00	—
	1st Albert C. Roessler cachet	—	—	300.00	—

1925-26

Scott Number	Description	Uncacheted Sgl	Blk	Cacheted Sgl	Blk
622	13¢ **Harrison**, 1/11/26, DC	35.00	65.00	—	—
	Indianapolis, IN	47.50	70.00	—	—
	North Bend, OH, Unofficial city (500)	250.00	400.00	—	—
	Other Unofficial city	325.00	—	—	—
623	17¢ **Wilson**, 12/28/25, DC	30.00	45.00	200.00	—
	New York, NY	30.00	45.00	200.00	—

1st Charles E. Nickles cachet   627   628

Scott Number	Description	Uncacheted Sgl	Blk	Cacheted Sgl	Blk
	Princeton, NJ	30.00	45.00	200.00	—
	Staunton, VA	30.00	45.00	200.00	—
	Bellefonte, PA, AMF Unofficial city	—	—	200.00	—
	Other unofficial city	50.00	—	—	—
	1st Charles E. Nickles cachet	—	—	400.00	—

1926

Scott Number	Description	Uncacheted Sgl	Blk	Cacheted Sgl	Blk
627	**2¢ Sesquicentennial,** 5/10/26, DC	14.00	20.00	80.00	—
	Boston, MA	14.00	20.00	80.00	—
	Philadelphia, PA	14.00	20.00	80.00	—
	Chester, PA, Unofficial city	—	—	40.00	—
	Valley Forge, PA, Unofficial city	20.00	—	60.00	—
	Other unofficial city	20.00	—	70.00	—
	1st Herbert H. Griffin cachet	—	—	150.00	—
	1st James H. Baxter cachet	—	—	70.00	—

Cacheted Sesquicentennial FDCs are most often found with Chester or Valley Forge unofficial cancels. Cacheted FDCs on this issue from official FDC cities are worth more than those from unofficial cities.

Scott Number	Description	Uncacheted Sgl	Blk	Cacheted Sgl	Blk
628	**5¢ Ericsson,** 5/29/26, DC	22.50	40.00	500.00	—
	Chicago, IL	22.50	40.00	500.00	—
	Minneapolis, MN	22.50	40.00	500.00	—
	New York, NY	22.50	40.00	500.00	—
	Unofficial city	40.00	—	—	—

The cacheted price given above is for a cachet of 2 crossed gold bars on a blue envelope. Any other cachet sells for one-quarter of the price listed.

Scott Number	Description	Uncacheted Sgl	Blk	Cacheted Sgl	Blk
629	**2¢ White Plains,** New York, NY, 10/18/26	6.25	15.00	50.00	—
	10/16/26 Predate	15.00	30.00	—	—
	New York, NY, International-Philatelic Exhibition Agency cancellation	6.25	15.00	50.00	—
	White Plains, NY (24,830)	6.25	15.00	50.00	—
	Washington, DC, 10/28/26	3.50	8.00	50.00	—
	Unofficial city	4.00	8.00	—	—
	1st Scott Stamp & Coin Co. cachet	—	—	60.00	—
630	**White Plains Sheet,** single or block from sheet	15.00	30.00	75.00	100.00
	Imprint strip of 10 (top or bottom)	—	100.00	—	—
	Full sheet (10/18/26)	1500.	—	—	—
	Full sheet, unofficial (10/18/26)	2000.	—	—	—
	Full sheet (10/28/26)	500.00	—	—	—
	Unofficial single	95.00	—	—	—

1926-34 *Imperf.*

Scott Number	Description	Uncacheted Sgl	Blk	Cacheted Sgl	Blk
631	**1½¢ Harding,** 8/27/26, DC	35.00	60.00	—	—

Cacheted prices are for covers with printed cachets. Covers with general purpose rubberstamp cachets sell at the uncacheted price. Rubberstamped Chamber of Commerce cachets sell for 1½ to 2 times the uncacheted price.

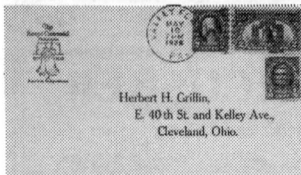

1st Herbert H. Griffin cachet

1st James H. Baxter cachet

1st Scott Stamp & Coin Co. cachet

629, 630

643

Scott Number	Description	Uncacheted Sgl	Blk	Cacheted Sgl	Blk
Perf. 11x10½					
☐☐ 632	1¢ Franklin, 6/10/27, DC	55.00	60.00	—	—
☐☐ 632a	1¢ Booklet, 11/2/27	800.00	—	—	—
☐☐ 633	1½¢ Harding, 5/17/27, DC	55.00	60.00	—	—
☐☐ 634	2¢ Washington, 12/10/26, DC	57.50	60.00	—	—
☐☐ 634A	2¢ Type 2, 12/20/28, Chicago, IL	700.00	—	—	—
☐☐ 635	3¢ Lincoln, 2/3/27, DC	47.50	75.00	—	—
☐☐ 635a	3¢ bright violet, 2/7/34, DC	22.50	35.00	35.00	—
☐☐ 636	4¢ Martha Washington, 5/17/27, DC	55.00	95.00	—	—
☐☐ 637	5¢ Roosevelt, 3/24/27, DC	55.00	95.00	—	—
☐☐ 638	6¢ Garfield, 7/27/27, DC	65.00	125.00	—	—
☐☐ 639	7¢ McKinley, 3/24/27, DC	67.50	125.00	—	—
☐☐	637, 639 on one cover	150.00	—	—	—
☐☐ 640	8¢ Grant, 6/10/27, DC	70.00	140.00	—	—
☐☐	632, 640 on one cover	150.00	—	—	—
☐☐ 641	9¢ Jefferson, 5/17/27, DC	85.00	150.00	—	—
☐☐	633, 636, 641 on one cover	250.00	—	—	—
☐☐ 642	10¢ Monroe, 2/3/27, DC	90.00	160.00	—	—
1927 Perf. 11					
☐☐ 643	2¢ Vermont, 8/3/27, DC	6.00	10.00	30.00	40.00
☐☐	Bennington, VT (50,000)	6.00	10.00	30.00	40.00
☐☐	Unofficial city	10.00	—	45.00	—
☐☐	1st Joshua R. Gerow Jr. cachet	—	—	175.00	—
☐☐	1st Haris R. Hunt cachet (643 or 644)	—	—	150.00	—
☐☐	1st Bradie Buchanan cachet	—	—	40.00	—
☐☐	1st S.S. Kurkjian cachet	—	—	250.00	—
☐☐ 644	2¢ Burgoyne, 8/3/27, DC	16.50	30.00	30.00	40.00
☐☐	Albany, NY	16.50	30.00	30.00	40.00
☐☐	Rome, NY	16.50	30.00	30.00	40.00
☐☐	Syracuse, NY	16.50	30.00	30.00	40.00
☐☐	Utica, NY	16.50	30.00	30.00	40.00
☐☐	Oriskany, NY, Unofficial city	40.00	—	—	—
☐☐	Schuylerville, NY, Unofficial city	—	—	175.00	—
☐☐	Other Unofficial cities	30.00	—	—	—

1st Joshua R. Gerow Jr. cachet

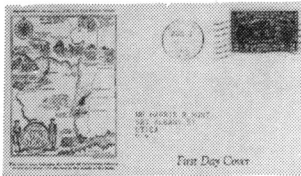

1st Haris R. Hunt cachet

1st Bradie Buchanan cachet

644

645

Scott Number	Description	Uncacheted Sgl	Blk	Cacheted Sgl	Blk
1928					
645	2¢ **Valley Forge,** 5/26/28, DC	5.00	10.00	40.00	50.00
	Cleveland, OH (town cancel)	100.00	175.00	150.00	—
	Lancaster, PA	5.00	10.00	40.00	50.00
	Norristown, PA (25,000)	5.00	10.00	40.00	50.00
	Philadelphia, PA	5.00	10.00	40.00	50.00
	Valley Forge, PA (70,000)	5.00	10.00	40.00	50.00
	West Chester, PA (15,000)	5.00	10.00	40.00	50.00
	Cleveland Midwestern Philatelic Sta. cancellation	5.00	10.00	40.00	50.00
	Other Unofficial city	10.00	—	50.00	—
	1st Joseph W. Stoutzenberg cachet	—	—	125.00	—
	1st Howard Davis Egolf cachet	—	—	100.00	—
	1st Adam K. Bert cachet	—	—	50.00	—
Perf. 11x10½					
646	2¢ **Molly Pitcher,** 10/20/28, DC	17.50	30.00	70.00	—
	Freehold, NJ (25,000)	17.50	30.00	70.00	—
	Red Bank, NJ	17.50	30.00	70.00	—
	Unofficial city	30.00	—	90.00	—
647	2¢ **Hawaii,** 8/13/28, DC	17.50	25.00	50.00	70.00
	Honolulu, HI	20.00	25.00	50.00	70.00
	Unofficial city	30.00	—	85.00	—
648	5¢ **Hawaii,** 8/13/28, DC	32.50	60.00	50.00	75.00
	Honolulu, HI	40.00	75.00	50.00	75.00
	Unofficial city	50.00	—	—	—
	647-48 set on one cover	60.00	75.00	125.00	—
Perf. 11					
649	2¢ **Aero Conf.,** 12/12/28, Green International Civil Aeronautic Conference slogan	10.00	15.00	30.00	40.00
	Black, Washington, DC, town cancel	15.00	25.00	30.00	40.00
	Unofficial city	20.00	—	—	—
650	5¢ **Aero Conf.,** 12/12/28, Green International Civil Aeronautic Conference slogan	15.00	25.00	30.00	40.00
	Black Washington, DC, town cancel	20.00	30.00	30.00	40.00
	Unofficial city	25.00	—	—	—
	Set on one cover, DC	27.50	—	—	—

1st Joseph W. Stoutzenberg cachet

1st Howard Davis Egolf cachet

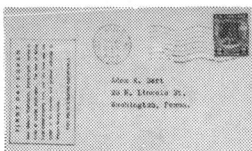

1st Adam K. Bert cachet

646

647

648

649

650

651

Scott Number	Description	Uncacheted Sgl	Uncacheted Blk	Cacheted Sgl	Cacheted Blk
1929					
651	2¢ **Clark,** Vincennes, IN, 2/25/29	7.50	10.00	25.00	35.00
	Unofficial city	15.00	—	30.00	—
	Washington, 2/26/29, first day of sale by Philatelic Agency	3.00	5.00	20.00	35.00
	Charlottesville, VA, 2/26/29	6.00	—	30.00	—
	1st Floyd D. Shockley cachet	—	—	25.00	—
	1st Harry C. Ioor cachet	—	—	150.00	—

Perf. 11x10½

653	½¢ **Hale,** 5/25/29, DC	—	30.00	—	—

Perf. 11

654	2¢ **Electric Light,** 6/5/29, Menlo Park, NJ (77,000)	13.00	13.00	25.00	30.00
	Orange, NJ, unofficial	—	—	30.00	—
	Other Unofficial city	—	—	30.00	35.00
	Washington, 6/6/29, first day of sale by Philatelic Agency	5.50	6.00	15.00	20.00
	1st Harry E. Klotzbach cachet	—	—	60.00	—

Perf. 11x10½

655	2¢ **Electric Light,** 6/11/29, DC	90.00	100.00	150.00	200.00

Perf. 10 Vertically

		Sgl	Pair	Sgl	Pair
656	2¢ **Electric Light,** 6/11/29, DC	100.00	125.00	175.00	200.00

1st Floyd D. Shockley cachet

1st Harry C. loor cachet

1st Harry E. Klotzbach cachet

653

654, 655, 656

657

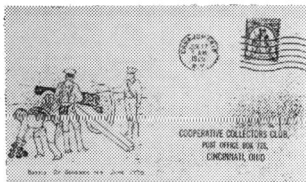

1st Robert C. Beazell cachet

1st A.C. Elliott cachet

Scott Number	Description	Uncacheted		Cacheted	
		Sgl	Pair	Sgl	Pair
☐☐ 656	Line pair	—	150.00	—	250.00
☐☐	655, 656 on one cover	175.00	—	300.00	—

Perf. 11

		Sgl	Blk	Sgl	Blk
☐☐ 657	2¢ **Sullivan,** Auburn, NY, 6/17/29 (5,000)	4.50	6.00	25.00	30.00
☐☐	Binghamton, NY (50,000)	4.50	6.00	25.00	30.00
☐☐	Canajoharie, NY (12,000)	4.50	6.00	25.00	30.00
☐☐	Canandaigua, NY	4.50	6.00	25.00	30.00
☐☐	Elmira, NY (11,000)	4.50	6.00	25.00	30.00
☐☐	Geneva, NY	4.50	6.00	25.00	30.00
☐☐	Geneseo, NY	4.50	6.00	25.00	30.00
☐☐	Horseheads, NY	4.50	6.00	25.00	30.00
☐☐	Owego, NY	4.50	6.00	25.00	30.00
☐☐	Penn Yan, NY	4.50	6.00	25.00	30.00
☐☐	Perry, NY	4.50	6.00	25.00	30.00
☐☐	Seneca Falls, NY (8,500)	4.50	6.00	25.00	30.00
☐☐	Waterloo, NY	4.50	6.00	25.00	30.00
☐☐	Watkins Glen, NY (6,500)	4.50	6.00	25.00	30.00
☐☐	Waverly, NY	4.50	6.00	25.00	30.00
☐☐	Loman, NY, Unofficial city	—	—	40.00	—
☐☐	Other Unofficial city	2.50	10.00	50.00	60.00
☐☐	Washington, DC, 6/18/29	2.50	5.00	20.00	25.00
☐☐	1st Robert C. Beazell cachet	—	—	300.00	—
☐☐	1st A.C. Elliott cachet	—	—	75.00	—

Cacheted prices are for covers with printed cachets. Covers with general purpose rubberstamp cachets sell at the uncacheted price. Rubberstamped Chamber of Commerce cachets sell for 1½ to 2 times the uncacheted price.

658, 668   669, 679

Kansas and Nebraska Overprints

The first day of sale for the complete series of 22 Kansas-Nebraska Overprints Scott 658 through 679 was May 1, 1929, at the Philatelic Agency in Washington, D.C.

There are also pre-May 1, 1929 (April), overprints canceled in 27 Kansas and 28 Nebraska towns. These are relatively scarce and command a price greater than the May 1, 1929, Washington, D.C., cancels.

Listed below are the earliest known cancels of these stamps at Kansas and Nebraska post offices in April 1929. Only a few of each are known to exist.

Scott Number			Description	Uncacheted Sgl	Blk	Cacheted Sgl	Blk
1929			**Regular Issues Kansas Overprints**				
☐☐	658	1¢	**Kansas,** 5/1/29, DC	27.50	—	—	—
			Newton, KS, 4/15/29	200.00	—	—	—
☐☐	659	1½¢	**Kansas,** 5/1/29, DC	27.50	—	—	—
☐☐			Colby, KS, 4/16/29	—	—	—	—
☐☐	660	2¢	**Kansas,** 5/1/29, DC	27.50	—	—	—
☐☐			Colby, KS, 4/16/29	—	—	—	—
☐☐			Dodge City, KS, 4/16/29	—	—	—	—
☐☐			Liberal, KS, 4/16/29	—	—	—	—
☐☐	661	3¢	**Kansas,** 5/1/29, DC	30.00	—	—	—
☐☐			Colby, KS, 4/16/29	—	—	—	—
☐☐	662	4¢	**Kansas,** 5/1/29, DC	32.50	—	—	—
☐☐			Colby, KS, 4/16/29	—	—	—	—
☐☐	663	5¢	**Kansas,** 5/1/29, DC	35.00	—	—	—
☐☐			Colby, KS, 4/16/29	—	—	—	—
☐☐	664	6¢	**Kansas,** 5/1/29, DC	42.50	—	—	—
☐☐			Newton, KS, 4/15/29	350.00	—	—	—
☐☐	665	7¢	**Kansas,** 5/1/29, DC	42.50	—	—	—
☐☐			Colby, KS, 4/16/29	—	—	—	—
☐☐	666	8¢	**Kansas,** 5/1/29, DC	80.00	—	—	—
☐☐			Newton, KS, 4/15/29	350.00	—	—	—
☐☐	667	9¢	**Kansas,** 5/1/29, DC	72.50	—	—	—
☐☐			Colby, KS, 4/16/29	—	—	—	—
☐☐	668	10¢	**Kansas,** 5/1/29, DC	85.00	—	—	—
☐☐			Colby, KS, 4/16/29	—	—	—	—
☐☐			658-668 set of 11 on one cover, DC, 5/1/29	800.00	—	—	—
☐☐			658, 664, 666, 4/15/29 Newton, KS	600.00	—	—	—

April canceled covers with Kansas overprint stamps are also known from Cape Henry, VA; Denver and Pueblo, CO; Kansas City, MO and Waynesboro, PA.

Nebraska Overprints

☐☐	669	1¢	**Nebraska,** 5/1/29, DC	27.50	—	—	—
☐☐			Beatrice, NE, 4/15/29	—	—	—	—
☐☐	670	1½¢	**Nebraska,** 5/1/29, DC	25.00	—	—	—
☐☐			Hartington, NE, 4/15/29	160.00	—	—	—
☐☐	671	2¢	**Nebraska,** 5/1/29, DC	25.00	—	—	—
☐☐			Auburn, NE, 4/15/29	—	—	—	—
☐☐			Beatrice, NE, 4/15/29	—	—	—	—
☐☐			Hartington, NE, 4/15/29	160.00	—	—	—
☐☐	672	3¢	**Nebraska,** 5/1/29, DC	32.50	—	—	—
☐☐			Beatrice, NE, 4/15/29	175.00	—	—	—
☐☐			Hartington, NE, 4/15/29	175.00	—	—	—

Scott Number	Description	Uncacheted Sgl	Blk	Cacheted Sgl	Blk
673	4¢ **Nebraska,** 5/1/29, DC	37.50	—	—	—
	Beatrice, NE, 4/15/29	175.00	—	—	—
	Hartington, NE, 4/15/29	175.00	—	—	—
674	5¢ **Nebraska,** 5/1/29, DC	37.50	—	75.00	—
	Beatrice, NE, 4/15/29	175.00	—	—	—
	Hartington, NE, 4/15/29	175.00	—	—	—
675	6¢ **Nebraska,** 5/1/29, DC	55.00	—	—	—
	Auburn, NE, 4/16/29	—	—	—	—
676	7¢ **Nebraska,** 5/1/29, DC	57.50	—	—	—
	Auburn, NE, 4/17/29	—	—	—	—
677	8¢ **Nebraska,** 5/1/29, DC	60.00	—	—	—
	Humbolt, NE, 4/17/29	—	—	—	—
	Pawnee City, NE, 4/17/29	—	—	—	—
678	9¢ **Nebraska,** 5/1/29, DC	62.50	—	—	—
	Cambridge, NE, 4/17/29	—	—	—	—
679	10¢ **Nebraska,** 5/1/29, DC	70.00	—	—	—
	Tecumseh, NE, 4/18/29	—	—	—	—
	669-679 set of 11 on one cover, DC, 5/1/29	850.00	—	—	—

April canceled covers with the Nebraska Overprint stamps are also known from Cleveland, OH; Kansas City, MO; and Washington, D.C. There also are 1¢ and 2¢ Nebraska overprints canceled April 6, 1929 (pre-date), from Syracuse, NE. Known and confirmed genuine by the Philatelic Foundation.

Perf. 11

Scott Number	Description	Uncacheted Sgl	Blk	Cacheted Sgl	Blk
680	2¢ **Fallen Timbers,** Erie, PA, 9/14/29	5.00	6.00	30.00	40.00
	Maumee, OH	5.00	6.00	30.00	40.00
	Perrysburg, OH	5.00	6.00	30.00	40.00
	Toledo, OH	5.00	6.00	30.00	40.00
	Waterville, OH (18,000)	5.00	6.00	30.00	40.00
	Fallen Timbers, PA	15.00	—	—	—
	Unofficial city	10.00	—	45.00	—
	Washington, DC, 9/16/29	5.00	6.00	20.00	25.00
681	2¢ **Ohio River,** Cairo, IL, 10/19/29	4.50	6.00	30.00	40.00
	Cincinnati, OH	4.50	6.00	30.00	40.00
	Evansville, IN (30,000)	4.50	6.00	30.00	40.00
	Homestead, PA (55,000)	4.50	6.00	30.00	40.00
	Louisville, KY	4.50	6.00	30.00	40.00
	Pittsburgh, PA (50,000)	4.50	6.00	30.00	40.00
	Wheeling, WV	4.50	6.00	30.00	40.00
	Unofficial city R.P.O.	6.00	—	40.00	—
	R.P.O. 10/18/29, pre-date	—	—	50.00	—
	Other Unofficial city	—	—	45.00	—
	Washington, DC, 10/21/29	4.50	6.00	20.00	25.00
	1st Delf Norona cachet	—	—	60.00	—

1930

Scott Number	Description	Uncacheted Sgl	Blk	Cacheted Sgl	Blk
682	2¢ **Massachusetts Bay Colony,** Boston, MA 4/8/30 (60,000)	5.25	6.00	30.00	40.00
	Salem, MA	5.25	6.00	30.00	40.00
	Unofficial city	9.00	—	45.00	55.00
	Washington, DC, 4/11/30	2.00	3.00	20.00	25.00
683	2¢ **Carolina-Charleston,** Charleston, SC, 4/10/30 (100,000)	5.50	7.00	30.00	40.00
	Unofficial city	9.00	—	—	—
	Washington, DC, 4/11/30	2.00	3.00	20.00	25.00
	682-683 on one cover, Washington, DC, 4/11/30	10.00	—	50.00	—

1st Delf Norona cachet

680

681

682

683

684, 686

685, 687

688

689

Scott Number	Description	Uncacheted Sgl	Blk	Cacheted Sgl	Blk

Perf. 11x10½

		Sgl	Blk	Sgl	Blk
☐☐ 684	1½¢ **Harding,** Marion, OH, 12/1/30	6.25	6.00	30.00	40.00
☐☐	Washington, DC, 12/2/30	2.50	4.00	25.00	30.00
☐☐ 685	4¢ **Taft,** Cincinnati, OH, 6/4/30	10.00	15.00	30.00	40.00
☐☐	Washington, DC, 6/5/30	4.00	7.00	25.00	30.00

Perf. 10 Vertically

		Pr	L.Pr.	Pr.	L.Pr.
☐☐ 686	1½¢ **Harding,** Marion, OH, 12/1/30	7.50	10.00	30.00	40.00
☐☐	Washington, DC, 12/2/30	3.00	4.00	25.00	30.00
☐☐	684, 686 on one cover, Marion, OH, 12/1/30	8.00	—	50.00	—
☐☐	684, 686 DC, 12/2/30	8.00	—	40.00	—
☐☐ 687	4¢ **Taft,** 9/18/30, DC	20.00	30.00	40.00	60.00

Perf. 11

		Sgl	Blk	Sgl	Blk
☐☐ 688	2¢ **Braddock,** Braddock, PA, 7/9/30 (50,000)	6.00	8.00	30.00	40.00
☐☐	Unofficial city	10.00	—	50.00	—
☐☐	Washington, DC 7/10/30	2.75	4.00	20.00	25.00
☐☐ 689	2¢ **Von Steuben,** New York, NY, 9/17/30	6.00	8.00	30.00	40.00
☐☐	Unofficial city	—	—	50.00	—
☐☐	Washington, DC, 9/18/30	2.75	4.00	20.00	25.00
☐☐	687, 689 DC Multiple	25.00	—	50.00	—

1931

		Sgl	Blk	Sgl	Blk
☐☐ 690	2¢ **Pulaski,** Brooklyn, NY, 1/16/31	5.00	6.00	30.00	35.00
☐☐	Buffalo, NY	5.00	6.00	30.00	35.00
☐☐	Chicago, IL	5.00	6.00	30.00	35.00
☐☐	Cleveland, OH	5.00	6.00	30.00	35.00
☐☐	Detroit, MI	5.00	6.00	30.00	35.00
☐☐	Gary, IN	5.00	6.00	30.00	35.00
☐☐	Milwaukee, WI	5.00	6.00	30.00	35.00
☐☐	New York, NY	5.00	6.00	30.00	35.00
☐☐	Pittsburgh, PA	5.00	6.00	30.00	35.00
☐☐	Savannah, GA	5.00	6.00	30.00	35.00

Prices for various cachet makers can be determined by using the Cachet Pricing Calculator found on pages 33 to 35.

1st Denys J. Truby cachet

690

Scott Number	Description	Uncacheted Sgl	Blk	Cacheted Sgl	Blk
□□	South Bend, IN	5.00	6.00	30.00	35.00
□□	Toledo, OH	5.00	6.00	30.00	35.00
□□	Unofficial city	10.00	—	50.00	—
□□	Washington, DC, 1/17/31	2.75	4.00	20.00	25.00
□□	1st Denys J. Truby cachet	—	—	70.00	—

Perf. 11x10½

□□ 692	11¢ **Hayes,** 9/4/31, DC	80.00	160.00	—	—
□□ 693	12¢ **Cleveland,** 8/25/31, DC	80.00	160.00	—	—
□□ 694	13¢ **Harrison,** 9/4/31, DC	85.00	175.00	—	—
□□	Woolrich, PA 9/4/31	600.00	—	—	—
□□ 695	14¢ **Indian,** 9/8/31, DC	83.00	175.00	—	—
□□ 696	15¢ **Liberty,** 8/27/31, DC	100.00	190.00	—	—

Perf. 10½x11

□□ 697	17¢ **Wilson,** 7/25/31, Brooklyn, NY	1750.	—	—	—
□□	Washington, DC, 7/27/31	325.00	650.00	—	—
□□ 698	20¢ **Golden Gate,** 9/18/31, DC	185.00	300.00	—	—
□□	Woolrich, PA, 9/4/31	250.00	—	—	—
□□ 699	25¢ **Niagara Falls,** 7/25/31, Brooklyn, NY	1750.	—	—	—
□□	Washington, DC, 7/27/31	350.00	700.00	—	—
□□	699 and 697 on one cover, Brooklyn, NY	3500.	—	—	—
□□ 700	30¢ **Bison,** 9/8/31, DC	275.00	500.00	—	—
□□ 701	50¢ **Arlington,** 9/4/31, DC	425.00	800.00	—	—
□□	Woolrich, PA, 9/4/31	900.00	—	—	—

1931

□□ 702	2¢ **Red Cross,** 5/21/31, DC	4.00	6.00	20.00	25.00
□□	Dansville, NY	4.00	6.00	20.00	25.00
□□	Unofficial city	6.00	—	40.00	—
□□	1st Edward G. Hacker cachet	—	—	150.00	—
□□ 703	2¢ **Yorktown,** 10/19/31, Wethersfield, CT	5.00	8.00	30.00	35.00
□□	Yorktown, VA	5.00	8.00	30.00	35.00
□□	Unofficial city	8.00	—	50.00	—
□□	1st Aero Print cachet	—	—	75.00	—
□□	1st Walter G. Crosby cachet	—	—	150.00	—
□□	1st Covered Wagon cachet	—	—	50.00	—
□□	Washington, DC, 10/20/31	3.00	4.00	20.00	30.00
□□	10/5/31 predate Wenatchee, WA (75) (AAMS #1146)	250.00	—	—	—
□□	Any predate Oct. 6 - Oct. 18	30.00	—	75.00	—

The POD experimented with a new stamp distribution method with the Yorktown stamp. This resulted in a number of pre-FDCs on this issue.

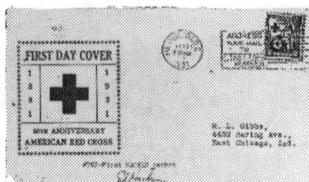

1st Edward G. Hacker cachet

1st Aero Print cachet

1st Covered Wagon cacnet

702

703

704

705

706

707

708

709

Scott Number	Description	Uncacheted Sgl	Blk	Cacheted Sgl	Blk

1932 Washington Bicentennial Issue

Scott Number	Description	Uncacheted Sgl	Blk	Cacheted Sgl	Blk
704	½¢ olive brown, 1/1/32, DC	5.00	8.00	15.00	18.00
705	1¢ green, 1/132, DC	5.50	10.00	15.00	18.00
706	1½¢ brown, 1/1/32, DC	5.50	10.00	15.00	18.00
707	2¢ carmine rose, 1/1/32, DC	5.50	10.00	15.00	18.00
708	3¢ deep violet, 1/1/32, DC	5.75	10.00	15.00	20.00
709	4¢ light brown, 1/1/32, DC	5.75	10.00	15.00	20.00
710	5¢ blue, 1/1/32, DC	6.00	12.00	15.00	20.00
711	6¢ red orange, 1/1/32, DC	6.75	12.00	15.00	20.00
712	7¢ black, 1/1/32, DC	6.75	12.00	15.00	20.00
713	8¢ olive bistre, 1/1/32, DC	6.75	12.00	15.00	20.00
714	9¢ pale red, 1/1/32, DC	7.75	15.00	15.00	20.00
715	10¢ orange yellow, 1/1/32, DC	10.00	12.00	15.00	20.00
	704 to 715, complete set of twelve on one cover, DC, 1/1/32	100.00	—	225.00	—
	1st Plimpton cachet (on any single)	—	—	25.00	—
	1st William T. Raley cachet (on any single)	—	—	30.00	—
	1st Frederick R. Rice cachet (on any single)	—	—	20.00	—

Add 100% for unofficial FD cancel on this issue.

1932

Scott Number	Description	Uncacheted Sgl	Blk	Cacheted Sgl	Blk
716	2¢ **Olympic Winter Games,** 1/25/32, Lake Placid, NY	7.50	7.50	15.00	20.00
	Unofficial city	—	—	20.00	—
	Washington, DC, 1/26/32	1.50	2.00	10.00	15.00
	1st Beverly Hills cachet	—	—	75.00	—

Cacheted prices are for covers with printed cachets. Covers with general purpose rubberstamp cachets sell at the uncacheted price. Rubberstamped Chamber of Commerce cachets sell for 1½ to 2 times the uncacheted price.

710

711

712

713

714

715

1st Frederick R. Rice cachet

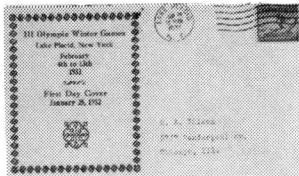
1st Beverly Hills cachet

1st Linprint cachet

716

717

718

Scott Number	Description	Uncacheted Sgl	Uncacheted Blk	Cacheted Sgl	Cacheted Blk
717	2¢ **Arbor Day,** 4/22/32, Nebraska City, NE	5.00	5.00	15.00	18.00
	Washington, DC, 4/23/32	1.50	2.00	7.00	10.00
	Adams, NY, 4/23/32	6.50	—	18.00	20.00
	1st Linprint cachet	—	—	15.00	—
718	3¢ **Olympic** Summer Games, 6/15/32, Los Angeles, CA	7.50	8.00	20.00	25.00
	Unofficial	—	—	30.00	—
	Washington, DC, 6/16/32	2.75	3.00	20.00	25.00
719	5¢ **Olympic** Summer Games, 6/15/32, Los Angeles, CA	9.50	10.00	20.00	25.00
	Unofficial	—	—	30.00	—
	Washington, DC, 6/16/32	2.75	3.00	20.00	25.00
	718-19 on one cover, Los Angeles, CA	16.00	20.00	25.00	30.00
	718-719 on one cover, DC	4.50	—	—	—
	718-19 on one cover, unofficial	—	—	35.00	—
720	3¢ **Washington,** 6/16/32, DC	10.00	12.00	25.00	35.00
720b	3¢ **Booklet pane,** 7/25/32, DC	100.00	—	125.00	—
720b	**Single**	30.00	—	40.00	—

Scott Number	Description	Sgl	Pr	Sgl	Pr
721	3¢ **Washington Coil,** Vertical, 6/24/32	20.00	25.00	35.00	40.00
722	3¢ **Washington Coil,** Horiz., 10/12/32	20.00	25.00	35.00	40.00
723	6¢ **Garfield Coil,** Vertical, 8/18/32, Los Angeles, CA	20.00	25.00	35.00	40.00
	Washington, DC, 8/19/32	6.00	8.00	20.00	25.00

Scott Number	Description	Sgl	Blk	Sgl	Blk
724	3¢ **William Penn,** 10/24/32, New Castle, DE	3.00	4.00	15.00	20.00
	Chester, PA	3.00	4.00	15.00	20.00
	Philadelphia, PA	3.00	4.00	15.00	20.00
	Unofficial city	—	—	30.00	—
	Washington, DC, 10/25/32	1.25	2.00	9.00	12.00
725	3¢ **Daniel Webster,** 10/24/32, Franklin, NH	3.00	4.00	15.00	20.00
	Exeter, NH	3.00	4.00	15.00	20.00
	Hanover, NH (70,000)	3.00	4.00	15.00	20.00

719

720, 720b, 721, 722

723

724

725

1st Anderson cachet

1st Henry Grimsland cachet

1st Brookhaven cachet

726

727, 752

728, 730, 766a

Scott Number	Description	Uncacheted Sgl	Uncacheted Blk	Cacheted Sgl	Cacheted Blk
	Marshfield, MA, unofficial	—	—	35.00	40.00
	Webster, MA, unofficial	—	—	40.00	—
	Any other unofficial city	—	—	30.00	—
725	Washington, DC, 10/25/32	1.25	2.00	9.00	12.00
	724-725 on one cover	5.00	8.00	25.00	—

1933

Scott Number	Description	Uncacheted Sgl	Uncacheted Blk	Cacheted Sgl	Cacheted Blk
726	3¢ **Gen. Oglethorpe,** 2/12/33, Savannah, GA (200,000)	3.00	4.00	15.00	20.00
	Any Georgia town, 2/13/33	3.00	—	9.00	12.00
	Washington, DC, 2/13/33	1.25	2.00	9.00	12.00
	1st Anderson cachet	—	—	150.00	—

Because 2/12/33 was a Sunday, second day Scott 726 FDCs were serviced.

Scott Number	Description	Uncacheted Sgl	Uncacheted Blk	Cacheted Sgl	Cacheted Blk
727	3¢ **Peace Proclamation,** 4/19/33, Newburgh, NY (349,571)	3.50	5.00	15.00	25.00
	Washington, DC, 4/20/33	1.20	2.00	9.00	12.00
	Unofficial city	—	—	30.00	—
	1st Henry Grimsland cachet	—	—	400.00	—
	1st Brookhaven cachet	—	—	75.00	—
728	1¢ **Century of Progress,** 5/25/33, Chicago, IL	3.00	4.00	12.00	15.00
	Chicago Ridge fancy cancel	10.00	12.00	40.00	60.00
	Any other unofficial	—	—	20.00	—
	Washington, DC, 5/26/33	1.00	2.00	9.00	12.00
729	3¢ **Century of Progress,** 5/25/33, Chicago, IL	3.00	4.00	12.00	15.00
	Chicago Ridge fancy cancel	10.00	12.00	40.00	60.00
	Any other unofficial	—	—	20.00	—
	Washington, DC, 5/26/33	1.00	2.00	9.00	12.00
	728, 729 on one cover	6.50	10.00	25.00	35.00

Total FDCs mailed May 25 - 232,251

729, 731, 767a

734

733, 735,
753, 768a

732

1st Albert B. Parsons cachet

Scott Number	Description	Uncacheted Sgl	Blk	Cacheted Sgl	Blk
☐☐ 730	1¢ **Am. Philatelic Society,** Sheet of 25, 8/25/33, Chicago, IL	120.00	—	175.00	—.
☐☐ 730a	1¢ **Am. Philatelic Soc., Imperf.,** 8/25/33, Chicago, IL	3.25	4.00	12.00	15.00
☐☐	Washington, DC, 8/28/33	1.25	2.00	9.00	12.00
☐☐ 731	3¢ **Am. Philatelic Soc.,** sheet of 25, 8/25/33, Chicago, IL	120.00		175.00	
☐☐ 731a	3¢ **A.P.S., single, imperf.,** Chicago, IL, 8/25/33	3.25	5.00	12.00	15.00
☐☐	Washington, DC, 8/28/33	1.25	2.00	9.00	12.00
☐☐	730a, 731a on one cover	5.50	9.00	20.00	30.00

Total FDCs mailed Aug. 25 - 65,218

☐☐ 732	3¢ **Nat'l Recovery Admin.,** 8/15/53, DC (65,000)	3.25	6.00	15.00	20.00
☐☐	Nira, IA, 8/17/33 (unofficial)	2.50	5.00	20.00	25.00
☐☐ 733	3¢ **Byrd Antarctic,** 10/9/33, DC	6.00	12.00	15.00	20.00
☐☐	1st Albert B. Parsons cachet	—	—	75.00	—
☐☐ 734	5¢ **Kosciuszko,** 10/13/33, Boston, MA (23,025)	5.50	8.00	15.00	20.00
☐☐	Buffalo, NY (14,981)	7.00	10.00	15.00	20.00
☐☐	Chicago, IL (26,306)	5.50	8.00	15.00	20.00
☐☐	Detroit, MI (17,792)	6.50	10.00	15.00	20.00
☐☐	Pittsburgh, PA (6,282)	37.50	48.00	60.00	70.00
☐☐	Kosciuszko, MS (27,093)	6.50	8.00	15.00	20.00
☐☐	St. Louis, MO (17,872)	6.50	10.00	15.00	20.00
☐☐	Washington, DC, 10/14/33	3.00	4.00	15.00	20.00
☐☐	Any unofficial	10.00	12.00	40.00	50.00

1934

☐☐ 735	3¢ **National Exhibition,** sheet of 6, Byrd Imperf., 2/10/34, New York, NY	55.00		60.00	
☐☐	**Washington, DC, 2/19/34**	27.50	—	—	—
☐☐ 735a	3¢ **National Exhibition,** single imperf., New York, NY, 2/10/34 (450,715)	6.00	8.00	15.00	20.00
☐☐	Washington, DC, 2/19/34	2.75	4.00	10.00	15.00
☐☐ 736	3¢ **Maryland Tercentenary,** 3/23/34, St. Mary's City, MD (148,785)	1.60	4.00	9.00	12.00
☐☐	Washington, DC, 3/24/34	.60	1.00	6.00	10.00
☐☐	1st Torkel Gundel cachet	—	—	150.00	—
☐☐	1st Top-Notch cachet	—	—	30.00	—
☐☐	1st Donald Kapner cachet	—	—	25.00	—
☐☐	1st Louis G. Nix cachet	—	—	50.00	—

Perf. 11x10½

☐☐ 737	3¢ **Mothers of America,** 5/2/34, any city	1.60	4.00	10.00	12.00

Perf. 11

☐☐ 738	3¢ **Mothers of America,** 5/2/34, any city	1.60	4.00	9.00	12.00
☐☐	737-738 Both printings on one cover	4.00	10.00	30.00	—

FDCs mailed at Washington May 2 total 183,359

1st Torkel Gundel cachet

1st Top-Notch cachet

1st Donald Kapner cachet

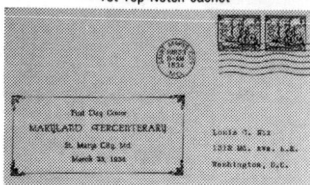
1st Louis G. Nix cachet

736

737, 738, 754

739, 755

740, 751, 756, 769a

741, 757

742, 750, 758, 770a

Scott Number	Description	Uncacheted Sgl	Uncacheted Blk	Cacheted Sgl	Cacheted Blk
739	3¢ **Wisconsin,** 7/7/34, Green Bay, WI (130,000)	1.60	4.00	12.00	15.00
	Washington, DC, July 9	.75	1.00	5.00	8.00
740	1¢ **Parks - Yosemite,** 7/16/34, Yosemite, CA (60,000)	2.75	4.00	8.00	10.00
	Washington, DC (26,219)	2.25	3.75	7.00	10.00
741	2¢ **Parks - Grand Canyon,** 7/24/34, Grand Canyon, AZ (75,000)	2.75	4.00	8.00	10.00
	Washington, DC (30,080)	2.25	3.75	7.00	10.00
742	3¢ **Parks - Mt. Rainier,** 8/3/34, Longmire, WA (64,500)	3.00	4.00	8.00	10.00
	Washington, DC (30,114)	2.50	3.75	7.00	10.00
743	4¢ **Parks - Mesa, Verde,** 9/25/34, Mesa Verde, CO (51,882)	3.50	5.00	8.00	10.00
	Washington, DC (21,729)	3.25	4.00	7.00	10.00
744	5¢ **Parks - Yellowstone,** 7/30/34, Yellowstone, WY (87,000)	3.50	5.00	8.00	10.00
	Washington, DC (32,150)	3.25	4.00	7.00	10.00
745	6¢ **Parks - Crater Lake,** 9/5/34, Crater Lake, OR (45,282)	4.25	6.00	8.00	10.00
	Washington, DC (19,161)	4.00	5.00	7.00	10.00
746	7¢ **Parks - Acadia,** 10/2/34, Bar Harbor, ME (51,312)	4.25	6.00	8.00	10.00
	Washington, DC (20,163)	4.00	5.00	7.00	10.00
747	8¢ **Parks - Zion,** 9/18/34, Zion, UT (43,650)	4.75	6.00	8.00	10.00
	Washington, DC (19,001)	4.25	5.00	7.00	10.00

743, 759

745, 761

747, 763

744, 760

1st Imperial cachet

746, 762

748, 764

749, 765

Scott Number	Description	Uncacheted Sgl	Blk	Cacheted Sgl	Blk
☐☐ 748	9¢ **Parks - Glacier Park,** 8/27/34, Glacier Park, MT (52,626)	4.75	7.00	8.00	10.00
☐☐	1st Imperial cachet	—	—	45.00	—
☐☐	Washington, DC (16,250)	4.50	6.00	7.00	10.00
☐☐ 749	10¢ **Parks - Smoky Mountains,** 10/8/34, Sevierville, TN (39,000)	11.00	11.00	15.00	18.00
☐☐	Washington, DC (18,368)	10.00	10.00	11.00	12.00
☐☐	Smokemont, TN, unofficial	—	—	20.00	—
☐☐	740-49 National Parks set complete, with Park cancels	—	—	100.00	115.00

Imperf.

☐☐ 750	3¢ **American Philatelic Society,** sheet of 6, 8/28/34, Atlantic City, NJ	55.00		60.00	
☐☐ 750a	3¢ **A.P.S., single,** 8/28/34, Atlantic City, NJ (40,000)	6.25	10.00	9.00	12.00
☐☐	Washington, DC, 9/4/34	4.00	6.00	8.00	10.00
☐☐ 751	1¢ **Trans-Mississippi Philatelic Expo.,** sheet of 6, 10/10/34, Omaha, NE	40.00		60.00	
☐☐ 751a	1¢ **Trans-Mississippi Phil. Expo., single,** 10/10/34, Omaha, NE, (125,000)	4.50	8.00	8.00	10.00
☐☐	Washington, DC, 10/15/34	2.00	3.00	6.00	8.00

1934 Special Printing (Farley's)

Nos. 752 to 771 inclusive issued 3/15/35

☐☐ 752	3¢ **Peace Commemoration,** DC	10.00	18.00	20.00	30.00
☐☐ 753	3¢ **Byrd,** DC	12.00	20.00	20.00	30.00
☐☐ 754	3¢ **Mothers of America,** DC	12.00	20.00	20.00	30.00
☐☐ 755	3¢ **Wisconsin Tercentenary,** DC	12.00	20.00	20.00	30.00
☐☐ 756	1¢ **Parks - Yosemite,** DC	12.00	20.00	20.00	30.00
☐☐ 757	2¢ **Parks - Grand Canyon,** DC	12.00	20.00	20.00	30.00
☐☐ 758	3¢ **Parks - Mount Rainier,** DC	13.00	20.00	20.00	30.00
☐☐ 759	4¢ **Parks - Mesa Verde,** DC	13.00	20.00	20.00	30.00

772

774

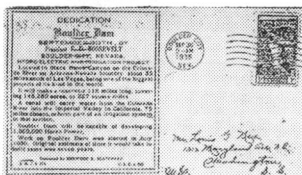
773

1st Winfred Milton Grandy cachet

1st William H. Espenshade cachet

1st Norwood B. Scatchard cachet

775

Scott Number	Description	Uncacheted Sgl	Uncacheted Blk	Cacheted Sgl	Cacheted Blk
760	5¢ Parks - Yellowstone, DC	13.00	20.00	20.00	30.00
761	6¢ Parks - Crater Lake, DC	13.00	22.00	20.00	30.00
762	7¢ Parks - Acadia, DC	13.00	22.00	20.00	30.00
763	8¢ Parks - Zion, DC	15.00	24.00	20.00	30.00
764	9¢ Parks - Glacier Park, DC	15.00	25.00	20.00	30.00
765	10¢ Parks - Smoky Mountains, DC	15.00	25.00	25.00	35.00
766a	1¢ Century of Progress, DC	11.00	15.00	20.00	30.00
766a	pane of 6		250.00		
767a	3¢ Century of Progress, DC	11.00	15.00	20.00	30.00
767a	pane of 6	—	250.00		
768a	3¢ Byrd, DC	13.00	18.00	20.00	30.00
768a	pane of 6	—	250.00		
769a	1¢ Parks - Yosemite, DC	8.00	11.00	20.00	30.00
769a	pane of 6	—	250.00		
770a	3¢ Parks - Mount Rainier, DC	10.00	15.00	20.00	30.00
770a	pane of 6	—	250.00		
771	16¢ Air Mail - special delivery, DC	25.00	30.00	35.00	45.00

Scott Number	Description	Cacheted Sgl	Blk	Pl Blk
772	3¢ Connecticut Tercentenary, 4/26/35, Hartford, CT (217,800)	11.00	12.00	18.00
	Washington, DC, 4/27/35	1.50	2.00	3.00
	1st Winfred Milton Grandy cachet	30.00	—	—
773	3¢ California Exposition, 5/29/35, San Diego, CA (214,042)	11.00	12.00	18.00
	Washington, DC, May 31	1.50	2.00	3.00
	1st William H. Espenshade cachet	40.00	—	—
774	3¢ Boulder Dam, 9/30/35, Boulder City, NV (166,180)	15.00	18.00	25.00
	Washington, DC, 10/1/35	2.25	3.00	4.00
	1st Norwood B. Scatchard cachet	60.00	—	—

776

777

778

1st John C. Sidenius cachet

1st Walter Czubay cachet

1st J. W. Clifford cachet

1st House of Farnam cachet

Scott Number	Description	Sgl	Cacheted Blk	Pl Blk
775	3¢ **Michigan Centenary,** 11/1/35, Lansing, MI (176,962)	11.00	12.00	18.00
	Washington, DC, 11/2/35	1.50	2.00	3.00
	1st Risko Art Studio cachet	75.00	—	—

1936

776	3¢ **Texas Centennial,** 3/2/36, Gonzales, TX (319,150)	15.00	18.00	20.00
	Washington, DC, 3/3/36	1.50	2.00	3.00
	1st John C. Sidenius cachet	50.00	—	—
	1st Walter Czubay cachet	60.00	—	—
777	3¢ **Rhode Island Tercentenary,** 5/4/36, Providence, RI (245,400)	10.00	12.00	18.00
	Washington, DC, 5/5/36	1.50	2.00	3.00
	1st J. W. Clifford cachet	30.00	—	—
778	**TIPEX souvenir sheet,** 5/9/36 (297,194) New York, NY (TIPEX cancellation)	20.00		
	Washington, DC, 5/11/36	3.50		
	1st House of Farnam cachet	500.00		
778a-d	Single from sheet	6.00		
782	3¢ **Arkansas Centennial,** 6/15/36, Little Rock, AR (376,693)	10.00	12.00	18.00
	Washington, DC, 6/16/36	1.25	2.00	3.00
783	3¢ **Oregon Territory Centennial,** 7/14/36, Astoria, OR (91,110)	10.00	12.00	18.00
	Daniel, WY (67,013)	10.00	12.00	18.00
	Lewiston, ID (86,100)	9.00	11.00	18.00
	Missoula, MT (59,883)	10.00	12.00	18.00
	Walla Walla, WA (106,150)	9.00	12.00	18.00

782

783

784

1st Historic Art cachet

785

786

787

788

789

790

791

792

793

794

Scott Number	Description	Sgl	Cacheted Blk	Pl Blk
	Washington, DC, 7/15/36	1.50	2.00	3.00
784	3¢ **Susan B. Anthony**, 8/26/36 DC (178,500)	20.00	22.00	25.00
	1st Historic Art cachet	35.00	—	—

1936-37

Scott Number	Description	Sgl	Cacheted Blk	Pl Blk
785	1¢ **Army**, 12/15/36, DC	6.00	8.00	15.00
786	2¢ **Army**, 1/15/37	6.00	8.00	15.00
787	3¢ **Army**, 2/18/37, DC	6.00	8.00	15.00
	1st William J. Von Ohlen cachet	60.00	—	—
788	4¢ **Army**, 3/23/37, DC	6.75	8.00	15.00
789	5¢ **Army**, 5/26/37, West Point, NY (160,000)	8.00	10.00	16.00
	Washington, DC, 5/27/37	1.50	2.00	3.00
	785-789 on one cover	25.00	—	—
790	1¢ **Navy**, 12/15/36, DC	6.00	8.00	15.00
791	2¢ **Navy**, 1/15/37, DC	6.00	8.00	15.00
792	3¢ **Navy**, 2/18/37, DC	6.00	8.00	15.00
793	4¢ **Navy**, 3/23/37, DC	6.75	8.00	15.00

FDCs postmarked in unofficial cities sell for 50% to 100% more than catalogue value.

1st Cachet Craft cachet

1st Pilgrim cachet

1st Fidelity Stamp Co. cachet

795

796

798

797

799

Scott Number	Description	Sgl	Cacheted Blk	Pl Blk
794	5¢ Navy, 5/26/37, Annapolis, MD (202,806)	8.00	10.00	16.00
	Washington, DC, 5/27/37	1.50	2.00	3.00
	790-794 on one cover	25.00	—	—
	785-794 on one cover	60.00	—	—

Covers for both 1¢ values total 390,749; 2¢ values total 292,570; 3¢ values total 320,888; 4¢ values total 331,000.

1937

Scott Number	Description	Sgl	Blk	Pl Blk
795	3¢ Ordinance of 1787, 7/13/37, Marietta, OH (130,531)	8.50	10.00	15.00
	New York, NY (125,134)	8.50	10.00	15.00
	Washington, DC. 7/14/37	1.35	2.00	3.00
	1st William S. Linto cachet	75.00	—	—
	1st Cachet Craft cachet	75.00	—	—
796	5¢ Virginia Dare, 8/18/37, Manteo, NC (226,730)	10.00	12.00	20.00
	Washington, DC, 8/19/37	2.00	3.00	4.00
	Dare, VA, unofficial	15.00	—	—
797	10¢ Souvenir Sheet, 8/26/37, Asheville, NC (164,215)	10.00	—	—
	Washington, DC, 8/28/37	2.00	—	—
798	3¢ Constitution, 9/17/37, Philadelphia, PA (281,478)	8.50	10.00	15.00
	Washington, DC, 9/18/37	1.50	2.00	3.00
	1st Pilgrim cachet	100.00	—	—
	1st Fidelity Stamp Co. cachet	10.00	—	—
799	3¢ Hawaii, 10/18/37, Honolulu, HI (320,334)	9.50	12.00	18.00
	Washington, DC, 10/19/37	1.50	2.00	3.00
800	3¢ Alaska, 11/12/37, Juneau, AK (230,370)	9.50	12.00	18.00
	Washington, DC, 11/13/37	1.50	2.00	3.00
801	3¢ Puerto Rico, 11/25/37, San Juan, PR (244,054)	9.50	12.00	18.00
	Washington, DC, 11/26/37	1.50	2.00	3.00

800   801   802

Scott Number	Description	Sgl	Cacheted Blk	Pl Blk
802	3¢ **Virgin Islands**, 12/15/37, Charlotte Amalie, VI (225,469)	9.50	12.00	18.00
	Washington, DC, 12/16/37	1.50	2.00	3.00

1938 Presidential Issue

			Sgl	Blk	Pl Blk
803	½¢ **Franklin**, 5/19/38, Philadelphia, PA (224,901)	—	1.25	3.00
	Washington, DC, 5/20/38	—	1.00	1.25
804	1¢ **Washington**, 4/25/38, DC (124,037)	2.00	2.50	6.00
804b	1¢ booklet pane, 1/27/39, DC	20.00	—	—
805	1½¢ **Martha Washington**, 5/5/38, DC (128,339)	2.00	2.50	6.00
806	2¢ **Adams**, 6/3/38, DC (127,806)	2.00	2.50	6.00
806b	2¢ booklet pane, 1/27/39, DC	20.00	—	—
807	3¢ **Jefferson**, 6/16/38, DC (118,097)	2.00	2.50	6.00
807a	3¢ booklet pane, 1/27/39, DC	24.00	—	—
	804b, 806b, 807a on one cover, 1/27/38, DC	60.00	—	—
808	4¢ **Madison**, 7/1/38 (118,765), DC	2.00	2.50	6.00
809	4½¢ **White House**, 7/11/38, DC (115,820)	2.50	3.00	8.00
810	5¢ **Monroe**, 7/21/38, DC (98,282)	2.25	3.00	8.00
811	6¢ **Adams**, 7/28/38, DC (97,428)	2.25	3.00	8.00
812	7¢ **Jackson**, 8/4/38, DC (98,414)	2.50	3.00	8.00
813	8¢ **Van Buren**, 8/11/38, DC (94,857)	2.50	3.00	8.00
814	9¢ **Harrison**, 8/18/38, DC (91,229)	2.65	3.50	8.00
815	10¢ **Tyler**, 9/2/38, DC (84,707)	2.75	3.50	8.00
816	11¢ **Polk**, 9/8/38, DC (63,966)	2.75	3.50	8.00
817	12¢ **Taylor**, 9/14/38, DC (62,935)	3.00	4.00	8.00
818	13¢ **Fillmore**, 9/22/38, DC (58,965)	3.00	4.00	8.00
819	14¢ **Pierce**, 10/6/38, DC (49,819)	3.25	4.00	10.00
820	15¢ **Buchanan**, 10/13/38, DC (52,209)	3.25	4.00	10.00
821	16¢ **Lincoln**, 10/20/38, DC (59,566)	3.50	5.00	10.00
822	17¢ **Johnson**, 10/27/38, DC (55,024)	3.75	5.00	10.00
823	18¢ **Grant**, 11/3/38, DC (53,124)	4.25	5.00	10.00
824	19¢ **Hayes**, 11/10/38, DC (54,124)	4.25	5.00	10.00
825	20¢ **Garfield**, 11/10/38, DC (51,971)	4.50	6.00	10.00
826	21¢ **Arthur**, 11/22/38, DC (44,367)	5.00	6.00	10.00
827	22¢ **Cleveland**, 11/22/38, DC (44,358)	5.25	6.00	10.00
828	24¢ **Harrison**, 12/2/38, DC (46,592)	5.25	6.00	10.00
829	25¢ **McKinley**, 12/2/38, DC (45,691)	6.50	8.00	10.00
830	30¢ **Roosevelt**, 12/8/38, DC (43,528)	10.00	12.00	25.00
831	50¢ **Taft**, 12/8/38, DC (41,984)	20.00	25.00	50.00
832	$1 **Wilson**, 8/29/38, DC (24,618)	55.00	60.00	75.00
832c	$1 **Wilson**, 8/31/54, DC (20,202)	30.00	40.00	50.00
833	$2 **Harding**, 9/29/38, DC (19,895)	125.00	150.00	250.00
834	$5 **Coolidge**, 11/17/38, DC (15,615)	200.00	275.00	400.00
	824,825 on one cover	35.00	—	—
	826,827 on one cover	35.00	—	—
	828,829 on one cover	40.00	—	—
	830,831 on one cover	40.00	—	—

These covers must have sheet selvage electric eye markings attached to stamps.

Prices for various cachet makers can be determined by using the Cachet Pricing Calculator found on pages 33 to 35.

804, 839, 848   815, 847

Scott Number	Description	Sgl	Cacheted Blk	Pl Blk
1938-42	**Presidential Electric Eye Issues**			
☐☐ **803**	½¢ Franklin, 9/8/41, DC	15.00	18.00	20.00
☐☐ **804**	1¢ Washington, 9/8/41, DC	15.00	18.00	20.00
22,000 covers for Scott 803, 804, and E15 Electric Eye				
☐☐ **805**	1½¢ Martha Washington, 1/16/41	15.00	18.00	20.00
Less than 10,000				
☐☐ **806**	2¢ Adams, 6/3/38, DC, Type I	15.00	18.00	30.00
☐☐ **806**	2¢ Adams, 4/5/39, DC, Type II	15.00	18.00	20.00
☐☐ **807**	3¢ Jefferson, 4/5/39, DC	15.00	18.00	30.00
28,500 covers for Scott 806 and 807 Electric Eye				
☐☐ **808**	4¢ Madison, 10/28/41, DC	15.00	18.00	30.00
☐☐ **809**	4½¢ White House, 10/28/41, DC	15.00	18.00	30.00
☐☐ **810**	5¢ Monroe, 10/28/41, DC	15.00	18.00	30.00
☐☐ **811**	6¢ Adams, 9/25/41, DC	15.00	18.00	30.00
☐☐ **812**	7¢ Jackson, 10/28/41, DC	15.00	18.00	30.00
☐☐ **813**	8¢ Van Buren, 10/28/41, DC	15.00	18.00	30.00
☐☐ **814**	9¢ Harrison, 10/28/41, DC	15.00	18.00	30.00
☐☐ **815**	10¢ Tyler, 9/25/41, DC	15.00	18.00	30.00
Covers of Scott 811 and 815 equal 7300				
☐☐ **816**	11¢ Polk, 10/8/41, DC	15.00	18.00	30.00
☐☐ **817**	12¢ Taylor, 10/8/41, DC	15.00	18.00	30.00
☐☐ **818**	13¢ Fillmore, 10/8/41, DC	15.00	18.00	30.00
☐☐ **819**	14¢ Pierce, 10/8/41, DC	15.00	18.00	30.00
☐☐ **820**	15¢ Buchanan, 10/8/41, DC	15.00	18.00	30.00
☐☐ **821**	16¢ Lincoln, 1/7/42, DC	20.00	25.00	40.00
☐☐ **822**	17¢ Johnson, 10/28/41, DC	20.00	25.00	40.00
16,200 covers of Scott 808-10 and 812-14, 822				
☐☐ **823**	18¢ Grant, 1/7/42, DC	20.00	25.00	40.00
☐☐ **824**	19¢ Hayes, 1/7/42, DC	20.00	25.00	40.00
☐☐ **825**	20¢ Garfield, 1/7/42, DC	20.00	25.00	40.00
☐☐ **826**	21¢ Arthur, 1/7/42, DC	20.00	25.00	40.00
☐☐ **827**	22¢ Cleveland, 1/28/42, DC	20.00	25.00	40.00
☐☐ **828**	24¢ Harrison, 1/28/42, DC	20.00	25.00	40.00
☐☐ **829**	25¢ McKinley, 1/28/42, DC	20.00	25.00	40.00
☐☐ **830**	30¢ Theodore Roosevelt, 1/28/42, DC	20.00	25.00	40.00
☐☐ **831**	50¢ Taft, 1/28/42, DC	20.00	25.00	40.00
Covers of Scott 827-31 equal 6700				
☐☐	803, 804, E15 on one cover	20.00	40.00	—
☐☐	806, 807 on one cover	12.00	25.00	—
☐☐	808-810, 812-814, 822 on one cover	60.00	85.00	—
☐☐	811, 815 on one cover	40.00	60.00	—
☐☐	816-820 on one cover	50.00	70.00	—
☐☐	821, 823-826 on one cover	60.00	85.00	—
☐☐	824-825 on one cover	60.00	85.00	—
☐☐	827-831 on one cover	60.00	85.00	—
1938				
☐☐ **835**	3¢ Constitution, 6/21/38, Phila., PA (232,873)	9.00	10.00	15.00
☐☐	Washington, DC, 6/16/38	1.50	2.00	3.00

835   836   837   838

1st Artcraft cachet   852   853   854

Scott Number	Description	Sgl	Cacheted Blk	Pl Blk
□□ 836	3¢ **Swedes and Finns,** 6/27/38, Wilmington, DE (225,617)	8.50	10.00	15.00
□□	Washington, DC, 6/28/38	1.50	2.00	3.00
□□ 837	3¢ **Northwest Sesqui.** 7/15/38, Marietta, OH (180,170)	8.50	10.00	15.00
□□	Washington, DC, 7/16/38	1.50	2.00	3.00
□□ 838	3¢ **Iowa,** 8/24/38, Des Moines, IA (209,860)	8.50	10.00	15.00
□□	Washington, DC, 8/25/38	1.50	2.00	3.00

1939 Coil Stamps *Perf. 10 Vertically*

		Sgl	Pr.	L.Pr.
□□ 839	1¢ 1/20/39, DC	—	7.00	10.00
□□ 840	1½¢ 1/20/39, DC	—	7.00	10.00
□□ 841	2¢ 1/20/39, DC	—	7.00	11.00
□□ 842	3¢ 1/20/39, DC	7.00	8.00	12.00
□□ 843	4¢ 1/20/39, DC	7.00	10.00	12.50
□□ 844	4½¢ 1/20/39, DC	7.00	10.00	12.50
□□ 845	5¢ 1/20/39, DC	7.00	11.00	14.00
□□ 846	6¢ 1/20/39, DC	10.00	16.00	17.00
□□ 847	10¢ 1/20/39, DC	12.00	22.00	25.00
□□	839 to 847 set of 9 on one cover, 1/20/39	40.00	125.00	175.00

Perf. 10 Horizontally

□□ 848	1¢ 1/27/39, DC	—	7.00	10.00
□□ 849	1½¢ 1/27/39, DC	—	9.00	10.00
□□ 850	2¢ 1/27/39, DC	—	11.00	12.00
□□ 851	3¢ 1/27/39, DC	6.00	13.50	15.00
□□	848-851 set of 4 on one cover, 1/27/39	24.00	55.00	65.00

1939

		Sgl	Blk	Pl Blk
□□ 852	3¢ **Golden Gate Expo.,** 2/18/39, San Francisco, CA (352,165)	7.50	9.00	14.00
□□ 853	3¢ **N.Y. World's Fair,** 4/1/39, New York, NY (585,565)	10.00	12.00	15.00
□□	1st Artcraft cachet	175.00	250.00	400.00
□□	1st Artcraft cachet, Unofficial city	500.00	—	—
□□ 854	3¢ **Washington Inauguration,** 4/30/39, New York, NY (395,644)	7.50	9.00	10.00
□□ 855	3¢ **Baseball Centennial,** 6/12/39, Cooperstown, NY (398,199)	25.00	26.00	30.00
□□ 856	3¢ **Panama Canal,** 8/15/39, USS Charleston, (230,974)	7.50	9.00	10.00

Uncacheted FDCs in this period sell for 10% of cacheted FDC prices.

855

856

858

857

859

864

869

874

879

884

889

Scott Number	Description	Sgl	Cacheted Blk	Pl Blk
☐☐ 857	3¢ **Printing Tercentenary,** 9/25/39, New York, NY (295,370)	7.50	9.00	10.00
☐☐ 858	3¢ **50th Statehood Anniversary,** Bismarck, ND, 11/2/39			
	(139,905)	7.00	9.00	10.00
☐☐	Pierre, SD, 11/2/39 (139,905)	7.00	9.00	10.00
☐☐	Helena, MT, 11/8/39 (130,273)	7.00	9.00	10.00
☐☐	Olympia, WA, 11/11/39 (150,429)	7.00	9.00	10.00

1940 Famous Americans

Scott Number	Description	Sgl	Cacheted Blk	Pl Blk
☐☐ 859	1¢ **Washington Irving,** 1/29/40, Tarrytown, NY (170,969)	2.00	3.00	4.00
☐☐ 860	2¢ **James Fenimore Cooper,** 1/29/40, Cooperstown, NY			
	(154,836)	2.00	3.00	4.00
☐☐ 861	3¢ **Ralph Waldo Emerson,** 2/5/40, Boston, MA (185,148)	2.00	3.00	4.00
☐☐ 862	5¢ **Louisa May Alcott,** 2/5/40, Concord, MA (134,325)	5.00	6.00	10.00
☐☐ 863	10¢ **Samuel L. Clemens,** 2/13/40, Hannibal, MO (150,492)	8.25	10.00	15.00
☐☐ 864	1¢ **Henry W. Longfellow,** 2/16/40, Portland, ME (160,508)	2.00	3.00	4.00
☐☐ 865	2¢ **John Greenleaf Whittier,** 2/16/40, Haverhill, MA			
	(148,423)	2.00	3.00	4.00
☐☐ 866	3¢ **James Russell Lowell,** 2/20/40, Cambridge, MA			
	(148,735)	2.00	3.00	4.00
☐☐ 867	5¢ **Walt Whitman,** 2/20/40, Camden, NJ (134,185)	4.50	6.00	10.00
☐☐ 868	10¢ **James Whitcomb Riley,** 2/24/40, Greenfield, IN			
	(131,760)	8.25	10.00	15.00
☐☐ 869	1¢ **Horace Mann,** 3/14/40, Boston, MA (186,854)	2.00	3.00	4.00
☐☐ 870	2¢ **Mark Hopkins,** 3/14/40, Williamstown, MA (140,286)	2.00	3.00	4.00
☐☐ 871	3¢ **Charles W. Eliot,** 3/28/40, Cambridge, MA (155,708)	2.00	3.00	4.00
☐☐ 872	5¢ **Frances E. Willard,** 3/28/40, Evanston, IL (140,483)	4.75	6.00	10.00
☐☐ 873	10¢ **Booker T. Washington,** 4/7/40, Tuskegee Institute, AL			
	(163,507)	8.25	10.00	15.00
☐ 874	1¢ **John James Audubon,** 4/8/40, St. Francisville, LA			
	(144,123)	2.00	3.00	4.00

1st Aristocrats cachet

1st Spartan cachet

894

896

895

897

898

899

900

Scott Number	Description	Sgl	Cacheted Blk	Pl Blk
875	2¢ **Dr. Crawford W. Long**, 4/8/40, Jefferson, GA (158,128)	2.00	3.00	4.00
876	3¢ **Luther Burbank**, 4/17/40, Santa Rosa, CA (147,033)	2.75	3.00	4.00
877	5¢ **Dr. Walter Reed**, 4/17/40, DC (154,464)	4.50	6.00	10.00
878	10¢ **Jane Addams**, 4/26/40, Chicago, IL (132,375)	8.25	10.00	15.00
879	1¢ **Stephen Collins Foster**, 5/3/40, Bardstown, KY (183,461)	2.00	3.00	4.00
880	2¢ **John Philip Sousa**, 5/3/40, DC (131,422)	2.00	3.00	4.00
881	3¢ **Victor Herbert**, 5/13/40, New York, NY (168,200)	2.00	3.00	4.00
882	5¢ **Edward A. MacDowell**, 5/13/40, Peterborough, NH (135,155)	4.50	6.00	10.00
883	10¢ **Ethelbert Nevin**, 6/10/40, Pittsburgh, PA (121,951)	7.75	10.00	15.00
884	1¢ **Gilbert Charles Stuart**, 9/5/40, Narragansett, RI (131,965)	2.00	3.00	4.00
885	2¢ **James A. McNeill Whistler**, 9/5/40, Lowell, MA (130,962)	2.00	3.00	4.00
886	3¢ **Augustus Saint-Gaudens**, 9/16/40, New York, NY (138,200)	2.00	3.00	4.00
887	5¢ **Daniel Chester French**, 9/16/40, Stockbridge, MA (124,608)	4.00	6.00	10.00
888	10¢ **Frederic Remington**, 9/30/40, Canton, NY (116,219)	7.75	10.00	15.00
889	1¢ **Eli Whitney**, 10/7/40, Savannah, GA (140,868)	2.00	3.00	4.00
890	2¢ **Samuel F.B. Morse**, 10/7/40, New York, NY (135,388)	2.00	3.00	4.00
891	3¢ **Cyrus Hall McCormick**, 10/14/40, Lexington, VA (137,415)	2.00	3.00	4.00
892	5¢ **Elias Howe**, 10/14/40, Spencer, MA (126,334)	5.00	6.00	10.00
893	10¢ **Alexander Graham Bell**, 10/28/40, Boston, MA (125,372)	13.50	20.00	35.00

1940

894	3¢ **Pony Express**, 4/3/40, St. Joseph, MO (194,589)	7.00	8.00	10.00
	Sacramento, CA (160,849)	7.00	8.00	10.00
	1st Aristocrats cachet	25.00	—	—
895	3¢ **Pan American Union**, 4/14/40 (182,401) DC	5.25	7.00	8.00
896	3¢ **Idaho Statehood**, 7/3/40, Boise, ID (156,429)	5.25	7.00	8.00
897	3¢ **Wyoming Statehood**, 7/10/40, Cheyenne, WY (156,709)	5.25	7.00	8.00
	1st Spartan cachet	30.00	—	—
898	3¢ **Coronado Expedition**, 9/7/40, Albuquerque, NM (161,012)	5.25	7.00	8.00
899	1¢ **Defense**, 10/16/40, DC	5.00	6.00	8.00
900	2¢ **Defense**, 10/16/40, DC	5.00	6.00	8.00

901

903

1st Fleetwood cachet

902

904

905

906

907

908

909

910

Scott Number	Description	Sgl	Cacheted Blk	Pl Blk
901	3¢ **Defense**, 10/16/40, DC	5.00	6.00	8.00
	899 to 901 on one cover (450,083)	15.00	18.00	20.00
902	3¢ **Thirteenth Amendment**, 10/20/40, World's Fair, NY (156,146)	6.00	8.00	12.00

1941

903	3¢ **Vermont Statehood**, 3/4/41, Montpelier, VT (182,423)	5.50	7.00	10.00
	1st Dorothy Knapp cachet	600.00	—	—
	1st Fleetwood cachet	80.00	—	—

1942

904	3¢ **Kentucky Statehood**, 6/1/42, Frankfort, KY (155,730)	5.00	7.00	10.00
	1st Signed Fleetwood cachet	50.00	—	—
905	3¢ **"Win the War"**, 7/4/42 DC (191,168)	4.75	6.00	9.00
906	5¢ **Chinese Commemorative**, 7/7/42, Denver, CO (168,746)	7.00	10.00	18.00

1943

907	2¢ **United Nations**, 1/14/43, DC (178,865)	4.25	6.00	8.00
908	1¢ **Four Freedoms**, 2/12/43, DC (193,800)	4.25	6.00	8.00
909	5¢ **Poland**, 6/22/43, Chicago, IL (88,170)	7.00	12.00	20.00
	Washington, DC (136,002)	5.75	8.00	15.00
	1st Smartcraft cachet	20.00	—	—
	1st Pent Arts cachet	25.00	—	—
910	5¢ **Czechoslovakia**, 7/12/'43, DC (145,112)	5.50	8.00	10.00
911	5¢ **Norway**, 7/27/43, DC (130,054)	5.00	8.00	10.00
912	5¢ **Luxembourg**, 8/10/43, DC (166,367)	5.00	8.00	10.00
913	5¢ **Netherlands**, 8/24/43, DC (148,763)	5.00	8.00	10.00
914	5¢ **Belgium**, 9/14/43, DC (154,220)	5.00	8.00	10.00
915	5¢ **France**, 9/28/43, DC (163,478)	5.00	8.00	10.00

Prices for various cachet makers can be determined by using the Cachet Pricing Calculator found on pages 33 to 35.

1st Smartcraft cachet   1st Pent Arts cachet

916   921   922

923   924   925

Scott Number	Description	Sgl	Cacheted Blk	Pl Blk
916	**5¢ Greece,** 10/12/43, DC (166,553)	5.00	8.00	10.00
917	**5¢ Yugoslavia,** 10/26/43, DC (161,835)	5.00	8.00	10.00
918	**5¢ Albania,** 11/9/43, DC (162,275)	5.00	8.00	10.00
919	**5¢ Austria,** 11/23/43, DC (172,285)	5.00	8.00	10.00
920	**5¢ Denmark,** 12/7/43, DC (173,784)	5.00	8.00	10.00
	909-920 on one cover	50.00	—	—

1944

Scott Number	Description	Sgl	Blk	Pl Blk
921	**5¢ Korea,** 11/2/44, DC (192,860)	6.50	9.00	15.00
	909-921 on one cover	60.00	—	—
922	**3¢ Railroad,** 5/10/44, Ogden, UT (151,324)	6.75	8.00	12.00
	Omaha, NE (171,000)	6.75	8.00	12.00
	San Francisco, CA (125,000)	6.75	8.00	12.00
923	**3¢ Steamship,** 5/22/44, Kings Point, NY (152,324)	4.50	6.00	8.00
	Savannah, GA (181,472)	4.50	6.00	8.00
924	**3¢ Telegraph,** 5/24/44, DC (141,907)	4.00	5.00	8.00
	Baltimore, MD (136,480)	4.00	5.00	8.00
925	**3¢ Philippines,** 9/27/44 (214,865), DC	4.00	5.00	8.00
926	**3¢ Motion Picture,** 10/31/44, Hollywood, CA (190,660)	4.00	5.00	8.00
	New York, NY (176,473)	4.00	5.00	8.00

1945

Scott Number	Description	Sgl	Blk	Pl Blk
927	**3¢ Florida,** 3/3/45, Tallahassee, FL (228,435)	4.00	5.00	8.00
928	**5¢ United Nations Conf.,** 4/25/45, San Francisco, CA (417,450)	4.00	5.00	8.00
929	**3¢ Iwo Jima,** 7/11/45, (391,650), DC	6.00	7.00	9.00

1945-1946

Scott Number	Description	Sgl	Blk	Pl Blk
930	**1¢ Roosevelt,** 7/26/45, Hyde Park, NY (390,219)	3.00	4.00	6.00
	1st Bi-Color Craft cachet	20.00	—	—
931	**2¢ Roosevelt,** 8/24/45, Warm Springs, GA (426,142)	3.00	4.00	6.00

926

927

928

930

929

1st Bi-Color Craft cachet

1st Fluegel Cover cachet

934

937

935

936

938

Scott Number	Description	Sgl	Cacheted Blk	Pl Blk
932	3¢ **Roosevelt,** 6/27/45, DC (391,650)	3.00	4.00	6.00
	1st Fluegel Cover cachet	60.00	—	—
933	5¢ **Roosevelt,** 1/30/46, DC (466,766)	4.00	4.50	6.00
	930-933 on one cover	12.00	—	—
934	3¢ **Army,** 9/28/45, DC (392,300)	4.00	5.00	6.00
935	3¢ **Navy,** 10/27/45, Annapolis, MD (460,352)	4.00	5.00	6.00
936	3¢ **Coast Guard,** 11/19/45, New York, NY (405,280)	4.00	5.00	6.00
937	3¢ **Alfred E. Smith,** 11/26/45, New York, NY (424,950)	4.00	5.00	6.00
938	3¢ **Texas,** 12/29/45, Austin, TX (397,860)	5.00	6.00	8.00

1946

939	3¢ **Merchant Marine,** 2/26/46, DC (432,141)	3.00	4.00	6.00
	Armed Forces combo 929, 934-6, 939, 2/26/46	8.00	—	—
940	3¢ **Honorable Discharge,** 5/9/46,DC (492,786)	3.00	4.00	6.00
	1st Artmaster cachet	12.00	—	—
	1st WCO cachet	20.00	—	—
	Armed Forces combo 929, 934-6, 939-40, 5/9/46	20.00	—	—
941	3¢ **Tennessee,** 6/1/46, Nashville, TN (463,512)	3.00	4.00	6.00
942	3¢ **Iowa,** 8/3/46, Iowa City, IA (517,505)	3.00	4.00	5.00
943	3¢ **Smithsonian,** 8/10/46, DC (402,448)	3.00	4.00	5.00
944	3¢ **Santa Fe,** 10/16/46, Santa Fe, NM (384,300)	3.00	4.00	5.00

939

940

941

942

1st Artmaster cachet

1st WCO cachet

943

944

946

945

947

948

949

950

951

Scott Number	Description	Sgl	Cacheted Blk	Pl Blk
1947				
☐☐ 945	3¢ **Thomas A. Edison,** 2/11/47, Milan, OH (632,473)	3.00	4.00	5.00
☐☐ 946	3¢ **Joseph Pulitzer,** 4/10/47, New York, NY (580,870)	3.00	4.00	5.00
☐☐ 947	3¢ **Stamp Centenary,** 5/17/47, New York, NY (712,873)	3.00	4.00	5.00
☐☐	1st Fulton cachet	25.00	—	—
☐☐ 948	5¢ **and 10¢ Centenary Exhibition Sheet,** 5/19/47, New York, NY (502,175)	5.00	—	—
☐☐ 949	3¢ **Doctors,** 6/9/47, Atlantic City, NJ (508,016)	2.00	3.00	4.00
☐☐ 950	3¢ **Utah,** 7/24/47, Salt Lake City, UT (456,416)	2.00	3.00	4.00
☐☐ 951	3¢ **"Constitution",** 10/21/47, Boston, MA (683,416)	2.00	3.00	4.00
☐☐	1st C. W. George cachet	40.00	—	—
☐☐ 952	3¢ **Everglades Park,** 12/5/47, Florida City, FL	2.00	3.00	4.00

FDCs postmarked in unofficial cities sell for 50% to 100% more than catalogue value.

1st Fulton cachet

1st C. W. George cachet

952

953

1st Jackson cachet

954

955

956

957

958

959

Scott Number	Description	Sgl	Cacheted Blk	Pl Blk
1948				
☐☐ 953	3¢ **Carver**, 1/5/48, Tuskegee Institute, AL (402,179)	2.00	3.00	4.00
☐☐	1st Ira Bennett cachet	50.00	—	—
☐☐	1st Jackson cachet	40.00	—	—
☐☐ 954	3¢ **California Gold**, 1/24/48, Coloma, CA (526,154)	2.00	3.00	4.00
☐☐ 955	3¢ **Mississippi Territory**, 4/7/48, Natchez, MS (434,804)	2.00	3.00	4.00
☐☐ 956	3¢ **Four Chaplains**, 5/28/48, DC (459,070)	2.00	3.00	4.00
☐☐ 957	3¢ **Wisconsin Centennial**, 5/29/48, Madison, WI (470,280)	2.00	3.00	4.00
☐☐ 958	5¢ **Swedish Pioneers**, 6/4/48, Chicago, IL (364,318)	2.00	3.00	4.00
☐☐ 959	3¢ **Women's Progress**, 7/19/48, Seneca, Falls, NY (401,923)	2.00	3.00	4.00
☐☐ 960	3¢ **William Allen White**, 7/31/48, Emporia, KS (385,648)	2.00	3.00	4.00
☐☐ 961	3¢ **U.S.-Canada Friendship**, 8/2/48, Niagara Falls, NY (406,467)	2.00	3.00	4.00
☐☐ 962	3¢ **Francis Scott Key**, 8/9/48, Frederick, MD (505,930)	2.00	3.00	4.00
☐☐ 963	3¢ **Salute to Youth**, 8/11/48, DC (347.070)	2.00	3.00	4.00
☐☐ 964	3¢ **Oregon Territory Establishment**, 8/14/48, Oregon City, OR (365,898)	2.00	3.00	4.00
☐☐ 965	3¢ **Harlan Fiske Stone**, 8/25/48, Chesterfield, NH (362,170)	2.00	3.00	4.00
☐☐ 966	3¢ **Palomar Observatory**, 8/30/48, Palomar Mountain, CA (401,365)	2.00	3.00	4.00
☐☐ 967	3¢ **Clara Barton**, 9/7/48, Oxford, MA (362,000)	1.50	2.00	3.00

960

961

962

963

964

965

966

967

968

969

970

971

972

973

974

Scott Number	Description	Cacheted		
		Sgl	Blk	Pl Blk
968	3¢ **Poultry Industry,** 9/9/48, New Haven, CT (475,000)	1.50	2.00	3.00
969	3¢ **Gold Star Mothers,** 9/21/48, DC (386,064)	2.00	3.00	4.00
970	3¢ **Fort Kearny,** 9/22/48, Minden, NE (429,633)	2.00	3.00	4.00
971	3¢ **Volunteer Firemen,** 10/4/48, Dover, DE (399,630)	2.00	3.00	4.00
972	3¢ **Indian Centennial,** 10/15/48, Muskogee, OK (459,528)	1.50	2.00	3.00
973	3¢ **Rough Riders,** 10/27/48, Prescott, AZ (399,198)	1.50	2.00	3.00
974	3¢ **Juliette Low,** 10/29/48, Savannah, GA (476,573)	1.50	2.00	3.00
975	3¢ **Will Rogers,** 11/4/48, Claremore, OK (450,350)	1.50	2.00	3.00
	1st Kolor Kover cachet	100.00	—	—
976	3¢ **Fort Bliss,** 11/5/48, El Paso, TX (421,000)	1.50	2.00	3.00
977	3¢ **Moina Michael,** 11/9/48, Athens, GA (374,090)	1.50	2.00	3.00
978	3¢ **Gettysburg Address,** 11/19/48, Gettysburg, PA (511,990)	1.50	2.00	3.00
979	3¢ **Am. Turners Soc.,** 11/20/48, Cincinnati, OH (434,090)	1.50	2.00	3.00
980	3¢ **Joel Chandler Harris,** 12/9/48, Eatonton, GA (426,199)	1.50	2.00	3.00

1949

981	3¢ **Minnesota Territory,** 3/3/49, St. Paul, MN (458,750)	1.50	2.00	3.00
982	3¢ **Washington and Lee Univ.,** 4/12/49, Lexington, VA (447,910)	1.50	2.00	3.00

975

976

977

978

979

980

981

982

983

984

986

985

987

988

989

Scott Number	Description	Sgl	Cacheted Blk	Pl Blk
☐☐ 983	3¢ **Puerto Rico Election,** 4/27/49, San Juan, PR (390,416)	1.50	2.00	3.00
☐☐ 984	3¢ **Annapolis,** 5/23/49, Annapolis, MD (441,802)	1.50	2.00	3.00
☐☐ 985	3¢ **G.A.R.,** 8/29/49, Indianapolis, IN (471,696)	1.50	2.00	3.00
☐☐ 986	3¢ **Edgar Allan Poe,** 10/7/49, Richmond, VA (371,020)	1.50	2.00	3.00

1950

Scott Number	Description	Sgl	Blk	Pl Blk
☐☐ 987	3¢ **Am. Bankers Assoc.,** 1/3/50, Saratoga Springs, NY (388,622)	1.50	2.00	3.00
☐☐ 988	3¢ **Samuel Gompers,** 1/27/50, DC (332,023)	1.50	2.00	3.00
☐☐ 989	3¢ **Nat. Capital Sesqui. (Freedom),** 4/20/50, DC (371,743)	1.50	2.00	3.00
☐☐ 990	3¢ **Nat. Capital Sesqui. (Executive),** 6/12/50, DC (376,789)	1.50	2.00	3.00
☐☐ 991	3¢ **Nat. Capital Sesqui. (Judicial),** 8/2/50, DC (324,007)	1.50	2.00	3.00
☐☐ 992	3¢ **Nat. Capital Sesqui. (Legislative),** 11/22/50, DC (352,215)	1.50	2.00	3.00
☐☐ 993	3¢ **Railroad Engineers,** 4/29/50, Jackson, TN (420,830)	1.50	2.00	3.00
☐☐ 994	3¢ **Kansas City Centenary,** 6/3/50, KS City, MO (405,390)	1.50	2.00	3.00
☐☐ 995	3¢ **Boy Scouts,** 6/30/50, Valley Forge, PA (622,972)	2.25	3.00	4.00
☐☐ 996	3¢ **Indiana Ter. Sesqui.,** 7/4/50, Vincennes, IN (359,643)	1.50	2.00	3.00
☐☐ 997	3¢ **California Statehood,** 9/9/50, Sacramento, CA (391,919)	1.50	2.00	3.00

Prices for various cachet makers can be determined by using the Cachet Pricing Calculator found on pages 33 to 35.

990

991

992

993

994

995

996

997

998

999

1000

1001

1002

1003

1004

Scott Number	Description	Sgl	Cacheted Blk	Pl Blk
1951				
☐☐ 998	3¢ **United Confederate Veterans,** 5/30/51, Norfolk, VA (374,235)	1.50	2.00	3.00
☐☐ 999	3¢ **Nevada Centennial,** 7/14/51, Genoa, NV (336,890)	1.50	2.00	3.00
☐☐ 1000	3¢ **Landing of Cadillac,** 7/24/51, Detroit, MI (323,094)	1.50	2.00	3.00
☐☐ 1001	3¢ **Colorado Statehood,** 8/1/51, Minturn, CO (311,568)	1.50	2.00	3.00
☐☐ 1002	3¢ **Am. Chemical Soc.,** 9/4/51, New York, NY (436,419)	1.50	2.00	3.00
☐☐ 1003	3¢ **Battle of Brooklyn,** 12/10/51, Brooklyn, NY (420,000)	1.50	2.00	3.00
☐☐	1st Velvatone cachet	40.00	—	—
1952				
☐☐ 1004	3¢ **Betsy Ross,** 1/2/52, Philadelphia, PA (314,312)	1.50	2.00	3.00
☐☐	1st Knoble/Bogert cachet	70.00	—	—
☐☐ 1005	3¢ **4-H Clubs,** 1/15/52, Springfield, OH (383,290)	1.50	2.00	3.00
☐☐ 1006	3¢ **B. & O. Railroad,** 2/28/52, Baltimore, MD (441,600)	2.00	3.00	4.00
☐☐ 1007	3¢ **Am. Automobile Assoc.,** 3/4/52, Chicago, IL (520,123)	1.25	1.50	3.00
☐☐ 1008	3¢ **NATO,** 4/4/52, DC (313,518)	1.25	1.50	3.00
☐☐ 1009	3¢ **Grand Coulee Dam,** 5/15/52, Grand Coulee, WA (341,680)	1.25	1.50	3.00
☐☐ 1010	3¢ **Lafayette,** 6/13/52, Georgetown, SC (349,102)	1.25	1.50	3.00

1st Velvatone cachet

1005

1006

1007

1008

1009

1011

1010

1012

1013

1014

1015

1016

1017

Scott Number	Description	Sgl	Cacheted Blk	Pl Blk
☐☐ 1011	3¢ **Mt. Rushmore Mem.,** 8/11/52, Keystone, SC (337,027)	1.25	1.50	3.00
☐☐ 1012	3¢ **Civil Engineers,** 9/6/52, Chicago, IL (318,483)	1.25	1.50	3.00
☐☐ 1013	3¢ **Service Women,** 9/11/52, Washington, DC (308,062)	1.25	1.50	3.00
☐☐ 1014	3¢ **Gutenberg Bible,** 9/30/52, DC (387,078)	1.25	1.50	3.00
☐☐ 1015	3¢ **Newspaper Boys,** 10/4/52, Philadelphia, PA (626,000)	1.25	1.50	3.00
☐☐ 1016	3¢ **Red Cross,** 11/21/52, New York, NY (439,252)	1.25	1.50	3.00

1953

☐☐ 1017	3¢ **National Guard,** 2/23/53, DC (387,618)	1.25	1.50	3.00
☐☐ 1018	3¢ **Ohio Sesquicentennial,** 3/2/53, Chillicothe, OH (407,983)	1.25	1.50	3.00
☐☐	1st Boerger cachet	25.00	—	—
☐☐ 1019	3¢ **Washington Territory,** 3/2/53, Olympia, WA (344,047)	1.25	1.50	3.00
☐☐ 1020	3¢ **Louisiana Purchase,** 4/30/53, St. Louis, MO (425,600)	1.25	1.50	3.00
☐☐ 1021	5¢ **Opening of Japan,** 7/14/53, DC (320,541)	1.25	1.50	3.00
☐☐	1st Overseas Mailers cachet	60.00	—	—
☐☐ 1022	3¢ **American Bar Assoc.,** 8/24/53, Boston, MA (410,036)	1.25	1.50	3.00
☐☐ 1023	3¢ **Sagamore Hill,** 9/14/53, Oyster Bay, NY (379,750)	1.25	1.50	3.00
☐☐ 1024	3¢ **Future Farmers,** 10/13/53, Kansas City, MO (424,193)	1.25	1.50	3.00

1st Boerger cachet

1st Overseas Mailers cachet

1018

1019

1020

1021

1022

1023

1024

1025

1026

1027

1028

1029

Scott Number	Description	Sgl	Cacheted Blk	Pl Blk
☐☐ 1025	3¢ **Trucking Industry,** 10/27/53, Los Angeles, CA (875,021)	1.25	1.50	3.00
☐☐ 1026	3¢ **Gen. G.S. Patton, Jr.,** 11/11/53, Fort Knox, KY (342,600)	1.25	1.50	3.00
☐☐ 1027	3¢ **New York City,** 11/20/53, New York, NY (387,914)	1.25	1.50	3.00
☐☐ 1028	3¢ **Gadsden Purchase,** 12/30/53, Tucson, AZ (363,250)	1.25	1.50	3.00

1954

☐☐ 1029	3¢ **Columbia University,** 1/4/54, New York, NY (550,745)	1.25	1.50	3.00

1954-68   Liberty Issue

☐☐ 1030	½¢ **Franklin,** 10/20/55, DC (223,122)		1.00	1.50
☐☐ 1031	1¢ **Washington,** 8/26/54, Chicago, IL (272,581)	1.00	1.50	2.00
☐☐ 1031A	1¼¢ **Palace,** 6/17/60, Santa Fe, NM	1.00	1.50	2.00
Total for Scott 1031A and 1054A - 501,848				
☐☐	1031A and 1054A on one cover	1.50	—	—
☐☐ 1032	1½¢ **Mount Vernon,** 2/22/56, Mount Vernon, VA (270,109)	1.00	1.50	2.00
☐☐ 1033	2¢ **Jefferson,** 9/15/54, San Francisco, CA (307,300)	1.00	1.50	2.00

1031, 1054   1033, 1055   1036, 1058   1060

1061   1062

1st Cascade cachet

1063   1065   1066

Scott Number	Description	Sgl	Cacheted Blk	Pl Blk
☐☐ 1034	2½¢ **Bunker Hill,** 6/17/59, Boston, MA (315,060)	1.00	1.50	2.00
☐☐ 1035	3¢ **Statue of Liberty,** 6/24/54, Albany, NY (340,001)	1.00	1.50	2.00
☐☐ 1035a	3¢ **Statue of Liberty,** Booklet Pane, 6/30/54	8.00	—	
☐☐ 1035b	3¢ **Statue of Liberty,** Luminescent, 7/6/66, DC	20.00	—	—
☐☐ 1036	4¢ **Lincoln,** 11/19/54, New York, NY (374,064)	1.00	1.50	2.00
☐☐ 1036a	4¢ **Lincoln,** Booklet Pane, 7/31/58, Wheeling, WV (135,825)	7.00	—	
☐☐ 1036b	4¢ **Lincoln,** Luminescent, 11/2/63, DC (500)	85.00	—	—
☐☐ 1037	4½¢ **Hermitage,** 3/16/59, Hermitage, TN (320,000)	1.00	1.50	2.00
☐☐ 1038	5¢ **Monroe,** 12/2/54, Fredericksburg, VA (255,650)	1.00	1.50	2.00
☐☐ 1039	6¢ **Roosevelt,** 11/18/55, New York, NY (257,551)	1.00	1.50	2.00
☐☐ 1040	7¢ **Wilson,** 1/10/56, Staunton, VA, (200,111)	1.00	1.50	2.00
☐☐ 1041	8¢ **Statue of Liberty,** 4/9/54, DC (340,077)	1.00	1.50	2.00
☐☐ 1042	8¢ **Statue of Liberty,** (Giori press), 3/22/58, Cleveland, OH, (223,899)	1.25	1.50	3.00
☐☐	1st Cascade cachet	25.00	—	
☐☐ 1042A	8¢ **Pershing,** 11/17/61, New York, NY (321,031)	1.25	1.50	3.00
☐☐ 1043	9¢ **The Alamo,** 6/14/56, San Antonio, TX (207,086)	1.50	1.50	3.00
☐☐ 1044	10¢ **Independence Hall,** 7/4/56, Phila., PA, (220,930)	1.25	1.50	3.00
☐☐ 1044b	10¢ **Independence Hall,** Luminescent, 7/6/66	20.00	—	
☐☐ 1044A	11¢ **Statue of Liberty,** 6/15/61, DC (238,905)	1.50	2.00	3.00
☐☐ 1044c	11¢ **Statue of Liberty,** Luminescent, 1/11/67	25.00	—	—
☐☐ 1045	12¢ **Harrison,** 6/6/59, Oxford, OH (225,869)	1.50	2.00	3.00
☐☐ 1045a	12¢ **Harrison,** Luminescent, 5/6/68	28.00	—	—
☐☐ 1046	15¢ **John Jay,** 12/12/58, DC (205,680)	1.50	2.00	3.00
☐☐ 1046a	15¢ **John Jay,** Luminescent, 7/6/66	30.00	—	—
☐☐ 1047	20¢ **Monticello,** 4/13/56, Charlottesville, VA (147,860)	1.75	3.00	4.00
☐☐ 1048	25¢ **Paul Revere,** 4/18/58, Boston, MA (196,530)	1.75	3.00	4.00
☐☐ 1049	30¢ **Robert Lee,** 9/21/55, Norfolk, VA (120,166)	1.75	3.00	4.00
☐☐ 1050	40¢ **John Marshall,** 9/24/55, Richmond, VA (113,972)	2.00	3.00	4.00

Prices for various cachet makers can be determined by using the Cachet Pricing Calculator found on pages 33 to 35.

1064

1067

1068

1069

Scott Number	Description	Cachetced Sgl	Blk	Pl Blk
☐☐ 1051	50¢ Susan Anthony, 8/25/55, Louisville, KY (110,220)	8.00	12.00	15.00
☐☐ 1052	$1 Patrick Henry, 10/7/55, Joplin, MO (80,191)	15.00	25.00	30.00
☐☐ 1053	$5 Alexander Hamilton, 3/19/56, Paterson, NJ (34,272)	80.00	100.00	125.00

1954-73 Coil Stamps

		Sgl.	Pr.	L.Pr.
☐☐ 1054	1¢ Washington, 10/8/54, Baltimore, MD (196,318)	—	1.25	2.00
☐☐ 1054A	1¼¢ Palace, 6/17/60, Santa Fe, NM	—	1.25	2.00
☐☐ 1055	2¢ Jefferson, 10/22/54, St. Louis, MO (162,050)	—	1.25	2.00
☐☐ 1055a	2¢ Jefferson, Luminescent, 5/6/68	—	15.00	18.00
☐☐ 1056	2½¢ Bunker Hill, 9/9/59, Los Angeles, CA (198,680)	1.25	2.00	3.00
☐☐ 1057	3¢ Statue of Liberty, 7/20/54, DC (137,139)	1.25	2.00	3.00
☐☐ 1058	4¢ Lincoln, 7/31/58, Mandan, ND (184,079)	1.25	2.00	3.00
☐☐ 1059	4½¢ The Hermitage, 5/1/59, Denver, CO (202,454)	1.75	2.00	3.00
☐☐ 1059A	25¢ Paul Revere, 2/25/65, Wheaton, MD (184,954)	1.50	3.00	4.00
☐☐ 1059b	25¢ 25¢ Paul Revere, luminescent 4/3/73, NY	18.00	—	—

1954

		Sgl	Blk	Pl Blk
☐☐ 1060	3¢ Nebraska Territory, 5/7/54, Nebraska City, NE (401,015)	1.25	1.50	3.00
☐☐ 1061	3¢ Kansas Territory, 5/31/54, Fort Leavenworth, KS (349,145)	1.25	1.50	3.00
☐☐ 1062	3¢ George Eastman, July 12, 1954, Rochester, NY (630,448)	1.25	1.50	3.00
☐☐ 1063	3¢ Lewis & Clark Expedition, 7/28/54, Sioux City, IA (371,557)	1.25	1.50	3.00

1955

☐☐ 1064	3¢ Pennsylvania Academy of Fine Arts, 1/15/55, Phila., PA (307,040)	1.25	1.50	3.00
☐☐ 1065	3¢ Land Grant Colleges, 2/12/55, East Lansing, MI (419,241)	1.25	1.50	3.00
☐☐ 1066	8¢ Rotary International, 2/23/55, Chicago, IL (350,625)	1.50	2.50	4.00
☐☐ 1067	3¢ Armed Forces Reserve, 5/21/55, DC (300,436)	1.25	1.50	3.00
☐☐ 1068	3¢ New Hampshire, 6/21/55, Franconia, NH (330,630)	1.25	1.50	3.00
☐☐ 1069	3¢ Soo Locks, 6/28/55, Sault Sainte Marie, MI (316,616)	1.25	1.50	3.00
☐☐ 1070	3¢ Atoms for Peace, 7/28/55, DC (351,940)	1.25	1.50	3.00
☐☐ 1071	3¢ Fort Ticonderoga, 9/18/55, Fort Ticonderoga, NY (342,946)	1.25	1.50	3.00
☐☐ 1072	3¢ Andrew W. Mellon, 12/20/55, DC, (278,897)	1.25	1.50	3.00

Uncacheted FDCs in this period sell for 10% of cacheted FDC prices.

1070

1071

1072

1073

1074

1076

1080

1077

1078

1082

1079

1081

1083

Scott Number	Description	Sgl	Cacheted Blk	Pl Blk
1956				
1073	3¢ **Benjamin Franklin,** 1/17/56, Phila., PA (351,260)	1.25	1.50	3.00
	Poor Richard Station	1.25	1.50	3.00
1074	3¢ **Booker T. Washington,** 4/5/56, Booker T. Washington			
	Birthplace, VA (272,659)	1.25	1.50	3.00
1075	11¢ **FIPEX Souvenir Sheet,** 4/28/56, N.Y., NY (429,327)	9.00		
1076	3¢ **FIPEX,** 4/30/56, New York, NY, (526,090)	1.25	1.50	3.00
1077	3¢ **Wildlife (Turkey),** 5/5/56, Fond du Lac, WI (292,121)	1.50	2.50	4.00
1078	3¢ **Wildlife (Antelope),** 6/22/56, Gunnison, CO, (294,731)	1.50	2.50	4.00
1079	3¢ **Wildlife (Salmon),** 11/9/56, Seattle, WA (346,800)	1.50	2.50	4.00
1080	3¢ **Pure Food and Drug Laws,** 6/27/56, DC (411,761)	1.25	1.50	3.00
1081	3¢ **Wheatland,** 8/5/56, Lancaster, PA (340,142)	1.25	1.50	3.00
1082	3¢ **Labor Day,** 9/3/56, Camden, NJ (338,450)	1.25	1.50	3.00
1083	3¢ **Nassau Hall,** 9/22/56, Princeton, NJ (350,756)	1.25	1.50	3.00
1084	3¢ **Devils Tower,** 9/24/56, Devils Tower, WY (285,090)	1.25	1.50	3.00
1085	3¢ **Children,** 12/15/56, DC, (305,125)	1.25	1.50	3.00
1957				
1086	3¢ **Alexander Hamilton,** 1/11/57, New York, NY (305,117)	1.25	1.50	3.00
1087	3¢ **Polio,** 1/15/57, DC, (307,630)	1.25	1.50	3.00
1088	3¢ **Coast & Geodetic Survey,** 2/11/57, Seattle, WA (309,931)	1.25	1.50	3.00
1089	3¢ **Architects,** 2/23/57, New York, NY (368,840)	1.25	1.50	3.00
1090	3¢ **Steel Industry,** 5/22/57, New York, NY (473,284)	1.25	1.50	3.00
1091	3¢ **Naval Review,** 6/10/57, U.S.S. Saratoga, Norfolk, VA			
	(365,923)	1.25	1.50	3.00

Cacheted FDC prices in this period are for unaddressed covers. Addressed covers sell for much less.

1084

1085

1086

1087

1090

1088

1089

1096

1091

1092

1093

1094

1095

1097

1098

1099

1100

Scott Number	Description	Sgl	Cacheted Blk	Pl Blk
☐☐ 1092	3¢ **Oklahoma Statehood,** 6/14/57, Oklahoma City, OK (327,172)	1.25	1.50	3.00
☐☐ 1093	3¢ **School Teachers,** 7/1/57, Phila., PA (375,986)	1.25	1.50	3.00
☐☐	"Philadelpia" error cancel	12.00	15.00	—
☐☐ 1094	4¢ **Flag,** 7/4/57, DC (523,879)	1.25	1.50	3.00
☐☐ 1095	3¢ **Shipbuilding,** 8/15/57, Bath, ME, (347,432)	1.25	1.50	3.00
☐☐ 1096	8¢ **Ramon Magsaysay,** 8/31/57, DC (334,558)	1.25	1.50	3.00
☐☐ 1097	3¢ **Lafayette Bicentenary,** 9/6/57, Easton, PA, (260,421)	1.25	1.50	3.00
☐☐	Fayetteville, NC (230,000)	1.25	1.50	3.00
☐☐	Louisville, KY (207,856)	1.25	1.50	3.00
☐☐ 1098	3¢ **Wildlife (Whooping Cranes),** 11/22/57, NY, NY, (342,970)	1.50	2.50	4.00
☐☐	New Orleans, LA (154,327)	1.50	2.50	4.00
☐☐	Corpus Christi, TX (280,990)	1.50	2.50	4.00
☐☐ 1099	3¢ **Religious Freedom,** 12/27/57, Flushing, NY, (357,770)	1.25	1.50	3.00

FDCs postmarked in unofficial cities sell for 50% to 100% more than catalogue value.

1104

1105

1106

1109

1107

1108

1110-11

1112

1115

1113

1114

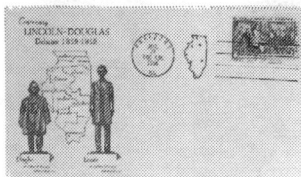
1st Western Cachets cachet

1116

1117-18

Scott Number	Description	Sgl	Cacheted Blk	Pl Blk
1958				
☐☐ 1100	**3¢ Gardening Horticulture,** 3/15/58, Ithaca, NY (451,292)	1.25	1.50	3.00
☐☐ 1104	**3¢ Brussels Exhibition,** 4/17/58, Detroit, MI (428,073)	1.25	1.50	3.00
☐☐ 1105	**3¢ James Monroe,** 4/28/58, Montross, VA (326,988)	1.25	1.50	3.00
☐☐ 1106	**3¢ Minnesota Statehood,** 5/11/58, Saint Paul, MN (475,552)	1.25	1.50	3.00
☐☐ 1107	**3¢ Int'l Geophysical Year,** 5/31/58, Chicago, IL (397,000)	1.25	1.50	3.00
☐☐ 1108	**3¢ Gunston Hall,** 6/12/58, Lorton, VA (349,801)	1.25	1.50	3.00
☐☐ 1109	**3¢ Mackinac Bridge,** 6/25/58, Mackinac Bridge, MI (445,605)	1.25	1.50	3.00
☐☐ 1110	**4¢ Simon Bolivar,** 7/24/58, DC	1.25	1.50	3.00
☐☐ 1111	**8¢ Simon Bolivar,** 7/24/58, DC	1.25	1.50	3.00
☐☐	1110 and 1111, set of two on one cover	3.00	—	—
Total of Scott 1110 and 1111 equals 708,777				
☐☐ 1112	**4¢ Atlantic Cable,** 8/15/58, New York, NY (365,072)	1.25	1.50	3.00
1958-1959				
☐☐ 1113	**1¢ Lincoln Sesqui.,** 2/12/59, Hodgenville, KY (379,862)	1.25	1.50	3.00
☐☐ 1114	**3¢ Lincoln Sesqui.,** 2/27/59, New York, NY (437,737)	1.25	1.50	3.00
☐☐ 1115	**4¢ Lincoln-Douglas Debates,** 8/27/58, Freeport, IL (373,063)	1.25	1.50	3.00
☐☐	1st Western Cachets cachet	15.00	—	—
☐☐ 1116	**4¢ Lincoln Sesqui.,** 5/30/59, DC (894,887)	1.25	1.50	3.00

1119   1122   1120   1121   1125-26

1123   1124

1127   1128   1129

1130   1131   1132

Scott Number	Description	Sgl	Cacheted Blk	Pl Blk
1958				
1117	4¢ **Lajos Kossuth**, 9/19/58, DC	1.25	1.50	3.00
1118	8¢ **Lajos Kossuth**, 9/19/58, DC	1.25	1.50	3.00
	1117-1118, set of two on one cover	3.00	—	—
Total for Scott 1117 and 1118 equals 722,188				
1119	4¢ **Freedom of Press**, 9/22/58, Columbia, MO (411,752)	1.25	1.50	3.00
1120	4¢ **Overland Mail**, 10/10/58, San Francisco, CA (352,760)	1.25	1.50	3.00
1121	4¢ **Noah Webster**, 10/16/58, West Hartford, CT (364,608)	1.25	1.50	3.00
1122	4¢ **Forest Conservation**, 10/27/58, Tucson, AZ (405,959)	1.25	1.50	3.00
1123	4¢ **Fort Duquesne**, 11/25/58, Pittsburgh, PA (421,764)	1.25	1.50	3.00
1959				
1124	4¢ **Oregon Statehood**, 2/14/59, Astoria, OR (452,764)	1.25	1.50	3.00
1125	4¢ **San Martin**, 2/25/59, DC	1.25	1.50	3.00
1126	8¢ **San Martin**, 2/25/59, DC	1.25	1.50	3.00
	1125-1126, set of two on one cover	3.00	—	—
Total for Scott 1125 and 1126 equals 910,208				
1127	4¢ **NATO**, 4/1/59, DC (361,040)	1.25	1.50	3.00
1128	4¢ **Arctic Explorations**, 4/6/59, Cresson, PA (397,770)	1.25	1.50	3.00
1129	8¢ **World Trade**, 4/20/59, DC (503,618)	1.25	1.50	3.00
1130	4¢ **Silver Centennial**, 6/8/59, Virginia City, NV (337,233)	1.25	1.50	3.00
1131	4¢ **St. Lawrence Seaway**, 6/26/59, Massena, NY (543,211)	1.25	1.50	3.00
1132	4¢ **Flag (49 stars)**, 7/4/59, Auburn, NY (523,773)	1.25	1.50	3.00
1133	4¢ **Soil Conservation**, 8/26/59, Rapid City, SD (400,613)	1.25	1.50	3.00
1134	4¢ **Petroleum Industry**, 8/27/59, Titusville, PA (801,859)	1.25	1.50	3.00
1135	4¢ **Dental Health**, 9/14/59, New York, NY (649,813)	1.25	1.50	3.00
1136	4¢ **Reuter**, 9/29/59, DC	1.25	1.50	3.00

1134

1133

1135

1136-37

1138

1138

1147-48

1139-44

1145

1146

1st Ritz cachet

SEATO
1151

1149

1150

Scott Number	Description	Sgl	Cacheted Blk	Pl Blk
☐☐ 1137	**8¢ Reuter,** 9/29/59 DC	1.25	1.50	3.00
☐☐	1136-1137, set of two on one cover	3.00	—	—

Total of Scott 1136 and 1137 equals 1,207,933

☐☐ 1138	**4¢ Dr. Ephraim McDowell,** 12/3/59, Danville, KY (344,603)	1.25	1.50	3.00

1960-61

☐☐ 1139	**4¢ Washington,** "Credo," 1/20/60, Mount Vernon, VA (438,335)	1.25	1.50	3.00
☐☐ 1140	**4¢ Franklin,** "Credo," 3/31/60, Phila., PA (497,913)	1.25	1.50	3.00
☐☐ 1141	**4¢ Jefferson,** "Credo," 5/18/60, Charlottesville, VA (454,903)	1.25	1.50	3.00
☐☐ 1142	**4¢ Francis Scott Key,** "Credo," 9/14/60, Baltimore, MD (501,129)	1.25	1.50	3.00
☐☐ 1143	**4¢ Lincoln,** "Credo," 11/19/60, New York, NY (467,780)	1.25	1.50	3.00
☐☐	1st Ritz cachet	20.00	—	—
☐☐ 1144	**4¢ Patrick Henry,** "Credo," 1/11/61, Richmond, VA (415,252)	1.25	1.50	3.00
☐☐ 1145	**4¢ Boy Scouts,** 2/8/60, DC (1,419,955)	1.50	2.00	3.00
☐☐ 1146	**4¢ Olympic** Winter Games, 2/18/60, Olympic Valley, CA (516,456)	1.25	1.50	3.00
☐☐ 1147	**4¢ Masaryk,** 3/7/60, DC	1.25	1.50	3.00
☐☐ 1148	**8¢ Masaryk,** 3/7/60, DC	1.25	1.50	3.00
☐☐	1147-1148, set of two on one cover	3.00	—	—

Total of Scott 1147 and 1148 equals 1,710,726

☐☐ 1149	**4¢ World Refugee Year,** 4/7/60, DC (413,298)	1.25	1.50	3.00
☐☐ 1150	**4¢ Water Conservation,** 4/18/60, DC (648,988)	1.25	1.50	3.00

1152

1154

1153

1155

1159-60

1156   1157   1158

1161

1163

1162   1164

1167

1165-66   1168-69   1170

Scott Number	Description	Sgl	Cacheted Blk	Pl Blk
1151	4¢ SEATO, 5/31/60, DC (514,926)	1.25	1.50	3.00
1152	4¢ American Woman, 6/2/60, DC (830,385)	1.25	1.50	3.00
1153	4¢ 50-Star Flag, 7/4/60, Honolulu, HI, (820,900)	1.25	1.50	3.00
1154	4¢ Pony Express Cent., 7/19/60, Sacramento, CA (520,223)	1.25	1.50	3.00
1155	4¢ Employ the Handicapped, 8/28/60, New York, NY (439,638)	1.25	1.50	3.00
1156	4¢ World Forestry Congress, 8/29/60, Seattle, WA (360,848)	1.25	1.50	3.00
1157	4¢ Mexican Indepen., 9/16/60, Los Angeles, CA (360,297)	1.25	1.50	3.00
1158	4¢ U.S.-Japan Treaty, 9/28/60, DC (545,150)	1.25	1.50	3.00
1159	4¢ Paderewski, 10/8/60, DC	1.25	1.50	3.00
1160	8¢ Paderewski, 10/8/60, DC	1.25	1.50	3.00
	1159-1160, set of two on one cover	3.00	—	—

Total of Scott 1159 and 1160 equals 1,057,438

Scott Number	Description	Sgl	Cacheted Blk	Pl Blk
1161	4¢ Robert A. Taft, 10/10/60, Cincinnati, OH (312,116)	1.25	1.50	3.00
1162	4¢ Wheels of Freedom, 10/15/60, Detroit, MI (380,551)	1.25	1.50	3.00
1163	4¢ Boy's Clubs, 10/18/60, New York, NY (435,009)	1.25	1.50	3.00
1164	4¢ Automated P.O., 10/20/60, Providence, RI (458,237)	1.25	1.50	3.00
1165	4¢ Mannerheim, 10/26/60, DC	1.25	1.50	3.00
1166	8¢ Mannerheim, 10/26/60, DC	1.25	1.50	3.00
	1165-1166, set of two on one cover	3.00	—	—

Total for Scott 1165 and 1166 equals 1,168,770

Scott Number	Description	Sgl	Cacheted Blk	Pl Blk
1167	4¢ Camp Fire Girls, 11/1/60, New York, NY (324,944)	1.25	1.50	3.00
1168	4¢ Garibaldi, 11/2/60, DC	1.25	1.50	3.00

1171   1172   1173   1174-75

1176   1177   1178-82

1183   1184   1185

Scott Number	Description	Sgl	Cacheted Blk	Pl Blk
☐☐ 1169	**Garibaldi,** 11/2/60, DC	1.25	1.50	3.00
☐☐	1168 and 1169, set of two on one cover	3.00	—	—
Total for Scott 1168 and 1169 equals 1,001,490				
☐☐ 1170	**4¢ Senator George,** 11/5/60, Vienna, GA (278,890)	1.25	1.50	3.00
☐☐ 1171	**4¢ Andrew Carnegie,** 11/25/60, New York, NY (318,180)	1.25	1.50	3.00
☐☐ 1172	**4¢ John Foster Dulles,** 12/6/60, DC (400,055)	1.25	1.50	3.00
☐☐ 1173	**4¢ Echo I,** 12/15/60, DC (583,747)	2.00	2.50	3.00

1961-64

		Sgl	Blk	Pl Blk
☐☐ 1174	**4¢ Gandhi,** 1/26/61, DC	1.25	1.50	3.00
☐☐ 1175	**8¢ Gandhi,** 1/26/61, DC	1.25	1.50	3.00
☐☐	1174-1175, set of two on one cover	3.00	—	—
Total for Scott 1174 and 1175 equals 1,013,515				
☐☐ 1176	**4¢ Range Conservation,** 2/2/61, Salt Lake City, UT (357,101)	1.25	1.50	3.00
☐☐ 1177	**4¢ Horace Greeley,** 2/3/61, Chappaqua, NY (359,205)	1.25	1.50	3.00
☐☐ 1178	**4¢ Fort Sumter,** 4/12/61, Charleston, SC (602,599)	2.00	2.50	4.00
☐☐ 1179	**4¢ Battle of Shiloh,** 4/7/62, Shiloh, TN (526,062)	2.00	2.50	4.00
☐☐ 1180	**5¢ Battle of Gettysburg,** 7/1/63, Gettysburg, PA (600,205)	2.00	2.50	4.00
☐☐ 1181	**5¢ Battle of Wilderness,** 5/5/64, Fredericksburg, VA (450,904)	2.00	2.50	4.00
☐☐ 1182	**5¢ Appomattox,** 4/9/65, Appomattox, VA (653,121)	2.00	2.50	4.00
☐☐ 1183	**4¢ Kansas Statehood,** 5/10/61, Council Grove, KS (480,561)	1.25	1.50	3.00
☐☐ 1184	**4¢ Senator Norris,** 7/11/61, DC (482,875)	1.25	1.50	3.00
☐☐ 1185	**4¢ Naval Aviation,** 8/20/61, San Diego, CA (416,391)	1.50	2.00	3.50
☐☐ 1186	**4¢ Workmen's Comp.,** 9/4/61, Milwaukee, WI (410,236)	1.25	1.50	3.00
☐☐ 1187	**4¢ Frederic Remington,** 10/4/61, DC (723,443)	1.25	1.50	3.00
☐☐ 1188	**4¢ China Republic,** 10/10/61, DC (463,900)	1.25	1.50	3.00
☐☐ 1189	**4¢ Naismith,** 11/6/61, Springfield, MA (479,917)	2.00	2.50	3.00
☐☐ 1190	**4¢ Nursing,** 12/28/61, DC (964,005)	1.25	1.50	3.00

Prices for various cachet makers can be determined by using the Cachet Pricing Calculator found on pages 33 to 35.

1186

1187

1188

1189

1190

1191

1192

1193

1195

1194

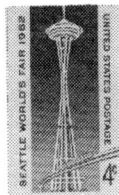
1196

1197

1198

1st Glory cachet

1st Marg cachet

Scott Number	Description	Sgl	Cacheted Blk	Pl Blk
1962				
☐☐ 1191	**4¢ New Mexico Statehood,** 1/6/62, Santa Fe, NM (365,330)	1.25	1.50	3.00
☐☐	1st Glory cachet	35.00	—	—
☐☐ 1192	**4¢ Arizona Statehood,** 2/14/62, Phoenix, AZ (508,216)	1.25	1.50	3.00
☐☐ 1193	**4¢ Project Mercury,** 2/20/62, Cape Canaveral, FL (3,000,000)	3.00	4.00	6.00
☐☐	Any city	7.00	8.00	9.00
☐☐	1st Marg cachet	25.00	—	—
☐☐ 1194	**4¢ Malaria Eradication,** 3/30/62, DC (554,175)	1.25	1.50	3.00
☐☐ 1195	**4¢ Charles Evans Hughes,** 4/11/62, DC (544,424)	1.25	1.50	3.00
☐☐ 1196	**4¢ Seattle World's Fair,** 4/25/62, Seattle, WA (771,856)	1.25	1.50	3.00
☐☐ 1197	**4¢ Louisiana Statehood,** 4/30/62, New Orleans, LA (436,681)	1.25	1.50	3.00
☐☐ 1198	**4¢ Homestead Act,** 5/20/62, Beatrice, NE (487,450)	1.25	1.50	3.00
☐☐ 1199	**4¢ Girl Scouts,** 7/24/62, Burlington, VT (634,347)	1.25	1.50	3.00

1199

1200

1201

1202

1203

1204

1205

1206

1207

1209, 1225

1231

1208

1213, 1229

1230

Scott Number	Description	Sgl	Cacheted Blk	Pl Blk
☐☐ 1200	4¢ **Brien McMahon,** 7/28/62, Norwalk, CT (384,419)	1.25	1.50	3.00
☐☐ 1201	4¢ **Apprenticeship,** 8/31/62, DC (1,003,548)	1.25	1.50	3.00
☐☐ 1202	4¢ **Sam Rayburn,** 9/16/62, Bonham, TX (401,042)	1.25	1.50	3.00
☐☐ 1203	4¢ **Dag Hammarskjold,** 10/23/62, New York, NY (500,683)	1.25	1.50	3.00
☐☐	4¢ **Hammarskjold Invert.,** 10/23/62, Brooklyn, NY, Vanderveer Sta.	2000.	—	—
☐☐ 1204	4¢ **Hammarskjold,** yellow inverted, 11/16/62, DC (c. 75,000)	8.00	10.00	15.00
☐☐ 1205	4¢ **Christmas,** 11/1/62, Pittsburgh, PA (491,312)	1.25	1.50	3.00
☐☐ 1206	4¢ **Higher Education,** 11/14/62, DC (627,347)	1.25	1.50	3.00
☐☐ 1207	4¢ **Winslow Homer,** 12/15/62, Gloucester, MA (498,866)	1.25	1.50	3.00

1963-1966

☐☐ 1208	5¢ **Flag,** 1/9/63, DC (696,185)	1.25	1.50	3.00
☐☐ 1208a	5¢ **Flag,** luminescent 8/25/66, DC	14.00	—	—

1962-66 Regular Issue

☐☐ 1209	1¢ **Jackson,** 3/22/63, New York, NY (392,363)	1.25	1.50	2.00
☐☐ 1209a	1¢ **Jackson,** luminescent, 7/6/66, DC	14.00	—	—
☐☐ 1213	5¢ **Washington,** 11/23/62, New York, NY (360,531)	1.25		
☐☐ 1213b	5¢ **Booklet Pane,** 11/23/62, New York, NY (111,452)	7.00		
☐☐ 1213c	5¢ **Washington,** luminescent, 10/28/63, Dayton, OH & DC	7.00	—	—
☐☐	5¢ **Booklet Pane,** luminescent, 10/28/63, Dayton, OH	110.00	—	
☐☐	Washington, DC (750)	115.00	—	
☐☐ 1225	1¢ **Coil,** 5/31/63, Chicago, IL (238,952)	—	pr 1.25	lp 1.50
☐☐ 1225a	1¢ **Coil,** luminescent, 7/6/66, DC	7.00		
☐☐ 1229	5¢ **Coil,** 11/23/62, New York, NY (184,627)	—	pr 1.25	lp 1.50

1232

EMANCIPATION PROCLAMATION
1233

1234

1235

1236

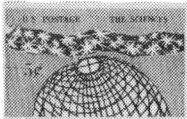
1237

1238

1239

1240

1241

1245

1st Cover Craft cachet

1242

Scott Number	Description	Sgl	Cacheted Pr	LPr
1229a	5¢ **Coil, luminescent,** 10/28/63, Dayton, OH & DC	25.00		
	1213b, 1213c, 1229a on one cover, 10/28/63, Dayton, OH	80.00		

1963

Scott Number	Description	Sgl	Blk	Pl Blk
1230	5¢ **Carolina Charter,** 4/6/63, Edenton, NC (426,200)	1.25	1.50	3.00
1231	5¢ **Food for Peace,** 6/4/63, DC	1.25	1.50	3.00
1232	5¢ **W. Virginia Statehood,** 6/20/63, Wheeling, WV (413,389)	1.25	1.50	3.00
1233	5¢ **Emancipation Procl.,** 8/16/63, Chicago, IL (494,886)	1.25	1.50	3.00
1234	5¢ **Alliance for Progress,** 8/17/63, DC (528,095)	1.25	1.50	3.00
1235	5¢ **Cordell Hull,** 10/5/63, Carthage, TN (391,631)	1.25	1.50	3.00
1236	5¢ **Eleanor Roosevelt,** 10/11/63, DC (860,155)	1.25	1.50	3.00
1237	5¢ **Science,** 10/14/63, DC (504,503)	1.25	1.50	3.00
1238	5¢ **City Mail Delivery,** 10/26/63, DC (544,806)	1.25	1.50	3.00
1239	5¢ **Red Cross,** 10/29/63, DC (557,678)	1.25	1.50	3.00
1240	5¢ **Christmas,** 11/1/63, Santa Claus, IN (458,619)	1.25	1.50	3.00
1240a	5¢ **Christmas, luminescent,** 11/2/63, DC (500)	80.00	—	—
1241	5¢ **Audubon,** 12/7/63, Henderson, KY (518,855)	1.25	1.50	3.00

1964

Scott Number	Description	Sgl	Blk	Pl Blk
1242	5¢ **Sam Houston,** 1/10/64, Houston, TX (487,986)	1.25	1.50	3.00
	Mr. Zip Imprint	10.00	15.00	—

Sam Houston was the first stamp to have Mr. Zip imprints. Zip singles and blocks on FDCs are scarce.

1243	5¢ **Charles Russell,** 3/19/64, Great Falls, MT (658,745)	1.25	1.50	3.00

1243

1244

1246

1248

1247

1249

1250

1251

1254-57

1252

1253

1258

1259

1261

1260

Scott Number	Description	Sgl	Cacheted Blk	Pl Blk
1244	5¢ **N.Y. World's Fair,** 4/22/64, World's Fair, NY (1,656,346)	1.25	1.50	3.00
	1st Sarzin Metallic cachet	20.00	—	—
1245	5¢ **John Muir,** 4/29/64, Martinez, CA (446,925)	1.25	1.50	3.00
1246	5¢ **John F. Kennedy,** 5/29/64, Boston, MA (2,003,096)	2.00	2.50	3.00
	Any city	2.00	2.50	3.00
	1st Cover Craft cachet	25.00	—	—
1247	5¢ **New Jersey Tercent.,** 6/15/64, Elizabeth, NJ (526,879)	1.25	1.50	3.00
1248	5¢ **Nevada Statehood,** 7/22/64, Carson City, NV (584,973)	1.25	1.50	3.00
1249	5¢ **Register & Vote,** 8/1/64, DC (533,439)	1.25	1.50	3.00
1250	5¢ **Shakespeare,** 8/14/64, Stratford, CT (524,053)	1.25	1.50	3.00
1251	5¢ **Drs. Mayo,** 9/11/64, Rochester, MN (674,846)	1.25	1.50	3.00
1252	5¢ **American Music,** 10/15/64, New York, NY (466,107)	1.25	1.50	3.00
1253	5¢ **Homemakers,** 10/26/64, Honolulu, HI (435,392)	1.25	1.50	3.00
1254-57	5¢ **Christmas,** (Se-tenant), 11/9/64, Bethlehem, PA (794,900)	1.25	1.50	3.00
1254a-57a	**Christmas,** luminescent (Se-tenant), Dayton, OH, 11/10/64	15.00	60.00	—
1258	5¢ **Verrazano-Narrows Bridge,** 11/21/64, Staten Island, NY (619,780)	1.25	1.50	3.00
1259	5¢ **Fine Arts,** 12/2/64, DC (558,046)	1.25	1.50	3.00
1260	5¢ **Amateur Radio,** 12/15/64, Anchorage, AK (452,255)	1.25	1.50	3.00

1267

1262

1263

1264

1268

1265

1266

1269

1270

1272

1271

1274

1276

1273

1278, 1299

1287

1275

Scott Number	Description	Sgl	Cacheted Blk	Pl Blk
1965				
☐☐ 1261	**5¢ Battle of New Orleans,** 1/8/65, New Orleans, LA (466,029)	1.25	1.50	3.00
☐☐ 1262	**5¢ Physical Fitness-Sokol,** 2/15/65, DC (864,848)	1.25	1.50	3.00
☐☐ 1263	**5¢ Cancer Crusade,** 4/1/65, DC (744,485)	1.25	1.50	3.00
☐☐ 1264	**5¢ Churchill,** 5/13/65, Fulton, MO (733,580)	1.25	1.50	3.00
☐☐ 1265	**5¢ Magna Carta,** 6/15/65, Jamestown, VA (479,065)	1.25	1.50	3.00
☐☐ 1266	**5¢ Int'l Cooperation Year,** 6/26/65, San Francisco, CA (402,925)	1.25	1.50	3.00
☐☐ 1267	**5¢ Salvation Army,** 7/2/65, New York, NY (634,228)	1.25	1.50	3.00
☐☐ 1268	**5¢ Dante,** 7/17/65, San Francisco, CA (424,893)	1.25	1.50	3.00
☐☐ 1269	**5¢ Herbert Hoover,** 8/10/65, West Branch, IA (698,182)	1.25	1.50	3.00
☐☐ 1270	**5¢ Robert Fulton,** 8/19/65, Clermont, NY (550,330)	1.25	1.50	3.00
☐☐ 1271	**5¢ Florida Settlement,** 8/28/65, St. Augustine, FL (465,000)	1.25	1.50	3.00
☐☐ 1272	**5¢ Traffic Safety,** 9/3/65, Baltimore, MD (527,075)	1.25	1.50	3.00
☐☐ 1273	**5¢ Copley,** 9/17/65, DC (613,484)	1.25	1.50	3.00
☐☐ 1274	**11¢ Int'l Telecommunication Union,** 10/6/65, DC (332,818)			

Scott Number	Description	Sgl	Cacheted Blk	Pl Blk
□□ 1275	5¢ **Adlai Stevenson**, 10/23/65, Bloomington, IL (755,656)	1.25	1.50	3.00
□□ 1276	5¢ **Christmas**, 11/2/65, Silver Bell, AZ (705,039)	1.25	1.50	3.00
□□ 1276a	5¢ **Christmas**, luminescent, 11/16/65, DC (300¢)	45.00	—	—

1965-1968   Prominent Americans Issue

□□ 1278	1¢ **Jefferson**, 1/12/68, Jeffersonville, IN	—	.75	1.00
□□ 1278a	1¢ **Jefferson**, Booklet Pane, 1/12/68, Jeffersonville, IN	3.00	—	
□□	Dull Gum, 3/1/71, DC	100.00	—	

Total for Scott 1278, 1278a and 1299 equals 655,680

□□ 1278b	1¢ **Jefferson**, Booklet pane of 4 plus 2 labels, 5/10/71, DC	18.00	—	—
□□ 1279	1¼¢ **Gallatin**, 1/30/67, Gallatin, MO (439,010)	—	.75	1.00
□□ 1280	2¢ **Wright**, 6/8/68, Spring Green, WI (460,427)	—	.75	1.00
□□ 1280a	2¢ **Wright**, Booklet Pane of 5 plus label, 1/8/68 Buffalo, NY (147,244)	4.00		
□□ 1280c	2¢ **Wright**, Booklet pane of 6, 5/7/71, Spokane, WA	18.00		
□□	Dull Gum, 10/31/75, Cleveland	100.00		
□□ 1281	3¢ **Parkman**, 9/16/67, Boston, MA (518,355)	—	.75	1.00
□□ 1282	4¢ **Lincoln**, 11/19/65, New York, NY (445,629)	—	.75	1.00
□□ 1282a	4¢ **Lincoln**, luminescent 12/1/65, Dayton, OH	35.00	—	—
□□	Washington, DC	32.50	—	—
□□ 1283	5¢ **Washington**, 2/22/66, DC (525,372)	.75	.85	1.00
□□ 1283a	5¢ **Washington**, luminescent, 2/23/66, Dayton, OH (c. 200)	75.00	—	—
□□	Washington, DC	22.50	—	—
□□ 1283B	5¢ **Washington**, Redrawn, 11/17/67, New York, NY (328,983)	.75	.85	1.00
□□ 1284	6¢ **Roosevelt**, 1/29/66, Hyde Park, NY (448,631)	1.00	1.25	2.00
□□ 1284a	6¢ **Tagged**, 12/29/66	20.00	—	—
□□ 1284b	6¢ **Roosevelt**, Booklet pane of 8, 12/28/67, DC	3.50		

312,330 first day cancellations were applied for Scott 1298 or 1284b

□□ 1284c	6¢ **Roosevelt**, Booklet pane of 5, 1/9/68, DC	125.00		
□□ 1285	8¢ **Einstein**, 3/14/66, Princeton, NJ (366,803)	1.25	1.50	3.00
□□ 1285a	8¢ **Einstein**, luminescent, 7/6/66, DC	16.00	—	—
□□ 1286	10¢ **Jackson**, 3/15/67, Hermitage, TN (255,945)	1.25	1.50	3.00
□□ 1286A	12¢ **Ford**, 7/30/68, Greenfield Village, MI (342,850)	1.25	1.50	3.00
□□ 1287	13¢ **Kennedy**, 5/29/67, Brookline, MA (391,195)	1.25	1.50	3.00
□□ 1288	15¢ **Holmes**, 3/8/68, DC (322,970)	1.25	1.50	3.00
□□ 1288B	15¢ **Redrawn**, for booklet pane, 6/14/78, Boston, MA (387,119)	1.25	1.50	3.00
□□ 1288c	**Booklet pane of 8**, 6/14/78, Boston, MA	5.00		
□□ 1289	20¢ **Marshall**, 10/24/67, Lexington, VA (221,206)	1.25	1.50	3.00
□□ 1289a	20¢ **Marshall**, luminescent, 4/3/73, New York, NY	15.00	—	—
□□ 1290	25¢ **Douglass**, 2/14/67, DC (213,730)	1.25	1.50	3.00
□□ 1290a	25¢ **Douglass**, luminescent, 4/3/73, New York, NY	20.00	—	—
□□ 1291	30¢ **Dewey**, 10/21/68, Burlington, VT (162,790)	1.50	2.50	4.00
□□ 1291a	30¢ **Dewey**, luminescent, 4/3/73, New York, NY	20.00	—	—
□□ 1292	40¢ **Paine**, 1/29/68, Philadelphia, PA (157,947)	1.75	3.00	5.00
□□ 1292a	40¢ **Paine**, luminescent, 4/3/73, New York, NY	20.00	—	—
□□ 1293	50¢ **Stone**, 8/13/68, Dorchester, MA (140,410)	4.00	5.00	10.00
□□ 1293a	50¢ **Stone**, luminescent, 4/3/73, New York, NY	25.00	—	—
□□ 1294	$1 **O'Neill**, 10/16/67, New London, CT (103,102)	9.00	12.00	20.00
□□ 1294a	$1 **O'Neill**, luminescent, 4/3/73, New York, NY	25.00	—	—
□□ 1295	$5 **Moore**, 12/3/66, Smyrna, DE (41,130)	70.00	100.00	150.00
□□ 1295a	$5 **Moore**, luminescent, 4/3/73, New York, NY	75.00	—	—

Total for 1059b, 1289a, 1290a, 1291a, 1292a, 1293a, 1294a, 1295a - 17,533 covers

Prices for various cachet makers can be determined by using the Cachet Pricing Calculator found on pages 33 to 35.

1306

1307

1308

1309

1310-11

1312

1313

National Park Service 1966-1966
1314

50TH ANNIVERSARY MARINE CORPS RESERVE
1315

GENERAL FEDERATION OF WOMEN'S CLUBS
1316

PLANT for a more BEAUTIFUL AMERICA
1318

1317

Scott Number	Description	Sgl	Cacheted Pr	L Pr
1966-1968	**Coil Stamps**			
☐☐ 1297	3¢ **Parkman,** 11/4/75, Pendleton, OR	—	1.25	2.00
☐☐ 1298	6¢ **Roosevelt,** perf. 10 horizontal, 12/28/67, DC	—	1.25	2.00
☐☐ 1299	1¢ **Jefferson,** 1/12/68, Jeffersonville, IN	—	1.25	2.00
☐☐ 1303	4¢ **Lincoln,** 5/28/66, Springfield, IL (322,563)	—	1.25	2.00
☐☐ 1304	5¢ **Washington,** 9/8/66, Cincinnati, OH	1.00	1.25	2.00
☐☐ 1304C	5¢ **Washington,** Redrawn, 3/31/81, eku, D.C. strip of 4	20.00	—	—
☐☐ 1305	6¢ **Perf. 10 vertically,** 2/28/68, DC (317,199)	1.00	1.25	2.00
☐☐ 1305E	15¢ 6/14/78, Boston, MA	1.00	1.25	2.00
☐☐	1288c, 1305E on one cover	8.00		
☐☐ 1305C	$1 **O'Neill Coil,** 1/12/73, Hempstead, NY (121,217)	4.00	6.00	8.00

		Sgl	Blk	Pl Blk
1966				
☐☐ 1306	5¢ **Migratory Bird Treaty,** 3/16/66, Pittsburgh, PA (555,485)	1.25	1.50	3.00
☐☐ 1307	5¢ **Humane Treatment of Animals,** 4/9/66, NY, NY (524,420)	1.25	1.50	3.00
☐☐ 1308	5¢ **Indiana Statehood,** 4/16/66, Corydon, IN (575,557)	1.25	1.50	3.00
☐☐ 1309	5¢ **Circus,** 5/2/66, Delavan, WI (754,076)	1.25	1.50	3.00
☐☐ 1310	5¢ **SIPEX,** 5/21/66, DC (637,802)	1.25	1.50	3.00
☐☐ 1311	5¢ **SIPEX,** Souvenir Sheet, 5/23/66, DC (700,882)	1.50		
☐☐ 1312	5¢ **Bill of Rights,** 7/1/66, Miami Beach, FL (562,920)	1.25	1.50	3.00
☐☐ 1313	5¢ **Polish Millennium,** 7/30/66, DC (712,603)	1.25	1.50	3.00
☐☐ 1314	5¢ **Nat'l Park Serv.,** 8/25/66, Yellowstone Nat'l Pk, WY (528,170)	1.25	1.50	3.00
☐☐ 1314a	5¢ **Nat'l Park Serv.,** luminescent, 8/26/66	25.00	—	—
☐☐ 1315	5¢ **Marine Corps Reserve,** 8/29/66, DC (585,923)	1.25	1.50	3.00
☐☐ 1315a	5¢ **Marine Corps Res.,** luminescent, 8/29/66, DC	25.00	—	—

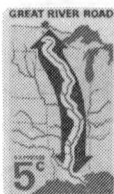
1319

1320

1321

1322

1323

1324

1325

1326

1327

1328

1330

1329

1331-32

Scott Number	Description	Sgl	Cacheted Blk	Pl Blk
☐☐ 1316	5¢ Gen'l Fed. of Women's Clubs, 9/12/66, NY, NY (383,334)	1.25	1.50	3.00
☐☐ 1316a	5¢ Gen'l Fed. of Women's Clubs, luminescent, 9/13/66, DC	25.00	—	—
☐☐ 1317	5¢ Johnny Appleseed, 9/24/66, Leominster, MA (794,610)	1.25	1.50	3.00
☐☐ 1317a	5¢ Johnny Appleseed, luminescent, 9/26/66, DC	25.00	—	—
☐☐ 1318	5¢ Beautification of America, 10/5/66, DC (564,440)	1.25	1.50	3.00
☐☐ 1318a	5¢ Beautification of America, luminescent, 10/5/66, DC	25.00	—	—
☐☐ 1319	5¢ Great River Road, 10/21/66, Baton Rouge, LA (330,933)	1.25	1.50	3.00
☐☐ 1319a	5¢ Great River Road, luminescent, 10/22/66, DC	25.00	—	—
☐☐ 1320	5¢ Savings Bonds - Servicemen, 10/26/66, Sioux City, IA, (444,421)	1.25	1.50	3.00
☐☐ 1320a	5¢ Savings Bonds - Servicemen, luminescent, 10/27/66, DC	25.00	—	—
☐☐ 1321	5¢ Christmas, 11/1/66, Christmas, MI (537,650)	1.25	1.50	3.00
☐☐ 1321a	5¢ Christmas, luminescent, 11/2/66, DC	10.00	—	—
☐☐ 1322	5¢ Mary Cassatt, 11/17/66, DC (593,389)	1.25	1.50	3.00
☐☐ 1322a	5¢ Mary Cassatt, luminescent, 11/17/66, DC	25.00	—	—

1967

☐☐ 1323	5¢ National Grange, 4/17/67, DC (603,460)	1.25	1.50	3.00
☐☐ 1324	5¢ Canada Centenary, 5/25/67, Montreal, Canada, (711,795)	1.25	1.50	3.00
☐☐ 1325	5¢ Erie Canal, 7/4/67, Rome, NY (784,611)	1.25	1.50	3.00
☐☐ 1326	5¢ Search for Peace, 7/5/67, Chicago, IL (393,197)	1.25	1.50	3.00
☐☐ 1327	5¢ Thoreau, 7/12/67, Concord, MA (696,789)	1.25	1.50	3.00
☐☐ 1328	5¢ Nebraska Statehood, 7/29/67, Lincoln, NE (1,146,957)	1.25	1.50	3.00

1333

1334

1335

1336

1338

1337

1339

1341

1342

1340

1343

1344

1345-54

1356

1355

Scott Number	Description	Sgl	Cacheted Blk	Pl Blk
☐☐ 1329	5¢ Voice of America, 8/1/67, DC (445,190)	1.25	1.50	3.00
☐☐ 1330	5¢ Davy Crockett, 8/17/67, San Antonio, TX (462,291)	1.25	1.50	3.00
☐☐ 1331-32	5¢ Space Accomplishments, 9/29/67, Kennedy Space Center, FL (667,267)	11.00	15.00	20.00
☐☐ 1333	5¢ Urban Planning, 10/2/67, DC (389,009)	1.25	1.50	3.00
☐☐ 1334	5¢ Finland Independence, 10/6/67, Finland, MN (408,532)	1.25	1.50	3.00
☐☐ 1335	5¢ Thomas Eakins, 11/2/67, DC (648,054)	1.25	1.50	3.00
☐☐ 1336	5¢ Christmas, 11/6/67, Bethlehem, GA (462,118)	1.25	1.50	3.00
☐☐ 1337	5¢ Mississippi Statehood, 12/11/67, Natchez, MS (379,612)	1.25	1.50	3.00

1968-1969

Scott Number	Description	Sgl	Cacheted Blk	Pl Blk
☐☐ 1338	6¢ Flag, 1/24/68, DC (412,120)	1.25	1.50	3.00
☐☐ 1338A	6¢ Flag coil, 5/30/69, Chicago, IL (248,434)	1.25 pr	1.50 lp	3.00
☐☐ 1338D	6¢ Flag, 8/7/70, DC (356,280)	1.25	1.50	3.00
☐☐ 1338F	8¢ Flag, 5/10/71, DC	1.25	1.50	3.00
☐☐ 1338G	8¢ Flag Coil, 5/10/71, DC	1.25 pr	1.50 lp	3.00
Total for Scott 1338F-G equals 235,543				
☐☐ 1339	6¢ Illinois Statehood, 2/12/68, Shawneetown, IL (761,640)	1.25	1.50	3.00
☐☐ 1340	6¢ Hemis Fair '68, 3/30/68, San Antonio, TX (469,909)	1.25	1.50	3.00
☐☐ 1341	$1 Airlift, 4/4/68, Seattle, WA (105,088)	10.00	15.00	20.00
☐☐ 1342	6¢ Youth-Elks, 5/1/68, Chicago, IL (354,711)	1.25	1.50	3.00

1357

1358

1360

1359

1361

1362

1363

1364

1365-68

1369

1370

1371

1372

1373

1374

1375

1380

Scott Number	Description	Sgl	Cacheted Blk	Pl Blk
☐☐ 1343	6¢ Law and Order, 5/17/68, DC (407,081)	1.25	1.50	3.00
☐☐ 1344	6¢ Register and Vote, 6/27/68, DC (355,685)	1.25	1.50	3.00
☐☐ 1345-54	6¢ Historic Flag Series of 10, 7/4/68, Pittsburgh, PA	12.50	15.00	30.00
☐☐	Set of 10 on one cover	15.00	—	—
Total for Scott 1345-1354 equals 2,924,962				
☐☐ 1355	6¢ Disney, 9/11/68, Marceline, MO (499,505)	1.50	1.75	3.00
☐☐ 1356	6¢ Marquette, 9/20/68, Sault Ste. Marie, MI (379,710)	1.25	1.50	3.00
☐☐ 1357	6¢ Daniel Boone, 9/26/68, Frankfort, KY (333,440)	1.25	1.50	3.00
☐☐ 1358	6¢ Arkansas River, 10/1/68, Little Rock, AR (358,025)	1.25	1.50	3.00
☐☐ 1359	6¢ Leif Erikson, 10/9/68, Seattle, WA (376,565)	1.25	1.50	3.00
☐☐ 1360	6¢ Cherokee Strip, 10/15/68, Ponca, OK (339,330)	1.25	1.50	3.00
☐☐ 1361	6¢ John Trumbull, 10/18/68, New Haven, CT (378,285)	1.25	1.50	3.00
☐☐ 1362	6¢ Waterfowl Conser., 10/24/68, Cleveland, OH, (349,719)	1.25	1.50	3.00
☐☐ 1363	6¢ Christmas, luminescent, 11/1/68, DC (739,055)	1.25	1.50	3.00
☐☐ 1363a	6¢ Christmas, no luminescence, 11/2/68, DC	10.00	—	—
☐☐ 1364	6¢ American Indian, 11/4/68, DC (415,964)	1.25	1.50	3.00

1376-79

PROFESSIONAL BASEBALL
1381

FOOTBALL
1382

U.S. 6¢ POSTAGE
DWIGHT D. EISENHOWER
1383

Christmas
1384

HOPE FOR THE CRIPPLED
1385

SIX CENTS
UNITED STATES POSTAGE
AMERICAN PAINTING
WILLIAM M. HARNETT
1386

EISENHOWER-USA
1393

U.S. 6¢
AMERICAN BALD EAGLE
1387-90

1391

Scott Number	Description	Sgl	Cacheted Blk	Pl Blk
1969				
☐☐ 1365-68 6¢	**Beautification of America,** (Se-tenant), 1/16/69, DC (1,094,184)	3.00	5.00	5.50
☐☐ 1369	6¢ **American Legion,** 3/15/69, DC (632,035)	1.25	1.50	3.00
☐☐ 1370	6¢ **Grandma Moses,** 5/1/69, DC (367,880)	1.25	1.50	3.00
☐☐ 1371	6¢ **Apollo 8,** 5/5/69, Houston, TX, (908,634)	4.00	5.00	8.00
☐☐ 1372	6¢ **W.C. Handy,** 5/17/69, Memphis, TN (390,216)	1.25	1.50	3.00
☐☐ 1373	6¢ **California Bicentenary,** 7/16/69, San Diego, CA (530,210)	1.25	1.50	3.00
☐☐ 1374	6¢ **J.W. Powell,** 8/1/69, Page, AZ (434,433)	1.25	1.50	3.00
☐☐ 1375	6¢ **Alabama Statehood,** 8/2/69, Huntsville, AL (485,801)	1.25	1.50	3.00
☐☐ 1376-79 6¢	**Botanical Congress,** (Se-tenant), 8/23/69, Seattle, WA (737,935)	3.00	7.00	7.50
☐☐ 1380	6¢ **Dartmouth Case,** 9/22/69, Hanover, NH (416,327)	1.25	1.50	3.00
☐☐ 1381	6¢ **Professional Baseball,** 9/24/69, Cincinnati, OH (414,942)	6.00	7.00	10.00
☐☐ 1382	6¢ **Intercollegiate Football,** 9/26/69, New Brunswick, NJ (414,860)	4.00	5.00	8.00
☐☐ 1383	6¢ **Dwight D. Eisenhower,** 10/14/69, Abilene, KS (1,009,560)	1.25	1.50	3.00
☐☐ 1384	6¢ **Christmas,** 11/3/69, Christmas, FL (555,550)	1.25	1.50	3.00
☐☐ 1384a	6¢ **Christmas,** Precancel, New Haven, Memphis, Baltimore, 11/4/69 (250)	20.00	—	—
☐☐ 1385	6¢ **Hope for Crippled,** 11/20/69, Columbus, OH (342,676)	1.25	1.50	3.00
☐☐ 1386	6¢ **William M. Harnett,** 12/3/69, Boston, MA (408,860)	1.25	1.50	3.00
1970-1974				
☐☐ 1387-90 6¢	**Natural History,** (Se-tenant), 5/6/70, NY, NY (834,260)	2.00	3.00	3.50

First day cancellations were applied to 834,260 covers bearing one or more of Scott 1387-1390.

1394, 1395, 1402

1392

1396

1399

1400

1405

1406

1407

1408

1409

1410-13

Scott Number	Description	Sgl	Cacheted Blk	Pl Blk
1391	6¢ **Maine Statehood,** 7/9/70, Portland, MD (472,165)	1.25	1.50	3.00
1392	6¢ **Wildlife Conservation,** 7/20/70, Custer, SD (309,418)	1.25	1.50	3.00
1393	6¢ **Eisenhower,** 8/6/70, DC	1.25	1.50	3.00
1393a	6¢ **Booklet,** pane of 8, 8/6/70, DC	4.00		
1393a	6¢ **Booklet,** experimental dull gum, 3/1/71, DC	75.00	—	—
1393b	6¢ **Booklet,** pane of 5 plus labels, 8/6/70, DC	3.00		
	1393a, 1393b (two different slogans in label) 3 panes on one FDC, 8/6/70, DC	10.00	—	—
1393D	7¢ **Franklin,** 10/20/72, Phila., PA (309,276)	1.25	1.50	3.00
1394	8¢ **Eisenhower,** 5/10/71, DC	1.25	1.50	3.00
1395	8¢ **Eisenhower,** 5/10/71, DC	1.25	1.50	3.00
1395a	8¢ **Booklet,** pane of 8, 5/10/71, DC	4.00		
1395b	8¢ **Booklet,** pane of 6, 5/10/71, DC	4.00		
	1395a, 1395b on one cover, 5/10/71, DC	6.00		
1395c	8¢ **Booklet,** pane of 4 plus labels, 1/28/72, Casa Grande, AZ	3.00		
1395d	8¢ **Booklet,** pane of 7 plus label, 1/28/72, Casa Grande, AZ	3.00		
	1395c, 1395d on one cover, 1/28/72, Casa Grande, AZ	4.00		
1396	8¢ **Postal Service Emblem,** 7/1/71, any city (est. 16,300,000)	1.25	1.50	3.00
	(7/1/71's any other city, specialized issue) Unofficials	—		
1397	14¢ **Fiorello H. LaGuardia,** 4/24/72, New York, NY (180,114)	1.50	1.75	3.00
1398	16¢ **Ernie Pyle,** 5/7/71, DC (444,410)	1.25	1.50	3.00
1399	18¢ **Elizabeth Blackwell,** 1/23/74, Geneva, NY (217,938)	1.50	1.75	3.00
1400	21¢ **Amedeo Giannini,** 6/27/73, San Mateo, CA (282,520)	1.50	1.75	3.00
1401	6¢ **Eisenhower Coil,** 8/6/70, DC	1.25 pr	1.75 lp	3.00
1402	8¢ **Eisenhower Coil,** 5/10/71, DC	1.25 pr	1.75 lp	3.00
1405	6¢ **Edgar Lee Masters,** 8/22/70, Petersburg, IL (372,804)	1.25	1.75	3.00
1406	6¢ **Woman Suffrage,** 8/26/70, Adams, MA (508,142)	1.25	1.75	3.00
1407	6¢ **South Carolina,** 9/12/70, Charleston, SC (533,000)	1.25	1.75	3.00
1408	6¢ **Stone Mt. Memorial,** 9/19/70, Stone Mountain, GA (558,546)	1.25	1.75	3.00
1409	6¢ **Fort Snelling,** 10/17/70, Fort Snelling, MN (497,611)	1.25	1.75	3.00

1415-18

1414

1419

1420

1421

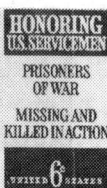
1422

1423

1424

1425

Scott Number		Description	Sgl	Cacheted Blk	Pl Blk
☐☐ 1410-13	6¢	Anti-Pollution, (Se-tenant), 10/28/70, San Clemente, CA (1,033,147)	2.00	4.25	5.00
☐☐ 1414	6¢	Christmas, 11/5/70, DC	1.25	1.75	3.00
☐☐ 1414a		Christmas, precanceled	10.00	—	—
☐☐ 1415-18	6¢	Christmas, (Se-tenant), 11/5/70, DC	1.25	1.75	3.00
☐☐ 1415a-18a		Precancel Christmas set	10.00	—	—
☐☐		1415a-1418a set of 4 on one cover	30.00		
☐☐		1414a-1418a set of 5 on one cover	35.00		

F.D. cancellation was applied to 2,014,450 covers bearing one or more Scott 1414-18 or 1414a-18a

☐☐ 1419	6¢	United Nations, 11/20/70, New York, NY (474,070)	1.25	1.75	3.00
☐☐ 1420	6¢	Pilgrims' Landing, 11/21/70, Plymouth, MA (629,850)	1.25	1.75	3.00
☐☐ 1421	6¢	Disabled Veterans, 11/24/70, Cincinnati or Montgomery, AL	1.25	1.75	3.00
☐☐ 1422	6¢	U.S. Servicemen, 11/24/70, Cincinnati or Montgomery, AL	1.25	1.75	3.00
☐☐		1421-1422 on one cover	2.00	2.50	4.00

476,610 covers were postmarked in Cincinnati; 336,451 in Montgomery.

1971

☐☐ 1423	6¢	Wool Industry, 1/19/71, Las Vegas, NV (379,911)	1.25	1.75	3.00
☐☐		1st Bazaar cachet	20.00	—	—
☐☐		1st Colorano Silk cachet	150.00	—	—
☐☐ 1424	6¢	MacArthur, 1/26/71, Norfolk, VA (720,035)	1.25	1.75	3.00
☐☐ 1425	6¢	Blood Donor, 3/12/71, New York, NY (644,497)	1.25	1.75	3.00
☐☐ 1426	8¢	Missouri Sesqui., 5/8/71, Independence, MO (551,000)	1.25	1.75	3.00
☐☐ 1427-30	8¢	Wildlife Conservation, (Se-tenant), 6/12/71, Avery Island, LA (679,483)	2.00	3.00	4.00
☐☐ 1431	8¢	Antarctic Treaty, 6/23/71, DC (419,200)	1.25	1.75	3.00
☐☐ 1432	8¢	American Revolution Bicent., 7/4/71, DC (434,930)	1.25	1.75	3.00
☐☐ 1433	8¢	John Sloan, 8/2/71, Lock Haven, PA (482,265)	1.25	1.75	3.00
☐☐ 1434-35	8¢	Space Achievement Decade, 8/2/71, Kennedy Space Center, FL (1,403,644) set	2.00	3.00	5.00
☐☐		Houston, TX (811,560) set	2.50	3.50	5.00
☐☐		Huntsville, AL (524,000) set	3.00	4.00	6.00
☐☐ 1436	8¢	Emily Dickinson, 8/28/71, Amherst, MA (498,180)	1.25	1.75	3.00

1st Bazaar cachet

1st Colorano Silk cachet

1426

1427-30

1433

1431

1434-35

1432

1436

1437

1438

1439

Scott Number	Description	Sgl	Cacheted Blk	Pl Blk
☐☐ 1437	8¢ San Juan, 9/12/71, San Juan, PR (510,668)	1.25	1.75	3.00
☐☐ 1438	8¢ Drug Abuse, 10/4/71, Dallas, TX (425,330)	1.25	1.75	3.00
☐☐ 1439	8¢ CARE, 10/27/71, New York, NY (402,121)	1.25	1.75	3.00
☐☐ 1440-43	8¢ Historic Preservation, (Se-tenant), 10/29/71, San Diego, CA (783,242)	2.00	3.00	4.00
☐☐ 1444-45	8¢ Christmas, 11/10/71, DC, either stamp	1.25	1.75	3.00
☐☐	1444-45 on one cover (348,038)	2.50	—	—

1972

☐☐ 1446	8¢ Sidney Lanier, 2/3/72, Macon, GA (394,800)	1.25	1.75	3.00
☐☐ 1447	8¢ Peace Corps, 2/11/72, DC (453,660)	1.25	1.75	3.00
☐☐ 1448-51	2¢ National Parks Centennial, (Se-tenant), 4/5/72, Hatteras, NC (505,697)	—	2.00	3.00
☐☐ 1452	6¢ National Parks, 6/26/72, Vienna, VA (403,306)	1.25	1.75	3.00
☐☐ 1453	8¢ National Parks, 3/1/72, Yellowstone National Park, WY	1.25	1.75	3.00
☐☐	Washington, DC (847,500)	1.25	1.75	3.00
☐☐ 1454	15¢ Nat'l Parks, 7/28/72, Mt. McKinley Nat'l Pk, AK (491,456)	2.00	2.50	3.00
☐☐ 1455	8¢ Family Planning, 3/18/72, New York, NY (691,385)	1.25	1.75	3.00

HISTORIC PRESERVATION
1440-43

Christmas
Georgetown, ca. 1308-1310
National Gallery of Art
1444

1445

SIDNEY LANIER
America's Poet
1446

Peace Corps
8¢
United States
1447

National Parks Centennial
8¢
Old Faithful, Yellowstone
1453

National Parks Centennial
1448-51

National Parks Centennial
1452

Family Planning
1455   UNITED STATES 8¢

National Parks Centennial
15¢
Mount McKinley, Alaska
1454

COLONIAL AMERICAN CRAFTSMEN
UNITED STATES POSTAGE 8 CENTS
1456-59

XX OLYMPIC SUMMER GAMES MUNICH 1972
1460-62

100th Anniversary of Mail Order
1468

P.T.A. 1897 1972
Parent Teacher Association U.S.
8¢
1463

UNITED STATES
8¢
• WILDLIFE CONSERVATION •
Cardinal
1464-67

Scott Number	Description	Sgl	Cacheted Blk	Pl Blk
☐☐ 1456-59	8¢ **Colonial Craftsmen,** (Se-tenant), 7/4/72, Williamsburg, VA	1.25	2.50	3.00
☐☐ 1460	6¢ **Olympics,** 8/17/72, DC	1.25	1.75	3.00
☐☐ 1461	8¢ **Winter Olympics,** 8/17/72, DC	1.25	1.75	3.00
☐☐ 1462	15¢ **Olympics,** 8/17/72, DC	2.00	2.50	3.00
☐☐	1460-62 and C85 on one cover	3.00	—	—
Total for Scott 1460-1462 and C85 is 7,536				
☐☐ 1463	8¢ **P.T.A.** 9/15/72, San Francisco, CA (523,454)	1.25	1.75	3.00
☐☐ 1464-67	8¢ **Wildlife,** (Se-tenant), 9/20/72, Warm Springs, OR (733,778)	3.00	4.00	5.00
☐☐ 1468	8¢ **Mail Order,** 9/27/72, Chicago, IL (759,666)	1.25	1.75	3.00
☐☐ 1469	8¢ **Osteopathy,** 10/9/72, Miami, FL (607,160)	1.25	1.75	3.00
☐☐ 1470	8¢ **Tom Sawyer,** 10/13/72, Hannibal, MO (459,013)	1.25	1.75	3.00
☐☐	1st Coulson cachet	20.00	—	—
☐☐ 1471-72	8¢ **Christmas,** 11/9/72, DC, either stamp	1.25	1.75	3.00
☐☐	1471-1472 on one cover (718,821)	2.50	—	—
☐☐ 1473	8¢ **Pharmacy,** 11/10/72, Cincinnati, OH (804,320)	1.25	1.75	3.00
☐☐ 1474	8¢ **Stamp Collecting,** 11/17/72, New York, NY (434,680)	1.25	1.75	3.00

FDCs postmarked in unofficial cities sell for 50% to 100% more than catalogue value.

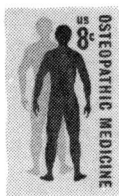  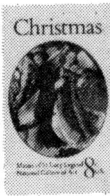  

1469   1470   1471   1472   1474

1st Coulson cachet   1473   1484-87

1475   1476-79   1480-83

1500-02   1488   1489-98   1499

Scott Number	Description	Sgl	Cacheted Blk	Pl Blk
1973				
☐☐ 1475	8¢ Love, 1/26/73, Phila., PA (422,492)	1.25	1.75	3.00
☐☐ 1476	8¢ Pamphleteer, 2/16/73, Portland, OR (431,784)	1.25	1.75	3.00
☐☐ 1477	8¢ Broadside, 4/13/73, Atlantic City, NJ (423,437)	1.25	1.75	3.00
☐☐ 1478	8¢ Post Rider, 6/22/73, Rochester, NY (586,850)	1.25	1.75	3.00
☐☐ 1479	8¢ Drummer, 9/28/73, New Orleans, LA (522,427)	1.25	1.75	3.00
☐☐ 1480-83	8¢ Boston Tea Party, (Se-tenant), 7/4/73, Boston, MA (897,870)	2.00	4.00	5.00
☐☐ 1484	8¢ George Gershwin, 2/28/73, Beverly Hills, CA (448,814)	1.25	1.75	3.00
☐☐ 1485	8¢ Robinson Jeffers, 8/13/73, Carmel, CA (394,261)	1.25	1.75	3.00
☐☐ 1486	8¢ Henry O. Tanner, 9/10/73, Pittsburgh, PA (424,065)	1.25	1.75	3.00
☐☐ 1487	8¢ Willa Cather, 9/20/73, Red Cloud, NE (435,784)	1.25	1.75	3.00
☐☐ 1488	8¢ Nicolaus Copernicus, 4/23/73, DC (734,190)	1.25	1.75	3.00
☐☐ 1489-98	8¢ Postal People, 4/30/73, any city, any single/block of 4/plate block	1.25	1.75	6.00
☐☐	Strip of 10 on one cover	7.00		
☐☐ 1499	8¢ Harry S. Truman, 5/8/73, Independence, MO (938,636)	1.25	1.75	3.00

1504-06

1507

1508

1503

1509, 1519

1510, 1520

1526

1511

1518

1525

1528

1529

1527

Scott Number	Description	Sgl	Cacheted Blk	Pl Blk
□□ 1500	6¢ Electronics, 7/10/73, New York, NY	1.25	1.75	3.00
□□ 1501	8¢ Electronics, 7/10/73, New York, NY	1.25	1.75	3.00
□□ 1502	15¢ Electronics, 7/10/73, New York, NY	1.25	1.75	3.00
□□	1500-1502 and C86 on one cover (1,197,700)	4.00	—	—
□□ 1503	8¢ Lyndon B. Johnson, 8/27/73, Austin, TX (701,490)	1.25	1.75	3.00
□□ 1504	8¢ Angus Cattle, 10/5/73, St. Joseph, MO (521,427)	1.25	1.75	3.00
□□ 1505	10¢ Chautauqua, 8/6/74, Chautauqua, NY (411,105)	1.25	1.75	3.00
□□ 1506	10¢ Wheat, 8/16/74, Hillsboro, KS (468,280)	1.25	1.75	3.00
□□ 1507-08	8¢ Christmas, 11/7/73, DC, either stamp	1.25	1.75	3.00
□□	1507-1508 on one cover (807,468)	2.50	—	—
□□ 1509	10¢ Crossed Flags, 12/8/73, San Francisco, CA	1.25	1.75	3.00

Total for Scott 1509 and 1519 is 341,528

□□ 1510	10¢ Jefferson Memorial, 12/14/73, DC	1.25	1.75	3.00
□□ 1510b	10¢ Booklet Pane of 5 plus labels, 12/14/73, DC	3.00		
□□ 1510c	10¢ Booklet Pane of 8, 12/14/73, DC	4.00		
□□ 1510d	10¢ Booklet Pane, Pane of 6, 8/5/74, Oakland, CA	4.00		
□□ 1511	10¢ Zip Code, 1/4/74, DC (335,220)	1.25	1.75	3.00
□□ 1518	6.3¢ Bell Coil, 10/1/74, DC (221,141)		pr 1.75 lp 3.00	
□□ 1519	10¢ Crossed Flags Coil, 12/8/73, San Francisco, CA	1.25 pr 1.75 lp 3.00		
□□ 1520	10¢ Jefferson Memorial Coil, 12/14/73, DC	1.25 pr 1.75 lp 3.00		

1974

□□ 1525	10¢ Veterans of Foreign Wars, 3/11/74, DC (543,598)	1.25	1.75	3.00
□□ 1526	10¢ Robert Frost, 3/26/74, Derry, NH (500,425)	1.25	1.75	3.00
□□ 1527	10¢ EXPO '74, 4/18/74, Spokane, WA (565,548)	1.25	1.75	3.00

Letters mingle souls

1530-37

1538-41

1542

1547

1543-46

1548

1550

1549

1551

1552

Scott Number	Description	Sgl	Cachet Blk	Pl Blk
1528 10¢ Horse Racing, 5/4/74, Louisville, KY (623,983)		1.25	1.75	3.00
1529 10¢ Skylab, 5/14/74, Houston, TX (972,326)		3.00	4.00	5.00
1530-37 10¢ UPU Centenary, 6/6/74, DC, any single/block of 4/pl block		1.25	1.75	4.25
Strip of 8 on one cover		7.00		
Total covers for Scott 1530-1537 is 1,374,765				
1538-41 10¢ Mineral Heritage, (Se-tenant), 6/13/74, Lincoln, NE (865,368)		1.50	3.00	4.00
1542 10¢ Kentucky Settlement, 6/15/74, Harrodsburg, KY (487,239)		1.25	1.75	3.00
1543-46 10¢ Continental Congress, (Se-tenant), 7/4/74, Phila., PA (2,124,957)		1.25	3.00	4.00
1547 10¢ Energy Conservation, 9/23/74, Detroit, MI (587,210)		1.25	1.75	3.00
1548 10¢ Sleepy Hollow, 10/10/74 North Tarrytown, NY (514,836)		1.25	1.75	3.00
1549 10¢ Retarded Children, 10/12/74, Arlington, TX (412,882)		1.25	1.75	3.00
1550-51 10¢ Christmas, 10/23/74, NY, NY (634,990) either stamp		1.25	1.75	3.00
1550-1551 on one cover (634,990)		2.50	—	—
1552 10¢ Christmas, 11/15/74, New York, NY (477,410)		1.25	1.75	3.00

1975

Scott Number	Description	Sgl	Blk	Pl Blk
1553 10¢ Benjamin West, 2/10/75, Swarthmore, PA (465,017)		1.25	1.75	3.00
1554 10¢ Paul L. Dunbar, 5/1/75, Dayton, OH (397,347)		1.25	1.75	3.00
1555 10¢ D.W. Griffith, 5/27/75, Beverly Hills, CA (424,167)		1.25	1.75	3.00
1556 10¢ Pioneer-Jupiter, 2/28/75, Mountain View, CA (594,896)		3.00	4.00	5.00
1557 10¢ Mariner 10, 4/4/75, Pasadena, CA (563,636)		3.00	4.00	5.00
1558 10¢ Collective Bargaining, 3/13/75, DC (412,329)		1.25	1.75	3.00
1559 8¢ Sybil Ludington, 3/25/75, Carmel, NY (394,555)		1.25	1.75	3.00
1560 10¢ Salem Poor, 3/25/75, Cambridge, MA (415,565)		1.25	1.75	3.00
1561 10¢ Haym Salomon, 3/25/75, Chicago, IL		1.25	1.75	3.00
1562 18¢ Peter Francisco, 3/25/75, Greensboro, NC		1.25	1.75	3.00
1559-1562 set on one cover, any city		10.00	—	—

Benjamin West
American artist
10 cents U.S. postage
1553

D.W. GRIFFITH
1555

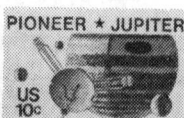
PIONEER ★ JUPITER
US 10¢
1556

Paul Laurence Dunbar
American poet
10 cents U.S. postage
1554

MARINER 10 ★ VENUS/MERCURY
US 10¢
1557

UNITED STATES
collective bargaining
out of conflict
10¢
1558

Bunker Hill 1775 by Trumbull
US Bicentennial 10¢
1564

Contributes to the Cause
8¢
Sybil Ludington ♦ Youthful Heroine
1559-62

Lexington & Concord 1775 by Sandham
US Bicentennial 10cents
1563

CONTINENTAL MARINES
US 10¢
1565-68

us 10¢ APOLLO SOYUZ 1975

APOLLO SOYUZ SPACE TEST PROJECT
10¢
1569-70

1st Gothic Covers cachet

USA 10¢
INTERNATIONAL WOMEN'S YEAR
1571

Scott Number	Description	Sgl	Cacheted Blk	Pl Blk
☐☐ **1563**	**10¢ Lexington-Concord,** (Rev. Bicentennial), 4/19/75, Lexington, MA or Concord, MA (975,020)	1.25	1.75	3.00
☐☐	Dual cancel	2.00	—	—
☐☐ **1564**	**10¢ Bunker Hill,** (Rev. Bicentennial), 6/17/75, Charlestown, MA, (557,130)	1.25	1.75	3.00
☐☐ **1565-68**	**10¢ Military Service,** (Se-tenant), (Rev. Bicentennial), 7/4/75, DC (1,134,831)	1.25	2.40	3.00
☐☐ **1569-70**	**10¢ Apollo-Soyuz,** 7/15/75, Kennedy Space Center, FL, either stamp (1,427,046)	1.25	2.50	3.50
☐☐	1569-1570 pair on one cover	6.00	—	—

Prices for various cachet makers can be determined by using the Cachet Pricing Calculator found on pages 33 to 35.

1572-75

1576

Gisslandse National Gallery
Christmas US postage

Merry Christmas!
Early Card by Louis Prang

1579-80

1577-78

1584

1592, 1617

1593

1596

1599, 1619

1608

United States 13c
1622, 1625

Scott Number	Description	Sgl	Cacheted Blk	Pl Blk
1571	10¢ Int'l Women's Year, 8/26/75, Seneca Falls, NY (476,769)	1.25	1.75	3.00
	1st Gothic Covers cachet	20.00	—	—
1572-75	10¢ Postal Service Bicent., 9/3/75, Phila., PA (969,000)	1.25	2.40	3.00
1576	10¢ World Peace through Law, 9/29/75, DC	1.25	1.75	3.00
1577-78	10¢ Banking-Commerce, 10/6/75, NY, NY (555,580), either stamp	1.25	1.75	3.00
	1577-1578 on one cover	2.50	—	—
1579-80	10¢ Christmas, 10/14/75, DC, either stamp	1.25	1.75	3.00
	1579-1580 on one cover (730,079)	2.50	—	—

1975-1981　Americana Regular Issue Series

1581	1¢ Inkwell & Quill, 12/8/77, St. Louis, MO	—	.75	1.00
1582	2¢ Speaker's Stand, 12/8/77, St. Louis, MO	—	.75	1.00
1584	3¢ Early Ballot Box, 12/8/77, St. Louis, MO	—	.75	1.00
1585	4¢ Books, Bookmark, & Eyeglasses, 12/8/77, St. Louis, MO	—	.75	1.00

Total for Scott 1581-1585 is 530,033

1590	9¢ Dome of the Capitol, Booklet Single, 3/11/77, New York, NY	1.50		
1591	9¢ Dome of the Capitol, 11/24/75, DC (190,117)	1.00	1.50	2.50
1592	10¢ Contemplation of Justice, 11/17/77, NY, NY (359,050)	1.00	1.50	2.50
1593	11¢ Early Am. Printing Press, 11/13/75, Phila., PA (217,755)	1.00	1.50	2.50
1594	12¢ Liberty's Torch, 4/8/81, Dallas, TX	1.00	1.50	2.50

Total for Scott 1594 and 1816 is 180,930

1595	13¢ Liberty Bell, Booklet Single, 10/31/75, Cleveland, OH	1.00		
1595a	13¢ Booklet, pane of 6, 10/31/75, Cleveland, OH	1.00		
1595b	13¢ Booklet, pane of 7 + label, 10/31/75, Cleveland, OH	1.00		
1595c	13¢ Booklet, pane of 8, 10/31/75, Cleveland, OH	1.00		
1595d	13¢ Booklet, pane of 5 + label, 4/2/76, Liberty, MO	1.00		
1596	13¢ Eagle & Shield, 12/1/75, Juneau, AK (418,272)	1.00	1.50	2.50
1597	15¢ Ft. McHenry Flag, 6/30/78, Baltimore, MD	1.00	1.50	2.50

1623

1629-31

1st Postmasters of America cachet

Scott Number	Description	Sgl	Cacheted Blk	Pl Blk
1598	15¢ **Ft. McHenry Flag,** booklet single, 6/30/78, Baltimore, MD	1.00	—	
1598a	15¢ **Booklet,** pane of 8, 6/30/78	3.00		

Total for Scott 1597-1598 and 1618C is 315,359

		Sgl	Blk	Pl Blk
1599	16¢ **Statue of Liberty's Head,** 3/31/78, New York, NY	1.00	1.50	2.50
1603	24¢ **Old North Church,** 11/14/75, Boston, MA (208,973)	1.00	1.50	2.50
1604	28¢ **Ft. Nisqually,** 8/11/78, Tacoma, WA (159,639)	1.25	1.75	3.00
1605	29¢ **Sandy Hook Lighthouse,** 4/14/78, Atlantic City, NJ (193,476)	1.25	1.75	3.00
1606	30¢ **Morris Township School No. 2,** 8/27/79, Devils Lake, ND (186,882)	1.25	1.75	3.00
1608	50¢ **Iron 'Betty' Lamp,** 9/11/79, San Juan, PR (159,540)	2.00	2.50	3.75
1610	$1 **Rush Lamp & Candle Holder,** 7/2/79, San Francisco, CA	3.50	5.00	8.00
1611	$2 **Kerosene Table Lamp,** 11/16/78, New York, NY (173,596)	6.00	10.00	12.00
1612	$5 **Railroad Lantern,** 8/23/79, Boston, MA (129,192)	18.00	35.00	40.00

Americana Series Coil Stamps

		Sgl	Pr	L Pr
1613	3.1¢ **Guitar,** 11/25/79, Shreveport, LA (230,403)	—	1.50	2.00
1614	7.7¢ **Saxhorns,** 11/20/76, New York, NY (285,290)	—	1.50	2.00
1615	7.9¢ **Drum,** 4/23/76, Miami, FL (193,270)	—	1.50	2.00
1615C	8.4¢ **Grand Piano,** 7/13/78, Interlochen, MI (200,392)	—	1.50	2.00
1616	9¢ **Dome of the Capitol,** 3/5/76, Milwaukee, WI (128,171)	—	1.50	2.00
1617	10¢ **Contemplation of Justice,** 11/4/77, Tampa, FL (184,954)		1.50	2.00
1618	13¢ **Liberty Bell,** 11/25/75, Allentown, PA (320,387)	1.00	1.50	2.00
1618C	15¢ **Ft. McHenry Flag,** 6/30/78, Baltimore, MD	1.00	1.50	2.00
1619	16¢ **Statue of Liberty's Head,** 3/31/78, New York, NY	1.00	1.50	2.00

1975-77

		Sgl	Blk	Pl Blk
1622	13¢ **Flag over Independence Hall,** 11/15/75, Phila., PA	1.00	1.50	2.50
1623	13¢ **Flag over Capitol,** booklet, single, perf. 11x10½, 3/11/77, New York, NY	1.50		
1623a	13¢ **Booklet,** pane of 7 + 1 1590, perf. 11x10½	35.00		
1623b	13¢ **Single,** from pane, perf. 10, 3/11/77, New York, NY	1.50		
1623c	13¢ **Booklet pane of 7 + 1 1590,** perf. 10	18.00		

Total for all versions of Scott 1623 is 242,208

		Sgl	Pr	L Pr
1625	13¢ **Flag over Independence Hall,** coil, 11/15/75, Phila., PA	1.00	1.50	—

Total for Scott 1622 and 1625 is 362,959

1976

		Sgl	Blk	Pl Blk
1629-31	13¢ **Spirit of '76,** 1/1/76, Pasadena, CA (Se-tenant), any stamp (1,013,067)	1.00	1.75	3.00
	1st Postmasters of America cachet	30.00	—	—
1632	13¢ **Interphil '76,** 1/17/76, Phila., PA (519,902)	1.00	1.50	2.50

1632

1633-82

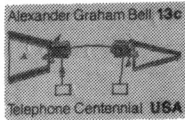
1683

1684

1685

1686

1687

1688

1691-94

1689

1st Metropolitan FDC Society cachet

1690

Scott Number	Description	Sgl	Cacheted Blk	Pl Blk
☐☐ 1633-82	13¢ **State Flags,** 2/23/76, DC, any single or block	1.75	2.00	—
☐☐	Complete set of 50	100.00		
☐☐	Complete pane on one cover	40.00		
☐☐ 1633-82	13¢ **State Flags,** 2/23/76, State capitals, any single or block	1.75	2.50	
☐☐	Complete set of 50	100.00		
☐☐ 1633-82	13¢ **State Flags,** 2/23/76, dual cancels (State & DC)	200.00		
☐☐ 1683	13¢ **Telephone,** 3/10/76, Boston, MA (662,515)	1.00	1.50	2.00
☐☐ 1684	13¢ **Commercial Aviation,** 3/19/76, Chicago, IL (631,555)	1.00	1.50	2.50
☐☐ 1685	13¢ **Chemistry,** 4/6/76, New York, NY	1.00	1.50	2.50
☐☐ 1686	13¢ **Bicentennial Souvenir Sheet of 5,** Surrender of Cornwallis, 5/29/76, Phila., PA	10.00		
☐☐ 1687	18¢ **Bicentennial Souvenir Sheet of 5,** Declaration of Independence, 5/29/76, Phila., PA	12.00		
☐☐ 1688	24¢ **Bicentennial Souvenir Sheet of 5,** Washington Crossing Delaware, 5/29/76, Phila., PA	12.00		
☐☐ 1689	31¢ **Bicentennial Souvenir Sheet of 5,** Washington at Valley Forge, 5/29/76, Phila., PA	15.00		
☐☐	1686-89 any single from sheet	1.00	1.50	2.50
☐☐ 1690	13¢ **Franklin,** 6/1/76, Phila., PA	1.00	1.50	2.50
☐☐	In Combo with Canadian issue, dual cancel	2.00	—	—
☐☐	1st Metropolitan FDC Society cachet	10.00	—	—
☐☐ 1691-94	13¢ **Declaration of Independence,** 7/4/76, Phila., PA (Se-tenant)	1.00		
☐☐	**Strip of 4**	—	3.00	—
☐☐ 1695-98	13¢ **Olympic Games,** 7/16/76, Lake Placid, NY (Se-tenant)	1.00	2.00	2.50

1695-98

1699

1700

1701

1702

1st Carrollton cachet

1704
US Bicentennial 13¢

1705

1st Doris Gold cachet

1710

Pueblo Art USA 13¢
1706-09

1st GAMM cachet

50th Anniversary
1st Spectrum cachet

Scott Number	Description	Cacheted		
		Sgl	Blk	Pl Blk
☐☐ 1699	**13¢ Clara Maass,** 8/18/76, Belleville, NJ	1.00	1.50	2.50
☐☐ 1700	**13¢ Adolph S. Ochs,** 9/18/76, New York, NY	1.00	1.50	2.50
☐☐ 1701	**13¢ Nativity,** 10/27/76, Boston, MA	1.00	1.50	2.50
☐☐ 1702	**13¢ 'Winter Pastime,'** 10/27/76, Boston, MA	1.00	1.50	2.50
	1701-1702 set on one cover	1.75	—	—
☐☐ 1703	**13¢ 'Winter Pastime,'** 10/27/76, Boston, MA (330,450)	1.00	1.50	
☐☐	1701-1703 set on one cover	2.00	—	—

1977

☐☐ 1704	**13¢ Washington,** 1/3/77, Princeton, NJ	1.00	1.50	2.50
☐☐	1st Carrollton cachet	20.00	—	—
☐☐ 1705	**13¢ Sound Recording,** 3/23/77, DC	1.00	1.50	2.50
☐☐ 1706-09	**13¢ Pueblo Pottery,** 4/13/77, Santa Fe, NM (Se-tenant)	1.00	1.75	2.50
☐☐	Santa Fe error in cancel	10.00	12.00	—

1st Tudor House cachet

1711

US Bicentennial 13¢
1716

1st Comic Cachets

1st Ham cachet

1712-15

1717-20

1721

US Bicentennial 13 cents
1722

1723-24

1725

Scott Number		Description	Sgl	Cacheted Blk	Pl Blk
☐☐ 1710	13¢	**Solo Flight**, 5/20/77, Garden City, NY	2.00	2.50	3.50
☐☐		1st Doris Gold cachet	50.00	—	—
☐☐		1st GAMM cachet	35.00	—	—
☐☐		1st Spectrum cachet	25.00	—	—
☐☐		1st Tudor House cachet	20.00	—	—
☐☐ 1711	13¢	**Colorado**, 5/21/77, Denver, CO	1.00	1.50	2.50
☐☐ 1712-15	13¢	**Butterflies**, 6/6/77, Indianapolis, IN (Se-tenant)	1.00	1.75	2.50
☐☐		1st Comic cachets	20.00	—	—
☐☐		1st Ham cachet	600.00	—	—
☐☐ 1716	13¢	**Lafayette**, 6/13/77, Charleston, SC	1.00	1.50	2.50
☐☐ 1717-20	13¢	**Skilled Hands**, 7/4/77, Cincinnati, OH (Se-tenant)	1.00	2.00	2.50
☐☐ 1721	13¢	**Peace Bridge**, 8/4/77, Buffalo, NY	1.00	1.50	2.50
☐☐		US and Canadian stamps on one cover	3.00	—	—
☐☐		Dual US and Canadian cancel	4.00	—	—
☐☐ 1722	13¢	**Herkimer**, 8/6/77, Herkimer, NY	1.00	1.50	2.50
☐☐ 1723-24	13¢	**Energy Conservation**, 10/20/77, DC (410,299), either stamp	1.00	2.00	2.50
☐☐		1723-1724 on one cover	1.50	—	—

Prices for various cachet makers can be determined by using the Cachet Pricing Calculator found on pages 33 to 35.

1726

1727

US Bicentennial 13 cents
1728

1729

1730

1734

1731

1732

1st Calhoun Collector's Society Gold Foil Cachet

1733

1735

1st Rob Cuscaden cachet

1st Western Silk Cachets

Scott Number	Description	Sgl	Cacheted Blk	Pl Blk
1725	13¢ Alta, CA, 9/9/77, San Jose, CA (709,457)	1.00	1.50	2.50
1726	13¢ Articles of Confederation, 9/30/77, York, PA (605,455)	1.00	1.50	2.50
1727	13¢ Talking Pictures, 10/6/77, Hollywood, CA (570,195)	1.00	1.50	2.50
1728	13¢ Surrender at Saratoga, 10/7/77, Schuylerville, NY (557,529)	1.00	1.50	2.50
1729	13¢ Christmas (Valley Forge), 10/21/77, Valley Forge, PA (583,139)	1.00	1.50	2.50
1730	13¢ Christmas (mailbox), 10/21/77, Omaha, NE (675,786)	1.00	1.50	2.50
	1729-30 on one cover	2.00	—	—
	1729-30 on one cover with dual cancel	3.00	—	—

1978

Scott Number	Description	Sgl	Cacheted Blk	Pl Blk
1731	13¢ Carl Sandburg, 1/6/78, Galesburg, IL	1.00	1.50	2.50
	1st Calhoun Collector's Society Gold Foil Cachet	35.00	—	—
	1st Rob Cuscaden cachet	15.00	—	—
	1st Western Silk cachets	35.00	—	—
1732-33	13¢ Captain Cook, 1/20/78, Honolulu, HI or Anchorage, AK, either stamp	1.00	1.50	2.50
	1732-1733 on one cover	2.50	—	—
	1732-33 on one cover with dual cancel	3.00	—	—
1734	13¢ Indian Head Penny, 1/11/78, Kansas City, MO (512,426)	1.25	1.75	2.50

1st F. Collins Cachet

1744

1749-52

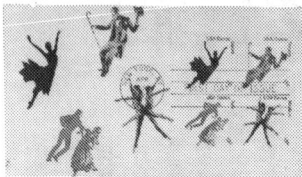

1st Andrews Cachet cachet

US Bicentennial 13c

1753

1754

1755

1756

Photography USA 15c

1758

1759

1st Softones cachet

1764-67

1760-63

Scott Number	Description	Sgl	Blk	Pl Blk
1978-80	**Regular Issues**			
☐☐ 1735 (15¢)	'A' & Eagle, non-denominated for rate-change, 5/22/78, Memphis, TN	1.00	1.50	2.50
☐☐	1st G. Peltin cachet	20.00	—	—
☐☐ 1736 (15¢)	'A', 5/22/78, Memphis, TN	1.00	1.50	2.50
☐☐ 1736a	Booklet, pane of 8, 5/22/78, Memphis, TN	4.00		
☐☐ 1737 15¢	Roses, single, 7/11/78, Shreveport, LA (445,003)	1.00	—	—
☐☐ 1737a	Booklet, pane of 8, 7/11/78, Shreveport, LA	4.00		
☐☐ 1738-42 15¢	Windmills Booklet, 5 different subjects, 2/7/80, Lubbock, TX, single	1.00	—	—
☐☐ 1742a	Booklet, pane of 10, 2/7/80, Lubbock, TX	4.00		
☐☐ 1743 (15¢)	'A' & Eagle coil, 5/22/78, Memphis, TN	1.00 pr	1.50 lp	2.50
Total for Scott 1735, 1736 and 1743 is 689,049				
☐☐ 1744 13¢	Harriet Tubman, 2/1/78, DC (493,495)	1.25	2.00	2.50
☐☐ 1745-48 13¢	American Quilts, 3/8/78 Charleston, WV (Se-tenant)	1.00	2.00	2.50
☐☐	1st F. Collins cachet	600.00	—	—

1770

1768

1769

International Year of the Child
1772

1771

1773

1st Bittings cachet

Einstein USA 15c
1774

Folk Art USA 15c
1775-8

1st DRC cachet

Architecture USA 15c
1779-82

Scott Number	Description	Sgl	Cacheted Blk	Pl Blk
1749-52 13¢	American Dance, 4/26/78, NY, NY (Se-tenant)	1.00	1.50	2.50
	1st Andrews Cachet	15.00	—	
1753 13¢	French Alliance, 5/4/78, York, PA	1.00	1.50	2.50
1754 13¢	Papanicolaou, 5/18/78, DC	1.00	1.50	2.50
1755 13¢	Jimmie Rodgers, 5/24/78, Meridian, MS	1.00	1.50	2.50
1756 15¢	Geo. M. Cohan, 7/3/78, Providence, RI	1.00	1.50	2.50
1757	CAPEX Souv. Sheet, 6/10/78 Toronto, Canada (1,994,067)	4.00		
	1757a-1757h single from sheet	1.00		
1758 15¢	Photography, 6/26/78, Las Vegas, NV	1.00	1.50	2.50
1759 15¢	Viking Missions, 7/20/78, Hampton, VA	1.25	1.75	2.50
	1st Softones cachet	20.00	—	
1760-63 15¢	American Owls, 8/26/78, Fairbanks, AK (Se-tenant)	1.00	2.00	2.50
1764-67 15¢	American Trees, 10/9/78, Hot Springs Nat'l Park, AR (Se-tenant)	1.00	2.00	2.50
1768 15¢	Christmas (Madonna), 10/18/78, DC	1.00	1.50	2.50
1769 15¢	Christmas (Hobby Horse), 10/18/78, Holly, MI	1.00	1.50	2.50
	1768-1769 on one cover	2.00	—	—
	1768-1769 dual cancel	3.00	—	—

1979

1770 15¢	Robert F. Kennedy, 1/12/79, DC (624,582)	1.00	1.50	2.50
	1st Bittings cachet	20.00	—	—
	1st DRC cachet	50.00	—	—
1771 15¢	Martin Luther King, Jr. 1/13/79, Atlanta, GA (726,149)	1.00	1.50	2.50
1772 15¢	Int'l Year of the Child, 2/15/79, Phila., PA, (716,782)	1.00	1.50	2.50
1773 15¢	John Steinbeck, 2/27/79, Salinas,CA (709,073)	1.00	1.50	2.50

1783-6   1787   1788   1789   1790

1795-8   1799   1800   1802

1801   1803   1804   1805-10   1811

1st Brennan cachet

1st Gill Craft cachet

Scott Number	Description	Sgl	Cacheted Blk	Pl Blk
☐☐ 1774	15¢ **Albert Einstein,** 3/4/79, Princeton, NJ (641,423)	1.00	1.50	2.50
☐☐ 1775-8	15¢ **Penn. Toleware,** 4/19/79, Lancaster, PA (Se-tenant)	1.00	2.00	2.50
☐☐ 1779-82	15¢ **Am. Architecture,** 6/4/79, Kansas City, MO (Se-tenant)	1.00	2.00	2.50
☐☐ 1783-6	15¢ **Endangered Flora,** 6/7/79, Milwaukee, WI (Se-tenant)	1.00	2.00	2.50
☐☐ 1787	15¢ **Seeing Eye Dogs,** 6/15/79, Morristown, NJ	1.00	1.50	
☐☐ 1788	15¢ **Special Olympics,** 8/9/79, Brockport, NY	1.00	1.50	2.50
☐☐ 1789	15¢ **John Paul Jones,** 9/23/79, Annapolis, MD, *Perf. 11x12*	1.00	1.50	2.50
☐☐ 1789a	15¢ **John Paul Jones,** *perf. 11*	1.00	1.50	2.50
Total for all Scott 1789 is 587,018				
☐☐ 1790	10¢ **Olympic Javelin,** 9/5/79, Olympia, WA (305,122)	1.25	1.75	2.50
☐☐ 1791-4	15¢ **Summer Olympics,** 9/28/79, L.A., CA (Se-tenant)	1.00	2.50	3.00
☐☐ 1795-8	15¢ **Winter Olympics,** 2/1/80, Lake Placid, NY (Se-tenant)	1.00	2.50	3.00
☐☐ 1799	15¢ **Christmas - Virgin & Child,** 10/18/79, DC (686,990)	1.00	1.50	2.50
☐☐ 1800	15¢ **Christmas - Santa Claus,** 10/18/79, North Pole, AK (511,829)	1.00	1.50	2.50
☐☐	1799-1800 on one cover	1.75	—	—
☐☐	1799-1800 on one cover, dual cancel	2.25	—	—
☐☐ 1801	15¢ **Will Rogers,** 11/4/79, Claremore, OK (1,643,151)	1.00	1.50	2.50

1818-20

1822

Frances Perkins
USA 15¢

1821

Emily Bissell
Crusader Against Tuberculosis
USA 15¢

1823

HELEN KELLER
ANNE SULLIVAN

1824

1825

1st American Postal Arts Society Cachet (Post/Art)

1st D.J. Graf Cachet

Scott Number		Description	Sgl	Cacheted Blk	Pl Blk
1802	15¢	Vietnam Veterans, 11/11/79, Arlington, VA (445,934)	1.50	2.00	3.00
		1st Brennan cachet	15.00	—	—

1980-81

1803	15¢	W.C. Fields, 1/29/80, Beverly Hills, CA (603,228)	1.00	1.50	2.50
		1st Gill Craft cachet	40.00	—	—
1804	15¢	Benjamin Banneker, 2/15/80, Annapolis, MD	1.00	1.50	2.50
1805-10	15¢	Nat'l Letter Writing Week, 2/25/80, DC, any single	1.00		
		Any vertical pair	1.50		
		Vertical strip of all 6	4.00		

Note: Marginal markings require 12 stamps, plate blocks 36, per Scott.

Coil Stamps

			Pr	L Pr
1811	1¢	Inkwell & Quill, 3/6/80, New York, NY	1.50	2.50
1813	3.5¢	Weaver Violins, 6/23/80, Williamsburg, PA	1.50	2.50
1816	12¢	Liberty's Torch, 4/8/81, Dallas, TX	1.50	2.50

Totals for Scott 1594 and 1816 is 280,930

1818	(18¢)	'B' & Eagle, 3/15/81, San Francisco, CA	1.00	1.50	2.50
1819	(18¢)	'B' & Eagle, single from pane, 3/15/81, San Francisco, CA	1.00	—	—
1819a		Booklet, pane of 8	3.00	—	—
1820	(18¢)	'B' & Eagle coil, 3/15/81, San Francisco, CA	1.00	1.50	2.50

Totals for Scott 1818-1820, U592 and UX88 is 511,688

1821	15¢	Frances Perkins, 4/10/80, DC	1.00	1.50	2.50
1822	15¢	Dolley Madison, 5/20/80, DC	1.00	1.50	2.50
		1st American Postal Arts Society Cachet (Post/Art)	35.00	—	—
		1st D.J. Graf Cachet	25.00	—	—
1823	15¢	Emily Bissell, 5/31/80, Wilmington, DE	1.00	1.50	2.50
1824	15¢	Helen Keller & Anne Sullivan, 6/27/80, Tuscumbia, AL	1.00	1.50	2.50
1825	15¢	Veterans Administration, 7/21/80, DC (634,101)	1.00	1.50	2.50
1826	15¢	Bernardo de Galvez, 7/23/80, New Orleans, LA (658,061)	1.00	1.50	2.50

1826

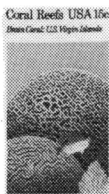

1827-30

1831

1832

1833

1834-7

1838-41

1842

1843

1845

1860

1866

1874

1875

Scott Number	Description	Sgl	Cacheted Blk	Pl Blk
1827-30	15¢ **Coral Reefs,** 8/26/80, Charlotte Amalie, VI (Se-tenant) (1,195,126)	1.00	2.00	2.50
1831	15¢ **Organized Labor,** 9/1/80, DC (759,973)	1.00	1.50	2.50
1832	15¢ **Edith Wharton,** 9/5/80, New Haven, CT (633,917)	1.00	1.50	2.50
1833	15¢ **Education,** 9/12/80, DC (672,592)	1.00	1.50	2.50
1834-7	15¢ **Pacific N/W Indian Masks,** 9/25/80, Spokane, WA (Se-tenant) (2,195,136)	1.00	2.00	2.50
1838-41	15¢ **Am. Architecture,** 10/9/80, NY, NY (Se-tenant) (2,164,721)	1.00	2.00	2.50
1842	15¢ **Christmas - Madonna & Child,** 10/31/80, DC	1.00	1.50	2.50
1843	15¢ **Christmas - Wreath & Toys,** 10/31/80, Christmas, MI	1.00	1.50	2.50
	1842-1843 on one cover	2.25	—	—
	1842-1843 on one cover, dual cancel	3.00	—	—

1980-85   Great Americans Series

1844	1¢ **Dorothea Dix,** 9/23/83, Hampden, ME (164,140)	—	1.00	1.50
1845	2¢ **Igor Stravinsky,** 11/18/82, New York, NY (501,719)	—	1.00	1.50
1846	3¢ **Henry Clay,** 7/13/83, DC (204,320)	—	1.00	1.50
1847	4¢ **Carl Schurz,** 6/3/83, Watertown, WI (165,010)	—	1.00	1.50
1848	5¢ **Pearl Buck,** 6/25/83, Hillsboro, WV (231,852)	—	1.00	1.50
1849	6¢ **Walter Lippman,** 9/19/85, Minneapolis, MN	1.00	1.50	2.50
1850	7¢ **Abraham Baldwin,** 1/25/85, Athens, GA (402,285)	1.00	1.50	2.50
1851	8¢ **Henry Knox,** 7/25/85, Thomaston, ME	1.00	1.50	2.50

Scott Number	Description	Sgl	Cacheted Blk	Pl Blk
☐☐ 1852	9¢ Sylvanus Thayer, 6/7/85, Braintree, MA	1.00	1.50	2.50
☐☐ 1853	10¢ Richard Russell, 5/31/84, Winder, GA	1.00	1.50	2.50
☐☐ 1854	11¢ Alden Partridge, 2/12/85, Northfield, VT (442,311)	1.00	1.50	2.50
☐☐ 1855	13¢ Crazy Horse, 1/15/82, Crazy Horse, SD	1.00	1.50	2.50
☐☐ 1856	14¢ Sinclair Lewis, 3/21/85, Sauk Centre, MN (308,612)	1.00	1.50	2.50
☐☐ 1857	17¢ Rachel Carson, 5/28/81, Springdale, PA (273,686)	1.00	1.50	2.50
☐☐ 1858	18¢ George Mason, 5/7/81, Gunston Hall, VA (461,937)	1.00	1.50	2.50
☐☐ 1859	19¢ Sequoyah, 12/27/80, Tahlequah, OK (241,325)	1.00	1.50	2.50
☐☐ 1860	20¢ Ralph Bunche, 1/12/82, New York, NY	1.00	1.50	2.50
☐☐ 1861	20¢ Thomas Gallaudet, 6/10/83, W. Hartford, CT	1.00	1.50	2.50
☐☐ 1862	20¢ Harry S. Truman, 1/26/84, DC	1.00	1.50	2.50
☐☐ 1863	22¢ John J. Audubon, 4/23/85, New York, NY	1.00	1.50	2.50
☐☐ 1864	30¢ Frank Laubach, 9/2/84, Benton, PA (118,974)	1.00	1.50	2.50
☐☐ 1865	35¢ Charles Drew, 6/3/81, DC (383,882)	1.50	2.50	3.50
☐☐ 1866	37¢ Robert Millikan, 1/26/82, Pasadena, CA	1.50	2.50	3.50
☐☐ 1867	39¢ Grenville Clark, 3/20/85, Hanover, NH	1.50	2.50	3.50
☐☐ 1868	40¢ Lillian Gilbreth, 2/24/84, Montclair, NJ	1.50	2.50	3.50
☐☐ 1869	50¢ Chester W. Nimitz, 2/22/85, Fredericksburg, TX (376,166)	1.50	2.50	3.50

1981

		Sgl	Blk	Pl Blk
☐☐ 1874	15¢ Everett Dirksen, 1/4/81, Pekin, IL	1.00	1.50	2.50
☐☐ 1875	15¢ Whitney Moore Young, Jr., 1/30/81, New York, NY	1.00	1.50	2.50
☐☐ 1876-9	18¢ Flowers, 4/23/81, Ft. Valley, GA (Se-tenant) (1,966,599)	1.00	1.50	2.50
☐☐ 1880-9	15¢ Wildlife Booklet, 5/14/81, Boise, ID, any single	1.00		
☐☐ 1889a	Complete pane, of 10 on one cover (1,641,749)	8.00		
☐☐ 1890	18¢ Flag, 'America the Beautiful (grain), 4/24/81, Portland, ME	1.00	1.50	2.50
☐☐ 1891	18¢ Flag, 'America the Beautiful' (sea) coil, 4/24/81, Portland, ME	1.00 pr	1.50 lp	2.50
☐☐ 1892	6¢ Field of Stars, 4/24/81, Portland, ME (from booklet only)	1.00		
☐☐ 1893	18¢ single, from booklet (mountain), 4/24/81, Portland, ME	1.00		
☐☐ 1893a	6 #1893 + 2 #1892, complete pane of 8	5.00		

Totals for all versions Scott 1890-1893 is 691,526

☐☐ 1894	20¢ Flag over Supreme Court, 12/17/81, DC	1.00	1.50	2.50
☐☐ 1895	20¢ Flag coil, 12/17/81, DC	1.00 pr	1.50 lp	2.50
☐☐ 1896	20¢ Flag over Supreme Court, 12/17/81, DC	1.00	1.50	2.50
☐☐ 1896a	20¢ Flag booklet pane of 6, 12/17/81, DC	8.00	—	—
☐☐	1894-6a on one cover (all singles/with booklet pane)	10.00	—	—
☐☐ 1896b	20¢ Flag booklet pane of 10, 6/1/82, DC	15.00	—	—

1981-84   Transportation Coils Series*

		Sgl	Pr	L Pr
☐☐ 1897	1¢ Omnibus, 8/19/83, Arlington, VA	—	1.50	11.00
☐☐ 1897A	2¢ Locomotive, 5/20/82, Chicago, IL (290,020)	—	1.50	11.00
☐☐ 1898	3¢ Handcar, 3/25/83, Rochester, NY (77,900)	—	1.50	12.00
☐☐ 1898A	4¢ Stagecoach, 8/19/82, Milwaukee, WI (152,940)	—	1.50	11.00
☐☐ 1899	5¢ Motorcycle, 10/10/83, San Francisco, CA (188,240)	—	1.50	12.50
☐☐ 1900	5.2¢ Sleigh, 3/21/83, Memphis, TN	—	1.50	30.00
☐☐	Combination with U604 envelope	—	1.50	30.00
☐☐ 1900a	5.2¢ Sleigh, precanceled, 3/21/83	—	125.00	
☐☐ 1901	5.9¢ Bicycle, 2/17/82, Wheeling, WV	—	1.50	30.00
☐☐ 1901a	5.9¢ Bicycle, precanceled, 2/17/82	150.00	150.00	
☐☐ 1902	7.4¢ Baby Buggy, 4/7/84, San Diego, CA	—	1.50	20.00
☐☐ 1902a	7.4¢ Baby Buggy, precanceled, 4/7/84	—	500.00	

*Note: Prices for FDC's with specific plate numbers may be found beginning on page 215.

Rose USA 18c
1876-9

1880-9
1949

1894

Mail Wagon 1880s USA 9.3c
1900

Fire Pumper 1860s USA 20c
1907

Exploring the Moon
USA 18c
1912-9

The Gift of Self
USA 18c
American Red Cross
1910

SAVINGS AND LOANS
USA 18c
1911

Professional Management
USA 18c
1920

Scott Number	Description	Sgl	Cacheted Blk	Pl Blk
☐☐ 1903	9.3¢ Mail Wagon, 12/15/81, Shreveport, LA	—	1.50	30.00
☐☐ 1903a	9.3¢ Mail Wagon, precanceled, 12/15/81	500.00	500.00	
☐☐ 1904	10.9¢ Hansom Cab, 3/26/82, Chattanooga, TN	—	1.50	30.00
☐☐ 1904a	10.9¢ Hansom Cab, precanceled, 3/26/82	500.00	500.00	
☐☐ 1905	11¢ Railroad Caboose, 2/3/84, Chicago, IL		1.50	20.00
☐☐ 1906	17¢ Electric Auto, 6/25/81, Dearborn, MI (239,458)	1.00	1.50	13.00
☐☐ 1907	18¢ Surrey, 5/18/81, Notch, MO, (207,801)	1.00	1.50	25.00
☐☐ 1908	20¢ Fire Pumper, 12/10/81, Alexandria, VA	1.00	1.50	25.00

1981-83

		Sgl	Blk	Pl Blk
☐☐ 1909	$9.35 Express Mail, 8/12/83, single, Kennedy Space Center, FL	50.00	—	—
☐☐	Flown on Shuttle (not FDC)	45.00	—	—
☐☐	Predate 8/2/83 single, D.C. only 3 exist	300.00	—	—
☐☐ 1909a	Booklet pane of 3 on one cover	125.00	—	—
☐☐ 1910	18¢ American Red Cross, 5/1/81, DC (874,972)	1.00	1.50	2.50
☐☐ 1911	18¢ Savings Loans, 5/8/81, Chicago, IL (740,910)	1.00	1.50	2.50
☐☐ 1912-9	18¢ Space Achievement, 5/21/81, Kennedy Space Center, FL (7,027,549)	1.50	6.00	—
☐☐ 1920	18¢ Professional Management, 6/18/81, Phila., PA (713,096)	1.00	1.50	2.50
☐☐ 1921-4	18¢ Wildlife Habitats (Se-tenant), 6/26/81, Reno, NV (2,327,609)	1.00	1.50	3.50
☐☐	1st Double A Cachet	15.00	—	—
☐☐ 1925	18¢ Int'l Year of the Disabled, 6/29/81, Milford, MI (714,244)	1.00	1.50	2.50
☐☐ 1926	18¢ Edna St. Vincent Millay, 7/10/81, Austerlitz, NY (725,978)	1.00	1.50	2.50
☐☐ 1927	18¢ Alcoholism, 8/19/81, DC	1.00	1.50	2.50
☐☐ 1928-31	18¢ Am. Architecture, 8/28/81, DC (Se-tenant) (1,998,208)	1.00	2.50	3.00
☐☐ 1932	18¢ 'Babe' Zaharias, 9/22/81, Pinehurst, NC	1.00	1.50	2.50
☐☐ 1933	18¢ Bobby Jones, 9/22/81, Pinehurst, NC	1.00	1.50	2.50
☐☐	1932-1933 on one cover	2.00	—	—
☐☐ 1934	18¢ Frederic Remington, 10/9/81, Oklahoma City, OK (1,367,099)	1.00	1.50	2.50
☐☐ 1935	18¢ James Hoban, 10/13/81, DC	1.00	1.50	2.50
☐☐ 1936	20¢ James Hoban, 10/13/81, DC	1.00	1.50	2.50
☐☐	1935-1936 on one cover	3.00	—	—
☐☐	1935-1936 on one cover with Irish Hoban stamp	8.00	—	—

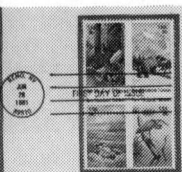

1st Double A Cachet

1921-4

1925

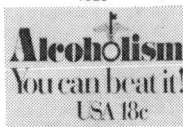

1927

1926   1932   1933   Architecture USA 18c

1928-31

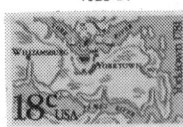

1934   1935-36   1937-38

Scott Number		Description	Sgl	Cacheted Blk	Pl Blk
1937	18¢	**Battle of Yorktown**, 10/16/81, Yorktown, VA	1.00	—	—
		Unofficial Cancel	2.00	—	—
1938	18¢	**Battle of the Virginia Capes**, 10/16/81, Yorktown, VA	1.00	—	—
		Unofficial Cancel	2.00	—	—
		1937-1938 on one cover. (Price for Pair, Blk, PBlk)	1.50	2.00	2.50
		Unofficial Cancel	3.00	3.50	4.00

Totals for Scott 1937-1938 is 1,098,278

1939	(20¢)	**Christmas - Botticelli**, 10/28/81, Chicago, IL (481,395)	1.00	1.50	2.50
		1st Court of Honor cachet	10.00	—	—
1940	(20¢)	**Christmas - Bear & Sleigh**, 10/28/81, Christmas Valley, OR (517,898)	1.00	1.50	2.50
		1939-1940 on one cover, one cancel	1.25	2.50	3.00
		1939-1940 on one cover, dual cancels	2.50	3.50	—
1941	20¢	**John Hanson**, 11/5/81, Frederick, MD (605,616)	1.00	1.50	2.50
1942-5	20¢	**Desert Plants**, 12/11/81, Tucson, AZ (Se-tenant) (1,770,187)	1.00	2.50	3.00
		1st Pugh Cachet	40.00	—	—
1946	(20¢)	**C Stamp**, 10/11/81, Memphis, TN	1.00	1.50	2.50
1947	(20¢)	**C Stamp coil**, 10/11/81, Memphis, TN	1.00 pr	1.50 lpr	2.50
1948	(20¢)	**C Stamp booklet**, 10/11/81, Memphis, TN, single	1.00		
		complete pane	5.00		

Totals Scott 1946-8, U594 and UX92 is 304,404

1982

1949	20¢	**Bighorn Sheep**, single from booklet, 1/8/82, Bighorn, MT	1.00		
1949a		**Booklet pane of 10**	10.00		

1st Court of Honor cachet

1939

John Hanson
President Continental Congress
USA 20c

1941

1st Pugh Cachet

1950

Domestic Mail

US Postage

1946 48

1st M.J. Philatelics cachet

1952

South Carolina
USA 20c

1953-2002

1940

1951

2003

Scott Number	Description	Sgl	Cacheted Blk	Pl Blk
1950	20¢ **Franklin D. Roosevelt**, 1/30/82, Hyde Park, NY	1.00	1.50	2.50
1951	20¢ **Love**, 2/1/82, Boston, MA	1.00	1.50	2.50
1952	20¢ **George Washington**, 2/22/82, Mount Vernon, VA	1.00	1.50	2.50
	1st M.J. Philatelics cachet	10.00	—	—
1953-2002	20¢ **State Birds & Flowers**, 4/14/82, DC, any single	1.25	1.75	—
	Complete set of 50	65.00		
	Complete pane on one cover	45.00		
1953-2002	20¢ **State Birds & Flowers**, 4/14/82, State Capitals, any single	1.75	2.50	—
	Complete set of 50	100.00		
2003	20¢ **Netherlands' Recognition**, 4/20/82, DC	1.00	1.50	2.50
	Combination with Dutch Stamp	5.00	—	—
2004	20¢ **Library of Congress**, 4/21/82, DC	1.00	1.50	2.50
2005	20¢ **Consumer Education Coil**, 4/27/82, DC	1.00 pr	1.50	lp20.00
2006-9	20¢ **Knoxville World's Fair**, 4/29/82, Knoxville, TN (Se-tenant)	1.00	2.50	3.00
2010	20¢ **Horatio Alger**, 4/30/82, Willow Grove, PA	1.00	1.50	2.50
2011	20¢ **Aging Together**, 5/21/82, Sun City, AZ (510,677)	1.00	1.50	2.50
2012	20¢ **The Barrymores**, 6/8/82, New York, NY	1.00	1.50	2.50

2004

2005

2006-9

2010

2011

2014

2012

2013

2017

2018

2015

2019-22

2023

2016

Scott Number	Description	Sgl	Cacheted Blk	Pl Blk
☐☐ 2013	20¢ **Dr. Mary Walker**, 6/10/82, Oswego, NY	1.00	1.50	2.50
☐☐ 2014	20¢ **International Peace Garden**, 6/30/82, Dunseith, ND	1.00	1.50	2.50
☐☐ 2015	20¢ **America's Libraries**, 7/13/82, Phila., PA	1.00	1.50	2.50
☐☐ 2016	20¢ **Jackie Robinson**, 8/2/82, Cooperstown, NY	4.00	5.00	6.00
☐☐ 2017	20¢ **Touro Synagogue**, 8/22/82, Newport, RI (517,264)	1.00	1.50	2.50
☐☐ 2018	20¢ **Wolf Trap**, 9/1/82, Vienna, VA	1.00	1.50	2.50
☐☐ 2019-22	20¢ **Am. Architecture**, 9/30/82, DC (Se-tenant) (1,552,567)	1.00	2.00	3.00
☐☐ 2023	20¢ **Francis of Assisi**, 10/7/82, San Francisco, CA (530,275)	1.00	1.50	2.50
☐☐ 2024	20¢ **Ponce de Leon**, 10/12/82, San Juan, PR	1.00	1.50	2.50
☐☐ 2025	13¢ **Christmas (Kitten & Puppy)**, 11/3/82, Danvers, MA	1.00	1.50	2.50
☐☐ 2026	20¢ **Christmas (Religious)**, 10/28/82, DC (462,982)	1.00	1.50	2.50
☐☐ 2027-30	20¢ **Christmas (Secular)**, 10/28/82, Snow, OK			
	(Se-tenant) (676,950)	1.00	2.50	3.00
☐☐	2026-2030, all 5, either city	2.00	—	—
☐☐	2026-2030 dual cancels	3.00	—	—

1983

	Description	Sgl	Blk	Pl Blk
☐☐ 2031	20¢ **Science & Industry**, 1/19/83, Chicago, IL	1.00	1.50	2.50
☐☐ 2032-5	20¢ **Ballooning**, 3/31/83, Albuquerque, NM & DC, either city			
	(Se-tenant)	1.00	2.50	3.00
☐☐	1st Post/Art Handpainted cachet	35.00	—	—
☐☐ 2036	20¢ **Swedish Trade Relations**, 3/24/83, Phila., PA	1.00	1.50	2.50
☐☐	Combination cover with Swedish issue	5.00	—	—

2024

2025

2026

2027-30

2036

2031

2032-5

2037

2039

2038

2041

2042

2040

2044

2046

2047

2043

Scott Number	Description	Sgl	Cacheted Blk	Pl Blk
2037	20¢ Civilian Conservation Corps, 4/5/83, Luray, VA	1.00	1.50	2.50
2038	20¢ Joseph Priestley, 4/13/83, Northumberland, PA	1.00	1.50	2.50
2039	20¢ Voluntarism, 4/20/83, DC	1.00	1.50	2.50
2040	20¢ German Immigration, 4/29/83, Germantown, PA	1.00	1.50	2.50
	Combination cover with German issue	5.00	—	—
2041	20¢ Brooklyn Bridge, 5/17/83, Brooklyn, NY	1.00	1.50	2.50
2042	20¢ Tennessee Valley Authority, 5/18/83, Knoxville, TN	1.00	1.50	2.50
2043	20¢ Physical Fitness, 5/14/83, Houston, TX	1.00	1.50	2.50
2044	20¢ Scott Joplin, 6/9/83, Sedalia, MO	1.00	1.50	2.50
2045	20¢ Medal of Honor, 6/7/83, DC	1.00	1.50	2.50
2046	20¢ Babe Ruth, 7/6/83, Chicago, IL	3.00	4.00	5.00
2047	20¢ Nathaniel Hawthorne, 7/8/83, Salem, MA	1.00	1.50	2.50
2048-51	13¢ Summer Olympics, 7/28/83, South Bend, IN (Se-tenant)	1.00	2.50	3.00
2052	20¢ Treaty of Paris, 9/2/83, DC	1.00	1.50	2.50
2053	20¢ Civil Service, 9/9/83, DC	1.00	1.50	2.50

Cacheted FDC prices in this period are for unaddressed covers. Addressed covers sell for much less.

USA 20c
Medal of Honor
2045

Olympics
USA
13c
2048-2051

Treaty of Paris 1783
US Bicentennial 20 cents
2052

METROPOLITAN OPERA
1883 1983 USA 20c
2054

USA
20c Charles Steinmetz
2055-2058

CIVIL SERVICE
1883
1983
USA 20c
2053

USA 20c
First American streetcar, New York City, 1832
2059-2062

Season's Greetings USA 20c
2064

Christmas USA 20c
Raphael, 1483-1520, National Gallery
2063

Martin Luther
1483-1983 USA 20c
2065

USA 20c
1959 1984 Alaska Statehood
2066

Olympics 84
USA
20c
2067-2070

FEDERAL DEPOSIT INSURANCE CORPORATION
2071

LO♥E
LO♥E
LO♥E
LO♥E
LO♥E
USA 20c
2072

Carter G. Woodson
Black Heritage USA 20c
2073

SOIL AND WATER CONSERVATION
USA 20c
2074

ACT OF 1934
USA 20c
2075

NATIONAL ARCHIVES
USA
2081

Scott Number	Description	Sgl	Cacheted Blk	Pl Blk
☐☐ 2054	20¢ Metropolitan Opera, 9/14/83, New York, NY	1.00	1.50	2.50
☐☐ 2055-8	20¢ Inventors, 9/21/83, DC (Se-tenant)	1.00	2.50	3.00
☐☐ 2059-62	20¢ Streetcars, 10/8/83, Kennebunkport, ME (Se-tenant)	1.00	2.50	3.00
☐☐ 2063	20¢ Christmas (Religious), 10/28/83, DC	1.00	1.50	2.50
☐☐ 2064	20¢ Christmas (Secular), 10/28/83, Santa Claus, IN	1.00	1.50	2.50
☐☐ 2065	20¢ Martin Luther, 11/11/83, DC	1.00	1.50	2.50

1984

Scott Number	Description	Sgl	Blk	Pl Blk
☐☐ 2066	20¢ Alaska Statehood, 1/3/84, Fairbanks, AK (816,591)	1.00	1.50	2.50
☐☐ 2067-70	20¢ Winter Olympics, 1/6/84, Lake Placid, NY (1,245,807)	1.00	2.50	3.00
☐☐ 2071	20¢ Federal Deposit Ins. Corp., 1/12/84, DC (536,329)	1.00	1.50	2.50
☐☐ 2072	20¢ Love, 1/31/84, DC	1.00	1.50	2.50

Hawaii Statehood 1959-1984
USA 20c
2080

2076-2079
USA 20c
Wild pink Arethusa bulbosa
2082-2085

USA 20c

Louisiana World Exposition USA 20c
Fresh water as a source of Life
2086

Health Research USA 20c
2087

USA 20c
2091

Preserving Wetlands 1934 1984
USA 20c
2092

DOUGLAS FAIRBANKS
Performing Arts USA 20c
2088

Jim Thorpe
USA 20c
2089

JOHN McCORMACK
Performing Arts USA 20c
2090

Roanoke Voyages North Carolina 1584
USA 20c
2093

Herman Melville
USA 20c
2094

Horace Moses
USA 20c
2095

SMOKEY
USA 20c
2096

Roberto Clemente
USA 20c
2097

Scott Number	Description	Sgl	Cacheted Blk	Pl Blk
2073	20¢ **Carter Woodson**, 2/1/84, DC	1.00	1.50	2.50
2074	20¢ **Soil & Water Conservation**, 2/6/84, Denver, CO	1.00	1.50	2.50
2075	20¢ **Credit Union Act**, 2/10/84, Salem, MA	1.00	1.50	2.50
2076-79	20¢ **Orchids**, 3/5/84, Miami, FL (se-tenant)	1.00	2.50	3.00
2080	20¢ **Hawaii Statehood**, 3/12/84, Honolulu, HI	1.00	1.50	2.50
2081	20¢ **National Archives**, 4/16/84, DC	1.00	1.50	2.50
2082-85	20¢ **Olympics**, 5/4/84, Los Angeles, CA (se-tenant)	1.00	2.50	3.00
2086	20¢ **Louisiana Exposition**, 5/11/84, New Orleans, LA	1.00	1.50	2.50
2087	20¢ **Health Research**, 5/17/84, New York, NY	1.00	1.50	2.50
2088	20¢ **Douglas Fairbanks**, 5/23/84, Denver, CO	1.00	1.50	2.50
2089	20¢ **Jim Thorpe**, 5/24/84, Shawnee, OK	1.00	1.50	2.50
2090	20¢ **John McCormack**, 6/6/84, Boston, MA	1.00	1.50	2.50
2091	20¢ **St. Lawrence Seaway**, 6/26/84, Massena, NY	1.00	1.50	2.50
2092	20¢ **Waterfowl Preservation Act**, 7/2/84, Des Moines, IA	1.00	1.50	2.50
2093	20¢ **Roanoke Voyages**, 7/13/84, Manteo, NC	1.00	1.50	2.50
2094	20¢ **Herman Melville**, 8/1/84, New Bedford, MA	1.00	1.50	2.50
2095	20¢ **Horace A. Moses**, 8/6/84, Bloomington, IN	1.00	1.50	—
2096	20¢ **Smokey the Bear**, 8/13/84, Capitan, NM	1.00	1.50	2.50
2097	20¢ **Roberto Clemente**, 8/17/84, Carolina, PR	1.00	1.50	2.50

2098-01

2102

2103

2104

2105

2106

2107

2108

2111

2110

2109

2117-21

2114

Scott Number	Description	Sgl	Cacheted Blk	Pl Blk
2098-01	20¢ Dogs, 9/7/84, New York, NY (1,157,373) (se-tenant)	1.00	2.50	3.50
2102	20¢ Crime Prevention, 9/26/84, DC (427,564)	1.00	1.50	2.50
2103	20¢ Hispanic Americans, 10/31/84, DC (416,796)	1.00	1.50	2.50
2104	20¢ Family Unity, 10/1/84, Shaker Heights, OH (400,659)	1.00	1.50	2.50
2105	20¢ Eleanor Roosevelt, 10/11/84, Hyde Park, NY (479,919)	1.00	1.50	2.50
2106	20¢ Nation of Readers, 10/16/84, DC (437,559)	1.00	1.50	2.50
2107	20¢ Christmas (Madonna), 10/30/84, DC (386,385)	1.00	1.50	2.50
2108	20¢ Christmas (Santa), 10/30/84, Jamaica, NY (430,843)	1.00	1.50	2.50
2109	20¢ Vietnam Vets Memorial, 11/10/84, DC (434,489)	1.00	1.50	2.50

1985

2110	22¢ Jerome Kern, 1/23/85, New York, NY (503,855)	1.00	1.50	2.50

Regular Issue

2111	22¢ 'D' Eagle, 2/1/85, Los Angeles, CA	1.00	1.50	2.50
2112	22¢ 'D' Eagle, coil, 2/1/85, Los Angeles, CA	1.00	pr1.50	lp12.00
2113	22¢ 'D' Eagle, booklet single, 2/1/85, Los Angeles, CA	1.00		
2113a	Booklet, 2/1/85, Los Angeles, CA	9.00		

First Day Cancel was applied to 513,027 covers bearing Scott Nos. 2111-2113

Definitives

2114	22¢ Flag over Capitol Dome, 3/29/85, DC	1.00	1.50	2.50
2115	22¢ Flag over Capitol Dome, coil, 3/29/85, DC	1.00	pr1.50	lp15.00
2115b	22¢ Flag over Capitol, pre-phosphored	—	pr 5.00	

First Day Cancel was applied to 268,161 covers bearing Scott Nos. 2114-2115.

2116	22¢ Flag over Capitol Dome, booklet single, 3/29/85, Waubeka, WI (234,318)	1.00		

Tricycle 1880s
6 USA

2127

USA $10.75

2122

Mary McLeod Bethune

Black Heritage USA 22

2137

Iceboat 1880s
USA
14

2134

Mallard Decoy

Folk Art USA 22

2138-41

22 USA

Winter Special Olympics

2142

22 USA

Rural
Electrification
Administration

2144

Scott Number	Description	Sgl	Cacheted Blk Pl Blk
☐☐ 2116a	**Booklet,** 3/29/85, Waubeka, WI	4.50	
☐☐ 2117-21	22¢ **Seashells,** 4/4/85, Boston, MA (426,290)	1.00	2.50
☐☐ 2121a	Booklet pane of 10	9.00	
☐☐ 2122	**$10.75 Eagle & Half Moon,** 4/29/85, San Francisco, CA	40.00	
☐☐ 2122a	Booklet pane of 3	100.00	

Transportation Issue

		Sgl	Pair
☐☐ 2123	3.4¢ **School Bus,** 6/8/85, Arlington, VA	1.50	11.00
☐☐ 2123a	3.4¢ **School Bus,** precanceled, 6/8/85	—	300.00
☐☐ 2124	4.9¢ **Buckboard,** 6/21/85, Reno, NV	1.50	12.50
☐☐ 2124a	4.9¢ **Buckboard,** precanceled, 6/21/85	—	250.00
☐☐ 2125	5.5¢ **Star Route Truck,** 11/1/86, Ft. Worth, TX	1.50	12.00
☐☐ 2125a	5.5¢ **Star Route Truck,** precanceled, 11/1/86	—	5.00
☐☐ 2126	6¢ **Tricycle,** 5/6/85, Childs, MD (151,494)	1.50	11.00
☐☐ 2126a	6¢ **Tricycle,** precanceled, 5/6/85	—	275.00
☐☐ 2127	7.1¢ **Tractor,** 2/6/87 Sarasota, FL	1.50	11.00
☐☐ 2127a	7.1¢ **Tractor,** precanceled, 2/6/87	—	5.00
☐☐ 2128	8.3¢ **Ambulance,** 6/21/85, Reno, NV	1.50	11.00
☐☐ 2128a	8.3¢ **Ambulance,** precanceled, 6/21/85	—	250.00
☐☐ 2129	8.5¢ **Tow Truck,** 1/24/87, Tucson, AZ	1.50	11.00
☐☐ 2129a	8.5¢ **Tow Truck,** precanceled, 1/24/87	—	5.00
☐☐ 2130	10.1¢ **Oil Wagon,** 4/18/85, Oil Center, NM	1.50	11.00
☐☐ 2130a	10.1¢ **Oil Wagon,** precanceled, 4/18/85	—	250.00
☐☐ 2131	11¢ **Stutz Super Bearcat,** 6/11/85, Baton Rouge, LA	1.50	11.00
☐☐ 2132	12¢ **Stanley Steamer,** 4/2/85, Kingfield, ME (173,998)	1.50	11.00
☐☐ 2132a	12¢ **Stanley Steamer,** precanceled, 4/2/85	—	2,000.
☐☐ 2133	12.5¢ **Pushcart,** 4/18/85, Oil Center, NM	1.50	11.00
☐☐ 2133a	12.5¢ **Pushcart,** precanceled, 4/18/85	—	250.00
☐☐ 2134	14¢ **Ice Boat,** 3/23/85, Rochester, NY (324,710)	1.50	11.00
☐☐ 2135	17¢ **Dog Sled,** 8/20/86, Anchorage, AK	1.50	12.50
☐☐ 2136	25¢ **Bread Wagon,** 11/22/86, Virginia Beach, VA	1.50	11.00

*Cacheted prices are for covers with printed cachets. Covers with general purpose rubberstamp cachets
sell at the uncacheted price. Rubberstamped Chamber of Commerce cachets sell for 1½ to 2 times the
uncacheted price.*

2143

2146

F.A. Bartholdi, Statue of Liberty Sculptor
2147

2152

2153

2145

2149

2150

2154

2155-58

2159

2160-63

2164

2165

2166

Scott Number	Description	Cacheted Sgl	Blk	Pl Blk
1985-86				
☐☐ 2137	22¢ **Mary McLeod Bethune,** 3/5/85, DC (413,244)	1.00	1.50	2.50
☐☐ 2138-41	22¢ **Duck Decoys,** 3/22/85, Shelburne, VT (932,249) (se-tenant)	1.00	1.50	2.75
☐☐ 2142	22¢ **Winter Special Olympics,** 3/25/85, Park City, UT (253,074)	1.00	1.50	2.50
☐☐ 2143	22¢ **Love,** 4/17/85, Hollywood, CA (283,072)	1.00	1.50	2.50
☐☐ 2144	22¢ **Rural Electrification Admin.,** 5/11/85, Madison, SD	1.00	1.50	2.50
☐☐ 2145	22¢ **Ameripex '86,** 5/25/85, Rosemont, IL	1.00	1.50	2.50
☐☐ 2146	22¢ **Abigail Adams,** 6/14/85, Quincy, MA	1.00	1.50	2.50
☐☐ 2147	22¢ **Frederic Auguste Bartholdi,** 7/18/85, New York, NY	1.00	1.50	2.50

Scott Number	Description	Sgl.	Pair
☐☐ 2149	18¢ Washington & Monument, 11/6/85, DC	1.50	
☐☐ 2149a	18¢ Washington & Monument, precanceled, 11/6/85	—	2,000.
☐☐ 2150	21.1¢ Sealed Envelopes, 10/22/85, DC	1.50	
☐☐ 2150a	21.1¢ Sealed Envelopes, precanceled, 10/22/85	—	5.00

		Sgl	Cacheted Blk	Pl Blk
☐☐ 2152	22¢ Korean War Veterans, 7/26/85, DC	1.00	1.50	2.50
☐☐ 2153	22¢ Social Security Act, 8/14/85, Baltimore, MD	1.00	1.50	2.50
☐☐ 2154	22¢ World War I Vets, 8/26/85, Milwaukee, WI	1.00	1.50	2.50
☐☐ 2155-58	22¢ Horses, 9/25/85, Lexington, KY (se-tenant)	1.00	1.50	2.75
☐☐ 2159	22¢ Public Education in America, 10/1/85, Boston, MA	1.00	1.50	2.50
☐☐ 2160-63	22¢ Int'l Youth Year, 10/7/85, Chicago, IL (se-tenant)	1.00	1.50	2.75
☐☐ 2164	22¢ Help End Hunger, 10/15/85, DC	1.00	1.50	2.50
☐☐ 2165	22¢ Christmas (Madonna & Child), 10/30/85, Detroit, MI	1.00	1.50	2.50
☐☐ 2166	22¢ Christmas (Poinsettia), 10/30/85, Nazareth, MI	1.00	1.50	2.50
☐☐ 2167	22¢ Arkansas Statehood, 1/3/86, Little Rock, AR (364,729)	1.00	1.50	2.50

1986-87 Great Americans Issue

☐☐ 2168	1¢ Margaret Mitchell, 9/17/86, New York, NY	1.00	1.50	2.50
☐☐ 2169	2¢ Mary Lyon, 2/28/87, S. Hadley, MA	1.00	1.50	2.50
☐☐ 2170	3¢ Dr. Paul Dudley White, 9/15/86, Washington, DC	1.00	1.50	2.50
☐☐ 2171	4¢ Father Flanagan, 7/14/86, Boys Town, NE	1.00	1.50	2.50
☐☐ 2172	5¢ Hugo Black, 2/27/86, Washington, DC (303,012)	1.00	1.50	2.50
☐☐ 2176	10¢ Red Cloud, 8/15/87, Red Cloud, NE	1.00	1.50	2.50
☐☐ 2177	14¢ Julia Ward Howe, 2/12/87, Boston, MA	1.00	1.50	2.50
☐☐ 2179	17¢ Belva Ann Lockwood, 6/18/86, Middleport, NY	1.00	1 50	2.50
☐☐ 2183	25¢ Jack London, 1/11/86, Glen Ellen, CA (358,686)	1.00	1.50	2.50
☐☐ 2191	56¢ John Harvard, 9/3/86, Boston, MA	2.00	3.00	4.00
☐☐ 2194	$1 Dr. Bernard Revel, 9/23/86, New York, NY	4.00	6.00	8.00
☐☐ 2195	$2 William Jennings Bryan, 3/19/86, Salem, IL			
	(123,430)	5.00	10.00	15.00
☐☐ 2196	$5 Francis Bret Harte, 8/25/87, Twain Harte, CA	8.00	25.00	30.00

1986

☐☐ 2198-2201	22¢ Stamp Collecting, 1/23/86, State College, PA			
	(se-tenant)	1.00		
☐☐ 2202	22¢ Love, 1/30/86, New York, NY	1.00	1.50	2.50
☐☐ 2203	22¢ Sojourner Truth, 2/4/86, New Paltz, NY (342,985)	1.00	1.50	2.50
☐☐ 2204	22¢ Republic of Texas, 3/2/86, San Antonio, TX	1.00	1.50	2.50
☐☐ 2205-09	22¢ Fish, 3/21/86, Seattle, WA (se-tenant)	1.00		
☐☐ 2209a	Booklet, 3/21/86, Seattle, WA	4.00		
☐☐ 2210	22¢ Public Hospitals, 4/11/86, New York, NY	1.00	1.50	2.50
☐☐ 2211	22¢ Duke Ellington, 4/29/86, New York, NY	1.00	1.50	2.50
☐☐ 2216-19	22¢ Presidential Souvenir Sheets of 9, 5/22/86,			
	Chicago, IL	5.00	—	—
☐☐	2216a-2219i	1.00	1.50	—
☐☐ 2220-23	22¢ Polar Explorers, 5/28/86, North Pole, AK (se-tenant)	1.00	1.50	2.50
☐☐	Set of 4	3.00	—	—
☐☐ 2224	22¢ Statue of Liberty, 7/4/86, New York, NY	.80	—	—
☐☐ 2226	2¢ Locomotive, Re-engraved coil, 3/6/87, Milwaukee, WI	1.00 pr	2.50	
☐☐ 2235-38	22¢ Navajo Art, 9/4/86 Window Rock, AZ (se-tenant)	1.00	1.50	2.50
☐☐	Set of 4	3.00	—	—
☐☐ 2239	22¢ T.S. Eliot, 9/26/86, St.Louis, MO	.80	—	—
☐☐ 2240-43	22¢ Woodcarved Figurines, 10/1/86, Washington, DC			
	(se-tenant)	1.00	1.50	2.50
☐☐	Set of 4	3.00	—	—
☐☐ 2244	22¢ Christmas (Madonna), 10/24/86, Washington, DC	1.00	1.50	2.50
☐☐ 2245	22¢ Christmas (Winter Village), 10/24/86, Snow Hill, MD	1.00	1.50	2.50

2167

Margaret Mitchell
USA 1
2168

Paul Dudley White MD
USA .3
2170

Father Flanagan USA
4
2171

Hugo L. Black
5 USA
2172

14 USA
Julia Ward Howe
2177

USA 17
2179

USA 25
Jack London
2183

John Harvard
USA 56
2191

Bernard Revel
USA $1
2194

Bryan $2
USA
William Jennings
2195

STAMP COLLECTING
USA 22
2198-2201

LOVE
USA 22
2202

Sojourner Truth 22
Black Heritage USA
2203

USA 22
San Jacinto 1836
Republic of Texas
2204

22 USA
Muskellunge
2205-09

Public Hospitals USA 22
H
2210

USA 22
Elisha Kent Kane
2220-23

USA 22
George Washington
2216a

John Tyler
USA 22
2217a

Duke Ellington USA
2211

Liberty
1886-1986
USA 22
2224

R.B. Hayes
USA 22
Rutherford B. Hayes
2218a

Warren G. Harding
USA 22
2219a

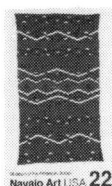
2235-38

2239

2240-43

2246

2244

2245

2247

2248

2249

2250

2251

2253

2255

2259

2264

Scott Number	Description	Sgl	Cacheted Blk	Pl Blk
1987				
☐☐ 2246	22¢ **Michigan**, 1/26/87, Lansing, MI	1.00	1.50	2.50
☐☐ 2247	22¢ **Pan Am Games**, 1/29/87, Indianapolis, IN	1.00	1.50	2.50
☐☐ 2248	22¢ **Love**, 1/30/87, San Francisco, CA	1.00	1.50	2.50
☐☐ 2249	22¢ **Jean Baptiste Point du Sable**, 2/20/87, Chicago, IL	1.00	1.50	2.50
☐☐ 2250	22¢ **Enrico Caruso**, 2/27/87, New York, NY	1.00	1.50	2.50
☐☐ 2251	22¢ **Girl Scouts of America**, 3/12/87, DC	1.00	1.50	2.50

1987-88	**Transportation Coils**	Sgl	Pair
☐☐ 2253	3¢ **Conestoga Wagon**, 2/29/88, Conestoga, PA	1.00	1.50
☐☐ 2255	5¢ **Milk Wagon**, 9/25/87, Indianapolis, IN	1.00	1.50
☐☐ 2259	10¢ **Canal Boat**, 4/11/87, Buffalo, NY	1.00	1.50
☐☐ 2264	17.5¢ **Mormon Wasp**, 9/25/87, Indianapolis, IN	1.00	1.50

1987		Sgl	Blk	Pl Blk
☐☐ 2267-74	22¢ **Special Occasions**, 4/20/87, Atlanta, GA	1.00		
☐☐ 2274a	Booklet pane of 10	5.00		
☐☐ 2275	22¢ **United Way**, 4/28/87, DC	1.00	1.50	2.50
☐☐ 2276	22¢ **Flag & Fireworks**, 5/9/87, Denver, CO	1.00	1.50	2.50
☐☐ 2276a	Booklet pane of 20	8.00		
☐☐ 2286-2335	22¢ **American Wildlife**, 6/13/87, Toronto, Ontario			
	(any single)	1.00		
☐☐	Complete Set	50.00		

2267-74

2275

2276

2286-2335

2336

2337

2338

2339

2340

2341

2342

Scott Number	Description	Sgl	Cacheted Blk	Pl Blk
1987-88				
☐☐ 2336	22¢ **Delaware Statehood Bicentennial,** 7/4/87, Dover, DE	1.00	1.50	2.50
☐☐ 2337	22¢ **Pennsylvania Statehood Bicentennial,** 8/26/87, Harrisburg, PA	1.00	1.50	2.50
☐☐ 2338	22¢ **New Jersey Statehood Bicentennial,** 9/11/87, Trenton, NJ	1.00	1.50	2.50
☐☐ 2339	22¢ **Georgia Statehood Bicentennial,** 1/6/88, Atlanta, GA	1.00	1.50	2.50
☐☐ 2340	22¢ **Connecticut Statehood Bicentennial,** 1/9/88, Hartford, CT	1.00	1.50	2.50
☐☐ 2341	22¢ **Massachusetts Statehood Bicentennial,** 2/6/88, Boston, MA	1.00	1.50	2.50
☐☐ 2342	22¢ **Maryland Statehood Bicentennial,** 2/15/88, Annapolis, MD	1.00	1.50	2.50
1987				
☐☐ 2349	22¢ **U.S.-Morocco Diplomatic Relations,** 7/17/87, DC	1.00	1.50	2.50
☐☐ 2350	22¢ **William Faulkner,** 8/3/87, Oxford, MS	1.00	1.50	2.50
☐☐ 2351-2354	22¢ **Lacemaking,** 8/14/87, Ypsilanti, MI	1.00	1.50	2.50
☐☐ 2354a	Set of 4	3.00		
☐☐ 2355-2359	22¢ **Drafting of the Constitution Bicentennial,** 8/28/87, DC	1.00		
☐☐ 2359a	Booklet pane of 5	4.00		

Friendship with Morocco 1787-1987
USA 22
2349

William Faulkner
USA 22
2350

Lacemaking USA 22
2351-54

U.S. Constitution
1787-1987 22 USA
2360

CPA
22 USA
2361

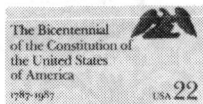
The Bicentennial of the Constitution of the United States of America
1787-1987   USA 22
2355-59

Stourbridge Lion 1829   USA 22
2362-66

CHRISTMAS 22 USA
Moroni, National Gallery
2367

USA 22 GREETINGS
2368

22 USA
2369

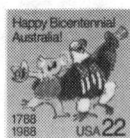
Happy Bicentennial Australia!
1788 1988 USA 22
2370

James Weldon Johnson 22
2371

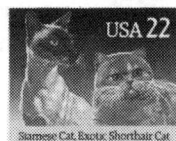
USA 22
Siamese Cat, Exotic Shorthair Cat
2372-75

22 USA
KNUTE ROCKNE
2376

	Scott Number	Description	Sgl	Cacheted Blk	Pl Blk
☐☐	2360	22¢ **Signing of the Constitution Bicentennial**, 9/17/87, Philadelphia, PA	1.00	1.50	2.50
☐☐	2361	22¢ **Certified Public Accounting**, 9/21/87, New York, NY	1.00	1.50	2.50
☐☐	2362-2366	22¢ **Locomotives**, 10/1/87, Baltimore, MD	1.00	1.50	2.50
☐☐	2366a	Booklet pane of 5	4.00		
☐☐	2367	22¢ **Christmas (Religious)**, 10/23/87, DC	1.00	1.50	2.50
☐☐	2368	22¢ **Christmas (Secular)**, 10/23/87, Anaheim, CA	1.00	1.50	2.50

1988

	Scott Number	Description	Sgl	Blk	Pl Blk
☐☐	2369	22¢ **1988 Winter Olympics**, 1/10/88, Anchorage, AK	1.00	1.50	2.50
☐☐	2370	22¢ **Australia Bicentennial**, 1/26/88, DC	1.00	1.50	2.50
☐☐	2371	22¢ **James Weldon Johnson**, 2/2/88, Nashville, TN	1.00	1.50	2.50
☐☐	2372-2375	22¢ **Cats**, 2/5/88, New York, NY	1.00	1.50	2.50
☐☐	2376	22¢ **Knute Kenneth Rockne**, 3/4/88, Notre Dame, IN	1.00	1.50	2.50

☐☐ _____
☐☐ _____
☐☐ _____
☐☐ _____
☐☐ _____
☐☐ _____
☐☐ _____
☐☐ _____
☐☐ _____
☐☐ _____
☐☐ _____
☐☐ _____
☐☐ _____
☐☐ _____
☐☐ _____
☐☐ _____
☐☐ _____
☐☐ _____
☐☐ _____
☐☐ _____
☐☐ _____
☐☐ _____
☐☐ _____
☐☐ _____
☐☐ _____
☐☐ _____
☐☐ _____
☐☐ _____
☐☐ _____
☐☐ _____
☐☐ _____
☐☐ _____
☐☐ _____
☐☐ _____
☐☐ _____
☐☐ _____
☐☐ _____
☐☐ _____
☐☐ _____

☐☐ _____
☐☐ _____
☐☐ _____
☐☐ _____
☐☐ _____
☐☐ _____
☐☐ _____
☐☐ _____
☐☐ _____
☐☐ _____
☐☐ _____
☐☐ _____
☐☐ _____
☐☐ _____
☐☐ _____
☐☐ _____
☐☐ _____
☐☐ _____
☐☐ _____
☐☐ _____
☐☐ _____
☐☐ _____
☐☐ _____
☐☐ _____
☐☐ _____
☐☐ _____
☐☐ _____
☐☐ _____
☐☐ _____
☐☐ _____
☐☐ _____
☐☐ _____
☐☐ _____
☐☐ _____
☐☐ _____
☐☐ _____
☐☐ _____
☐☐ _____

We Invite You To Join . . .

THE AMERICAN
FIRST DAY COVER SOCIETY

The FIRST and ONLY not-for-profit, non-commercial, International Society devoted exclusively to First Day Covers and First Day Cover collecting.

FIRST DAYS . . . IS THE AWARD WINNING OFFICIAL PUBLICATION OF THE AMERICAN FIRST DAY COVER SOCIETY.
FDC collecting is a hands-on hobby of personal involvement — much more than simple collecting. It encourages the individual collector to fully develop his range of interests so that his collection is a reflection of his personal tastes. FDCs will encourage your creativity to reach full expression by adapting cachets or cancellations or using combinations (related stamps). In this hobby uniqueness is the rule, not the exception.
BUT . . . FIRST DAYS IS AVAILABLE ONLY TO MEMBERS OF THE AFDCS.
It's just ONE of the many benefits of membership. Whether you are interested in topical areas of collecting, working on serious research or just learning more about the hobby in general, this is the organization for you.

FIRST DAYS
IMPORTANT FEATURES

- Classic U.S. First Day Covers Research
- Auction Notes
- First Day Activity Reports
- Combinations Column with Suggestions
- Question Box
- How To Obtain Foreign Covers
- Unofficials, Cancellation Varieties
- Cover Exchange
- Topical Checklists of Popular Subjects
- First Cachets
- Handdrawn Cachets & Colored Designs
- Comprehensive FDC Marketplace
- Do-it-yourself Articles

...tMounts

120	120
	111
107	106
105	
	100
	89
84	82
80	
	74
70	68
66	
61	63
	57
55	52
50	48
44	
40	41
	39
36	
	33
31	30
28	27
25	24
22	20
0	0

ScottMount Scale

Carefully position the stamp along the horizontal base line with perforations barely touching and roughly centered along the upright bar. The cross-line closest to the top perforations indicates the size mount to be used.

□□ _____
□□ _____
□□ _____
□□ _____
□□ _____
□□ _____
□□ _____
□□ _____
□□ _____
□□ _____
□□ _____
□□ _____
□□ _____
□□ _____
□□ _____
□□ _____
□□ _____
□□ _____
□□ _____
□□ _____
□□ _____
□□ _____
□□ _____
□□ _____
□□ _____
□□ _____
□□ _____
□□ _____
□□ _____
□□ _____

IMPORTANT NOTICE

Cachet prices in this catalogue are for an average cacheted First Day Cover. Some FDC's, depending on the cachet, can sell for many times the catalogue price, while others sell for less.

The Cachet Pricing Calculator lists cachetmakers, the dates they produced FDC's and a market value multiplier. The Calculator can be found on pages 33 thru 35 of this catalogue.

☐☐ _____
☐☐ _____
☐☐ _____
☐☐ _____
☐☐ _____
☐☐ _____
☐☐ _____
☐☐ _____
☐☐ _____
☐☐ _____
☐☐ _____
☐☐ _____
☐☐ _____
☐☐ _____
☐☐ _____
☐☐ _____
☐☐ _____
☐☐ _____
☐☐ _____
☐☐ _____
☐☐ _____
☐☐ _____
☐☐ _____
☐☐ _____
☐☐ _____
☐☐ _____
☐☐ _____
☐☐ _____
☐☐ _____
☐☐ _____
☐☐ _____
☐☐ _____
☐☐ _____
☐☐ _____
☐☐ _____
☐☐ _____
☐☐ _____
☐☐ _____
☐☐ _____

AIRMAIL

| C1-C3 | C7-C9 | C10 |

			Uncacheted		Cacheted	
Scott Number	Description		Sgl	Blk	Sgl	Blk

1918

☐☐ C1	6¢ **Jenny,** 12/10/18, DC		17500.00	—	—	—
☐☐	Washington, DC, 12/16/18		2000.00	—	—	—
☐☐	Philadelphia, PA 12/16/18		2000.00	—	—	—
☐☐	New York, NY, 12/16/18		2000.00	—	—	—
☐☐ C2	16¢ **Jenny,** 7/11/18, DC		22500.00	—	—	—
☐☐	Washington, DC, 7/15/18		800.00	—	—	—
☐☐	Philadelphia, PA, 7/15/18		800.00	—	—	—
☐☐	New York, NY, 7/15/18		800.00	—	—	—
☐☐ C3	24¢ **Jenny,** 5/13/18, DC		27500.00	—	—	—
☐☐	Washington, DC, 5/15/18		750.00	—	—	—
☐☐	Philadelphia, PA, 5/15/18		750.00	—	—	—
☐☐	New York, NY, 5/15/18		750.00	—	—	—

*The earliest date listed under C1-C3 is the First Day. The other date is
the First Flight for the three different air mail rates of 1918*

1923

☐☐ C4	8¢ **Propeller,** 8/15/23, DC		350.00	1000.	—	—
☐☐ C5	16¢ **Insignia,** 8/17/23, DC		750.00	1600.	—	—
☐☐ C6	24¢ **Biplane,** 8/21/32, DC		900.00	3000.	—	—

1926-1927

☐☐ C7	10¢ **Map,** 2/13/26, DC		65.00	150.00	—	—
☐☐	Chicago, IL		75.00	160.00	—	—
☐☐	Cleveland, OH		135.00	200.00	—	—
☐☐	Dearborn, MI		135.00	200.00	—	—
☐☐	Detroit, MI		75.00	160.00	—	—
☐☐	Unofficial City		135.00	—	—	—

FDCs flown on CAM on 2/15/26 sell for 25% more than prices listed.

☐☐ C8	15¢ **Map,** 9/18/26, DC		75.00	150.00	250.00	—
☐☐ C9	20¢ **Map,** 1/25/27, DC		115.00	175.00	—	—
☐☐	New York, NY		125.00	200.00	—	—
☐☐	1st Albert E.Gorham cachet		—	—	250.00	—
☐☐ C10	10¢ **Lindbergh,** 6/18/27, DC		25.00	40.00	125.00	—
☐☐	Detroit, MI		35.00	55.00	125.00	—
☐☐	Little Falls, MN		35.00	55.00	125.00	—
☐☐	St. Louis, MO		25.00	40.00	125.00	—
☐☐	Air Mail Field, Chicago, Unofficial		150.00	—	—	—
☐☐	Any other Unofficial City		150.00	—	125.00	—
☐☐	1st Milton Mauck cachet		—	—	150.00	—
☐☐ C10a	**Booklet,** 5/26/28, DC		925.00	—		
☐☐ C10a	**Single from booklet,** DC		90.00	—		
☐☐ C10a	**Booklet,** Cleveland Mid. Phil. Sta.		900.00	—		
☐☐ C10a	**Single,** Cleveland Mid. Phil. Sta.		80.00	—		
☐☐ C10a	**Booklet,** plus 645 Valley Forge, Cleveland Mid. Phil. Sta.		1000.00	—		
☐☐ C10a	**Single,** plus 645 Valley Forge		150.00	—		

*Lindbergh booklet FDCs and C10a plus 645 FDCs are both known on
Garfield Perry Shield Eagle and Biplane general purpose cacheted
envelopes. These sell for a 10% to 20% premium over uncacheted FDCs.*

C11

C12, C16, C17, C19

C13, C15

C18

C20-C22

C23

C24

C25, C35

C32

Scott Number	Description	Uncacheted		Cacheted	
		Sgl	Blk	Sgl	Blk
1928					
☐☐ **C11 5¢ Beacon,** 7/25/28, DC (pair)		50.00	60.00	150.00	—
☐☐ With single stamp and postage due stamp		175.00	—	250.00	—
☐☐ Unofficial city (pair)		200.00	—	250.00	—
☐☐ Single stamp with no postage due		200.00	—	350.00	—
1930					
☐☐ **C12 5¢ Winged Globe,** 2/10/30, DC		20.00	22.00	70.00	—
☐☐ **C13 65¢ Zeppelin,** 4/19/30, DC		1850.	3000.	2700.	5400.
☐☐ **C14 $1.30 Zeppelin,** 4/19/30, DC		1400.	2500.	2000.	4000.
☐☐ **C15 $2.60 Zeppelin,** 4/19/30, DC		2000.	3000.	3000.	6000.
☐☐ C13-15 complete set on one cover		13,500.	—	—	—
☐☐ C13-15 complete set of pl# sgl on one cover		18,000.	—	—	—
FDCs flown on Zeppelin flights sell for a premium					
1931-1935					
☐☐ **C16 5¢ Winged Globe,** 8/19/31, DC		200.00	300.00	—	—
☐☐ **C17 8¢ Winged Globe,** 9/26/32, DC		20.00	30.00	40.00	60.00
☐☐ **C18 50¢ Zeppelin,** 10/2/33, New York, NY (3,500)		275.00	450.00	350.00	500.00
☐☐ Akron, OH, 10/4/33		425.00	650.00	475.00	675.00
☐☐ Washington, DC, 10/5/33		375.00	500.00	425.00	525.00
☐☐ Miami, FL, 10/6/33		250.00	375.00	275.00	400.00
☐☐ Chicago, IL, 10/7/33		375.00	500.00	425.00	675.00
FDCs flown on a Zeppelin flight are more desirable and sell for a premium.					
☐☐ **C19 6¢ Winged Globe,** 7/1/34, DC		10.00	15.00	35.00	45.00
☐☐ Unofficial City		20.00	—	—	—
☐☐ Baltimore, MD, 6/30/34		200.00	—	500.00	—
☐☐ New York, NY		650.00	—	1000.	—
☐☐ **C20 25¢ China Clipper,** 11/22/35 San Francisco, CA (15,000)		10.00	15.00	35.00	45.00
☐☐ Washington, DC (10,910)		15.00	20.00	40.00	50.00

C33, C37, C39, C41   C34   C38   C40

C42   C45   C46

C47   C48, C50   C49   C51, C52, C60, C61

Scott Number	Description	Uncacheted Sgl	Blk	Cacheted Sgl	Blk
1937-1939					
☐☐ C21 20¢	China Clipper, 2/15/37, DC	12.00	15.00	40.00	50.00
☐☐ C22 50¢	China Clipper, 2/15/37, DC	15.00	18.00	45.00	55.00
☐☐	Both on one cover	20.00	30.00	75.00	100.00
Total for Scott C21 and C22 equals 40,000					
☐☐ C23 6¢	Eagle Holding Shield, 5/14/38, Dayton, OH				
	(116,443)	5.00	8.00	20.00	30.00
☐☐	St. Petersburg, FL (95,121)	5.00	8.00	20.00	30.00
☐☐ C24 30¢	Winged Globe, 5/16/39, NY, NY (63,634)	12.00	15.00	50.00	60.00

		Cacheted Sgl	Blk	Pl Blk
1941-1944				
☐☐ C25	6¢ Plane, 6/25/41, DC (99,986)	2.50	4.00	8.00
☐☐ C25a	6¢ Booklet, 3/18/43 (50,216)	40.00		
☐☐ C25a	Single, from booklet	8.00		
☐☐ C26	8¢ Plane, 3/21/44, DC (147,484)	4.00	5.00	8.00
☐☐ C27	10¢ Plane, 8/15/41, Atlantic City, NJ (87,712)	8.00	12.00	15.00
☐☐ C28	15¢ Plane, 8/19/41, Baltimore, MD (74,000)	12.00	20.00	30.00
☐☐ C29	20¢ Plane, 8/27/41, Phila., PA (66,225)	12.00	20.00	30.00
☐☐ C30	30¢ Plane, 9/25/41, Kansas City, MO (57,175)	17.00	25.00	35.00
☐☐ C31	50¢ Plane, 10/29/41, St. Louis, MO (54,580)	45.00	50.00	70.00

		Sgl	Blk	Pl Blk
1946-1949				
☐☐ C32	5¢ Skymaster, 9/25/46, DC, (Total for C32 and			
	UC14, 396,639)	2.00	4.00	6.00
☐☐	1st William W. Bayless cachet	15.00	—	—
☐☐ C33	5¢ DC-4, 3/26/47, DC (342,634)	2.00	4.00	6.00
☐☐ C34	10¢ Pan Am. Bldg., 8/30/47, DC (265,773)	2.00	4.00	6.00
☐☐ C35	15¢ N.Y. Skyline, 8/20/47, New York, NY	2.75	4.00	6.00
☐☐ C36	25¢ Bay Bridge, 7/30/47, San Francisco, CA (201,762)	3.50	7.00	10.00
☐☐ C37	5¢ DC-4, Coil, 1/15/48, DC (192,084)	1.00 pr	2.00 lp	4.00
☐☐ C38	5¢ Map, 7/31/48, New York, NY (371,265)	1.75	3.00	4.00
☐☐ C39	6¢ DC-4, 1/18/49, DC (266,790)	1.50	3.00	4.00
☐☐ C39a	6¢ Booklet, 11/18/49, New York, NY	10.00		
☐☐ C40	6¢ Alexandria, 5/11/49, Alexandria, VA (386,717)	1.25	3.00	4.00
☐☐ C41	6¢ DC-4, Coil, 8/25/49, DC (240,386)	1.00 pr	1.25 lp	4.00

C53   C55

C54

C56

C57, C59, C62, C63   C64-C65   C67

C68

C66   C69   C70

Scott Number	Description	Sgl	Cacheted Blk	Pl Blk
☐☐ C42	10¢ P.O. Bldg., 11/18/49, New Orleans, LA (270,000)	1.75	3.00	4.00
☐☐ C43	15¢ Globe & Doves, 10/7/49, Chicago, IL (246,833)	2.25	5.00	8.00
☐☐ C44	25¢ Boeing, 11/30/49, Seattle, WA (220,215)	2.75	5.00	8.00
☐☐ C45	6¢ Wright Bros., 12/17/49, Kitty Hawk, NC (378,585)	3.75	5.00	8.00

1952-54

☐☐ C46	80¢ Diamond Head, 3/26/52, Honolulu, HI (89,864)	20.00	30.00	60.00
☐☐ C47	6¢ Powered Flight, 5/29/53, Dayton, OH, (359,050)	1.50	3.00	4.00
☐☐ C48	4¢ Eagle, 9/3/54, Phila., PA (295,720)	1.25	3.00	4.00

1957-1959

☐☐ C49	6¢ Air Force, 8/1/57, DC (356,683)	2.00	3.00	4.00
☐☐ C50	5¢ Eagle, 7/31/58, Colorado Springs, CO (207,954)	1.25	3.00	4.00
☐☐ C51	7¢ Blue Jet, 7/31/58, Phila., PA (204,401)	1.25	3.00	4.00
☐☐ C51a	7¢ Booklet, 7/31/58, San Antonio, TX (119,769)	11.00	—	—
☐☐ C52	7¢ Blue Jet Coil, 7/31/58, Miami, FL (181,603)	1.25 pr	3.00 lp	4.00
☐☐ C53	7¢ Alaska, 1/3/59, Juneau, AK (489,752)	1.25	3.00	4.00
☐☐ C54	7¢ Balloon, 8/17/59, Lafayette, IN (383,556)	1.25	3.00	4.00
☐☐ C55	7¢ Hawaii, 8/21/59, Honolulu, HI, (533,464)	1.25	3.00	4.00
☐☐ C56	10¢ Pan Am. Games, 8/27/59, Chicago, IL (302,206)	1.25	3.00	4.00

1960-1966

☐☐ C57	10¢ Liberty Bell, 6/10/60, Miami, FL (246,509)	2.00	3.00	5.00
☐☐ C58	15¢ Statue of Liberty, 11/20/59, New York, NY (259,412)	2.00	3.00	5.00
☐☐ C59	25¢ Lincoln, 4/22/60, San Francisco, CA (211,235)	2.00	3.00	5.00
☐☐ C59a	25¢ Lincoln, luminescent, 12/29/66, DC (3,000)	25.00	—	—
☐☐ C60	7¢ Red Jet, 8/12/60, Arlington, VA (247,190)	1.25	3.00	4.00
☐☐ C60a	7¢ Booklet, 8/19/60, St. Louis, MO (143,363)	11.00		
☐☐ C61	7¢ Jet Coil, 10/22/60, Atlantic City, NJ (197,995)	1.25 pr	3.00 lp	4.00
☐☐ C62	13¢ Liberty Bell, 6/28/61, New York, NY (316,166)	1.25	3.00	4.00
☐☐ C62a	13¢ Liberty Bell, luminescent, 2/15/67, DC	25.00	—	—
☐☐ C63	15¢ Statue of Liberty, 1/13/61, Buffalo, NY (192,976)	1.25	3.00	4.00
☐☐ C63a	15¢ Statue of Liberty, luminescent, Jan. 1967, DC	25.00	—	—

C71   C72-C73   C74   C77

C84   1st Readers Digest cachet   C78, C82

C79, C83

Scott Number	Description	Sgl	Cacheted Blk	Pl Blk
☐☐ C64	8¢ Capitol, 12/5/62, DC (288,355)	1.25	3.00	4.00
☐☐ C64a	8¢ Capitol, luminescent, 8/1/63, Dayton, OH (262,720)	1.25	3.00	4.00
☐☐ C64b	8¢ Booklet, 12/5/62, DC (146,835)	3.00		
☐☐ C65	8¢ Capitol Coil, 12/5/62, DC (220,173)	1.25 pr	3.00	lp 4.00
☐☐ C65a	8¢ Capitol Coil, luminescent, 1/14/65, New Orleans, LA	25.00	—	—
☐☐ C66	15¢ Blair, 5/3/63, Silver Spring, MD (260,031)	1.50	3.00	4.00
☐☐ C67	6¢ Bald Eagle, 7/12/63, Boston, MA (268,265)	1.25	3.00	4.00
☐☐ C67a	6¢ Bald Eagle, luminescent, 2/15/67, DC	15.00	—	—
☐☐ C68	8¢ Earhart, 7/24/63, Atchison, KS (437,996)	3.00	4.00	5.00
☐☐ C69	8¢ Goddard, 10/5/64, Roswell, NM (421,020)	3.00	4.00	5.00

1967-1969

☐☐ C70	8¢ Alaska, 3/30/67, Sitka, AK (554,784)	1.25	3.00	4.00
☐☐ C71	20¢ Audubon, 4/26/67, New York, NY (227,930)	2.50	4.00	5.00
☐☐ C72	10¢ 50-Star Runway, 1/5/68, San Fran., CA	1.25	3.00	4.00
☐☐ C72b	10¢ Booklet, pane of 8, 1/5/68, DC	4.00		
☐☐ C72c	10¢ Booklet, pane of 5 plus Mail Early Tab, 1/6/68, DC	150.00		
☐☐ C72c	10¢ Booklet, pane of 5 plus Zip tab, 1/6/68, DC	150.00		
☐☐ C73	10¢ 50-Star Runway, Coil 1/5/68, San Fran., CA	1.25 pr	3.00	lp 4.00

Total for Scott C72-C73 is 814,140

☐☐ C74	10¢ Jenny, 5/15/68, DC (521,084)	1.75	3.00	4.00
☐☐	1st Readers Digest cachet	15.00	—	—
☐☐ C75	20¢ "USA," 11/22/68, New York, NY (276,244)	1.25	3.00	4.00
☐☐ C76	10¢ First Man on Moon, 9/9/69, DC (8,743,070)	3.50	8.00	12.00

1971-1974

☐☐ C77	9¢ Delta Plane, 5/15/71, Kitty Hawk, NC	1.00	2.00	3.00

Total for Scott C77 and UXC10 is 379,442

☐☐ C78	11¢ Jet, 5/7/71, Spokane, WA	1.00	2.00	3.00
☐☐ C78a	11¢ Booklet, 5/7/71, Spokane, WA	3.00		
☐☐ C79	13¢ Winged Envelope, 11/16/73, New York, NY (282,550)	1.00	2.00	3.00
☐☐ C79a	13¢ Booklet, 12/27/73, Chicago, IL	3.00		
☐☐ C80	17¢ Statue of Liberty, 7/13/71, Lakehurst, NJ (172,269)	1.00	2.00	3.00
☐☐ C81	21¢ USA, 5/21/71, DC (293,140)	1.00	2.00	3.00
☐☐ C82	11¢ Jet Coil, 5/7/71, Spokane, WA	1.00 pr	2.00	lp 3.00

Total for Scott C78, C78a and C82 is 464,750

C75, C81

FIRST MAN ON THE MOON
C76

C85

Progress in Electronics
C86

C87

C88

C89

C90

28¢
USAirmail
Blanche Stuart Scott
Pioneer Pilot
C99

Philip Mazzei
Patriot Remembered
USAirmail
40¢
C98

Glenn Curtiss
Aviation Pioneer
USAirmail 35¢
C100

C105-8

C101-4

Scott Number	Description	Sgl	Cacheted Blk	Pl Blk
☐☐ C83	13¢ **Winged Air Envelope Coil,** 12/27/73, Chicago, IL	1.00 pr	2.00 lp	3.00
Total for Scott C79a and C83 is 204,756				
☐☐ C84	11¢ **City of Refuge,** 5/3/72, Honaunau, HI (364,816)	1.00	2.00	3.00
☐☐ C85	11¢ **Olympics,** 8/17/72, DC	1.00	2.00	3.00
☐☐ C86	11¢ **Electronics,** 7/10/73, New York, NY	1.00	2.00	3.00
Total for set Scott 1500-2 and C86 is 1,197,700				
☐☐ C87	18¢ **Statue of Liberty,** 1/11/74, Hempstead, NY	1.00	2.00	3.00
☐☐	1st James Hogg cachet	15.00	—	—
☐☐ C88	26¢ **Mt. Rushmore,** 1/2/74, Rapid City, SD	1.00	2.00	3.00
☐☐ C89	25¢ **Plane and Globe,** 1/2/76, Honolulu, HI	1.50	3.00	5.00
☐☐ C90	31¢ **Plane, globe and flag,** 1/2/76, Honolulu, HI	1.50	3.00	5.00
☐☐	C88 & C90 on one cover	3.00	—	—
☐☐ C91	31¢ **Wright Bros.,** 9/23/78, Dayton, OH	1.50	3.00	5.00
☐☐ C92	31¢ **Wright Bros.,** 9/23/78, Dayton, OH	1.50	3.00	5.00
☐☐	C91 & C92 on one cover	3.00	—	—
☐☐ C93	21¢ **Octave Chanute Airmail,** 3/29/79, Chanute, KS	1.25	3.00	5.00
☐☐ C94	21¢ **Octave Chanute Airmail,** 3/29/79, Chanute, KS	1.25	3.00	5.00
☐☐	C93 & C94 on one cover	3.50	—	—
☐☐ C95-6	25¢ **Wiley Post,** 11/20/79, Oklahoma City, OK, either stamp	1.25	—	—
☐☐	C95 & C96 on one cover	2.25	3.00	—
☐☐ C97	31¢ **Olympic Games,** High Jump, 11/1/79, Colorado Springs, CO	1.25	1.75	2.50

Cacheted FDC prices in this period are for unaddressed covers. Addressed covers sell for much less.

C113

C114

C115

C116

Scott Number	Description	Sgl	Cacheted Blk	Pl Blk
1980-1983				
☐☐ C98	40¢ Philip Mazzei, 10/13/80, DC	2.00	3.50	5.00
☐☐ C99	28¢ Blanche Stuart Scott, 12/30/80, Hammondsport, NY	1.50	1.75	3.00
☐☐ C100	35¢ Glenn Curtiss, 12/30/80, Hammondsport, NY	1.50	1.75	3.00
☐☐	C99 & C100 on one cover	4.00	—	—
☐☐ C101-4	28¢ Olympics, 6/17/83, San Antonio, TX (Se-tenant)	1.25	1.75	2.50
☐☐ C105-8	40¢ Olympics, 4/8/83, Los Angeles, CA (Se-tenant)	2.00	3.50	6.00
☐☐ C109-C112	35¢ Olympics, 11/4/83, Colorado Springs, CO (Se-tenant)		2.00	4.50 5.00
☐☐ C113	33¢ Alfred Verville, 2/13/84, Garden City, NY	2.00	4.50	5.00
☐☐ C114	39¢ Lawrence & Elmer Sperry, 2/13/85, Garden City, NY	2.00	4.50	5.00
☐☐ C115	44¢ Transpacific Air Mail, 2/15/85, San Francisco, CA (269,229)	2.00	4.50	5.00
☐☐ C116	44¢ Junipero Serra, 8/22/85, San Diego, CA	2.00	4.50	5.00

AIRMAIL SPECIAL DELIVERY

CE1-CE2

E1

E12-E13, E15-E18

E14, E19

E22-E23

FA1

E20-E21

Scott Number	Description	Sgl	Cacheted Blk	Pl Blk
1934				
☐☐ CE1	**16¢ Great Seal,** 8/30/34, Chicago, IL (AAMS Convention Sta.)			
	(41,213)	25.00	35.00	40.00
☐☐	Washington, DC, 8/31/34	18.00	20.00	25.00
1936				
☐☐ CE2	**16¢ Great Seal,** 2/10/36, DC (72,981)	20.00	30.00	35.00

SPECIAL DELIVERY

		Sgl	Blk	Pl Blk
☐☐ E1	**10¢ Messenger,** at SD offices, Oct. 1, 1885	8000.00		
☐☐ E2	**10¢ Messenger,** at any PO, eku Oct. 22, 1888	—	—	
☐☐ E3	**10¢ Orange,** Columbian issue, eku Feb. 11, 1893	—	—	
☐☐ E4	**10¢ Bureau,** unwmkd, eku Nov. 21, 1894	—	—	
☐☐ E5	**10¢ Bureau,** wmk USPS, eku Oct. 3, 1895 (unverified)	—	—	
☐☐ E5	**10¢ Bureau,** Plt. #882 variety, eku Dec. 5, 1899	—	—	
☐☐ E6	**10¢ Bicycle,** *Perf. 12* dbl-ln wmk, eku 1/22/03	—	—	
☐☐ E7	**10¢ Mercury,** eku 12/14/08	—	—	
☐☐ E8	**10¢ Bicycle,** *perf. 12,* sgl-ln wmk, eku 2/13/11	—	—	
☐☐ E9	**10¢ Bicycle,** *perf. 10,* sgl-ln wmk, eku 10/26/14	—	—	
☐☐ E10	**10¢ Bicycle,** *perf. 10,* unwmk, eku 11/4/16	—	—	
☐☐ E11	**10¢ Bicycle,** *perf. 11,* unwmk, eku 5/2/17	—	—	
☐☐ E12	**10¢ Motorcycle,** *perf. 11,* 7/12/22	550.00	—	
☐☐ E13	**15¢ Motorcycle,** *perf. 11,* 4/11/25	275.00	375.00	
☐☐ E14	**20¢ P.O. Truck,** *perf. 11,* 4/25/25	150.00	225.00	
☐☐ E15	**10¢ Motorcycle,** 11/29/27, DC	100.00	150.00	
☐☐ E15	**10¢ Electric Eye,** 9/8/41, DC	25.00	35.00	

Prices given for Scott E15 Electric Eye are for covers with sheet selvage with Electric Eye markings. Covers with printed cachets sell for 50% more than uncacheted covers.

| ☐☐ E16 | **15¢ Motorcycle,** 8/13/31, DC | 135.00 | 200.00 | |
| ☐☐ | Easton, PA, 8/6/31 | 1000.00 | — | |

8/6/31 is the earliest known use of Scott E16. 8/13/31 is the first day of sale at the Philatelic Agency.

ln = line
eku = earliest known use

Scott Number	Description	Cacheted Sgl	Blk
☐☐ E17	13¢ Motorcycle, 10/30/44	12.00	18.00
☐☐ E18	17¢ Motorcycle, 10/30/44	12.00	18.00
☐☐	13¢ & 17¢ values both on one cover	15.00	—

Total for Scott E17 and E18 is 158,863

☐☐ E19	20¢ P.O. Truck, 11/30/51, DC (33,193)	5.00	8.00
☐☐ E20	20¢ Letter, 10/13/54, Boston, MA (194,043)	3.00	5.00
☐☐ E21	30¢ Letter, 9/3/57, Indianapolis, IN (111,451)	3.00	5.00
☐☐ E22	45¢ Arrows, 11/21/69, New York, NY (192,391)	4.00	6.00
☐☐ E23	60¢ Arrows, 5/10/71, Phoenix, AZ (129,562)	4.00	6.00

CERTIFIED MAIL/REGISTRATION

☐☐ FA1	15¢ Certified Mail, 6/6/55, (176,308)	4.00	6.00
☐☐ F1	10¢ Registry, 12/1/11	8000.00	—

SPECIAL HANDLING

QE1-QE4   Q2   J68   J88

		Cacheted Sgle	Uncacheted Sgle	Blk
☐☐ QE1	10¢ Special Handling, 6/25/28	200.00	55.00	75.00
☐☐ QE2	15¢ Special Handling, 6/25/28	200.00	55.00	75.00
☐☐ QE3	20¢ Special Handling, 6/25/28	200.00	55.00	75.00
☐☐ QE4	25¢ Special Handling, 4/11/25	300.00	225.00	275.00

PARCEL POST

Parcel Post Service (4th class) began Jan. 1, 1913, and these stamps were issued for that service only. The 1¢, 2¢, 4¢ and 5¢ are known with Jan. 1, 1913 postmarks - the 2¢ undoubtedly for 4th class usage, the others possible but unproven. Beginning July 1, these stamps could be used for any purpose, thus a few 1st class FDC's were prepared for some of the lower denominations.

		4th Class (1/1/13)	1st Class (7/1/13)
☐☐ Q1	1¢ Post Office Clerk	—	800.00

Scott Q1 known on picture postcard

☐☐ Q2	2¢ City Carrier	—	800.00
☐☐ Q3	3¢ Railway Mail Clerk	—	2500.
☐☐ Q4	4¢ Rural Carrier	—	2500.
☐☐ Q5	5¢ Mail Train	—	2500.

OFFICIALS

		Sgl	Blk
☐☐ O127	1¢ Great Seal, 1/12/83, DC	1.00	1.50
☐☐ O128	4¢ Great Seal, 1/12/83, DC	1.00	1.50
☐☐ O129	13¢ Great Seal, 1/12/83, DC	1.00	1.50
☐☐ O129A	14¢ Great Seal, 5/15/85	1.00	1.50
☐☐ O130	17¢ Great Seal, 1/12/83, DC	1.00	1.50
☐☐ O132	$1 Great Seal, 1/12/83, DC	5.00	9.00
☐☐ O133	$5 Great Seal, 1/12/83, DC	9.00	20.00
☐☐ O135	20¢ Great Seal Coil, 1/12/83, DC	1.00	lp 30.00
☐☐	O127-35 on one cover	15.00	—
☐☐	O127-35 on Official postal card (UZ2) or envelope (UO73)	18.00	—
☐☐ O136	22¢ 5/15/85	1.00	1.50

Scott Number	Description	4th Class (1/1/13)	1st Class (7/1/13)
☐☐ O138	14¢ **Great Seal,** 2/4/85, DC	1.00	1.50
☐☐ O139	22¢ **Great Seal,** 2/4/85, DC	1.00	lp 30.00

POSTAGE DUE

Single

☐ J68	½¢ **Postage Due,** 4/13/25, none known to exist	
☐	4/15/25 eku	450.00
☐ J88	½¢ **Red and Black,** Postage Due, 6/19/59	50.00
☐ J89	1¢ **Red and Black,** Postage Due, 6/19/59	50.00
☐ J90	2¢ **Red and Black,** Postage Due, 6/19/59	50.00
☐ J91	3¢ **Red and Black,** Postage Due, 6/19/59	50.00
☐ J92	4¢ **Red and Black,** Postage Due, 6/19/59	50.00
☐ J93	5¢ **Red and Black,** Postage Due, 6/19/59	100.00
☐ J94	6¢ **Red and Black,** Postage Due, 6/19/59	100.00
☐ J95	7¢ **Red and Black,** Postage Due, 6/19/59	100.00
☐ J96	8¢ **Red and Black,** Postage Due, 6/19/59	100.00
☐ J97	10¢ **Red and Black,** Postage Due, 6/19/59	100.00
☐ J98	30¢ **Red and Black,** Postage Due, 6/19/59	100.00
☐ J99	50¢ **Red and Black,** Postage Due, 6/19/59	100.00
☐ J100	$1 **Red and Black,** Postage Due, 6/19/59	150.00
☐ J101	$5 **Red and Black,** Postage Due, 6/19/59	150.00
☐ J102	11¢ **Red and Black,** Postage Due, 1/2/78	5.00
☐ J103	13¢ **Red and Black,** Postage Due, 1/2/78	5.00
☐ J104	17¢ **Red and Black,** Postage Due, 6/10/85	5.00

POSTAL NOTES

Last day covers of this service also exist, dated 3/31/51. These sell for $10.00.

☐ PN1	1¢ **Black Postal Notes,** 2/1/45, on complete 3 part money order form	30.00
☐ PN1-18	1¢ to 90¢ **Postal Notes,** 2/1/45 on 18 money order forms	300.00

POSTAL SAVINGS

☐ PS11	10¢ **Red Postal Savings,** 5/1/41, any city	175.00

REVENUES

These examples of Revenue First Days are postmarked with fiscal rather than postal cancellations.

☐ R154	1¢ **Green,** Franklin, July 1, 1898	1000.00
☐ R155	2¢ **Washington,** July 1, 1898	1000.00
☐ R166	4¢ **Rose Battleship,** July 1, 1898	1000.00

DUCKS

RW53 - DeRosset Duck FDC

The following are not postage stamp items, however, they are listed here only for collector's interest.

☐ RW3	$1 **Canada Geese,** 7/1/36, Warren, NJ	700.00
☐ RW43	$5 **Canada Geese,** 7/1/76, any city	75.00
☐ RW46	$7.50 **Green-winged Teal,** 7/1/79, any city	50.00
☐ RW47	$7.50 **Mallards,** 7/1/80, any city	75.00
☐ RW48	$7.50 **Ruddy Ducks,** 7/1/81, any city	75.00

Scott Number	Description	Single
☐ RW49 $7.50 **Canvas Backs,** 7/1/82, any city		55.00
☐ RW50 $7.50 **Pintail,** 7/1/83, any city		45.00
☐ RW51 $7.50 **Wigeons,** 7/1/84, any city		45.00
☐ RW52 $7.50 **Cinnamon Teal,** 7/1/85, any city		40.00
☐ RW53 $7.50 **Fulvous Whistling Duck,** 7/1/86, any city		35.00
☐ RW54 $10 **Redheads,** 7/1/87, any city		35.00

☐☐ _____
☐☐ _____
☐☐ _____
☐☐ _____
☐☐ _____
☐☐ _____
☐☐ _____
☐☐ _____
☐☐ _____
☐☐ _____
☐☐ _____
☐☐ _____
☐☐ _____
☐☐ _____
☐☐ _____
☐☐ _____
☐☐ _____
☐☐ _____
☐☐ _____
☐☐ _____
☐☐ _____
☐☐ _____
☐☐ _____
☐☐ _____
☐☐ _____
☐☐ _____
☐☐ _____
☐☐ _____
☐☐ _____
☐☐ _____

ENVELOPES

Sizes of U.S. Envelope First Day's are as follows: Size 5 - 89x160mm, Size 6¾ - 92x165mm, Size 7 - 98x225mm, Size 7½ - 99x190mm, Size 8 and 10 - 105x240mm, Size 13 - 95x171mm. Where a paper difference is shown, the watermark of 'Standard Quality' is similar to Watermark 28 and 'Extra Quality' is similar to Watermark 29.

After 1950 add 10% for hand cancels.

U481, U436-9, U529-31

U522

U523-28

U532-4, U536, U544

U541-2

U543

U546

				Uncach'd	Cach'd
☐☐	U221	3¢	**Centennial,** green, May 10, 1876, Centennial cancel, size 3, wmk 3	3500.00	—
☐☐	U227	2¢	**Washington,** Oct. 2, 1883, eku, size 5, wmk 6	350.00	—
☐☐	U293	2¢	**U.S. Grant Lettersheet,** Aug. 18, 1886	—	—
☐☐	U429	2¢	**Washington,** 1/2/31, size 7½, wmk 29	75.00	—
☐☐			Size 7½, wmk 30a	75.00	—
☐☐	U436a	3¢	**Washington,** white paper, extra quality, 6/16/32, DC, size 5, die 1, wmk 29	75.00	—
☐☐			Size 8, die 1, wmk 29	18.00	—
☐☐	U436e	3¢	**Washington,** white paper, extra quality, 6/16/32, DC, size 5, die 7, wmk 29	12.00	50.09
☐☐			Size 13, die 7, wmk 29	75.00	—
☐☐	U436f	3¢	**Washington,** white paper, extra quality, 6/16/32, DC, size 5, die 9, wmk 29	12.00	50.00
☐☐			Size 13, die 9, wmk 29	18.00	—
☐☐	U437a	3¢	**Washington,** amber paper, 7/13/32, DC, size 5, wmk 28, standard quality	50.00	—
☐☐			7/19/32, DC, size 5, wmk 29, extra quality	35.00	—
☐☐	U439	3¢	**Washington,** blue paper, 7/13/32, DC, size 5, wmk 28, standard quality	40.00	—
☐☐			Size 13, wmk 28, standard quality	65.00	—
☐☐			9/9/32, DC, size 8, wmk 28, standard quality	85.00	—
☐☐	U439a	3¢	**Washington,** blue paper, 7/19/32, DC, extra quality, size 5, wmk 29	40.00	—
☐☐	U481	1½¢	**Washington,** 3/19/25, DC, size 5, wmk 27	35.00	—
☐☐			Size 5, wmk 27 with 553, 582 & 598	150.00	—
☐☐			Size 8, wmk 27	70.00	—
☐☐			Size 13, wmk 26	50.00	—
☐☐			Size 8, wmk 27 with 553, 582 & 598	125.00	—
☐☐			Size 13, wmk 26 with 553	60.00	—
☐☐	U495	1½¢	**on 1¢ green Franklin,** 6/1/25, DC, size 5	50.00	—
☐☐			6/3/25, DC, size 8	65.00	—
☐☐			6/2/25, DC, size 13	60.00	—

Scott Number	Description	Uncach'd	Cach'd
☐☐ U515 1½¢	on 1¢ green Franklin, 8/1/25, Des Moines, IA, size 5, die 1	50.00	—
☐☐ U521 1½¢	on 1¢ green Franklin, 10/22/25, DC, size 5, die 1, wmk 25	100.00	—
☐☐ U522a 2¢	Liberty Bell, 7/27/26, Phila., PA, size 5, wmk 27	20.00	30.00
☐☐	7/27/26, DC, size 5, wmk 27	30.00	40.00
☐☐	7/27/26, unofficial city, size 5, wmk 27	35.00	45.00
☐☐ U523 1¢	Mount Vernon, 1/1/32, DC, size 5, wmk 29	10.00	16.00
☐☐	Size 8, wmk 29	12.50	18.50
☐☐	Size 13, wmk 29	10.00	16.00
☐☐ U524 1½¢	Mount Vernon, 1/1/32, DC, size 5, wmk 29	10.00	16.00
☐☐	Size 8, wmk 29	12.50	18.50
☐☐	Size 13, wmk 29	10.00	16.00
☐☐ U525 2¢	Mount Vernon, 1/1/32, DC, size 5, wmk 29	8.00	15.00
☐☐	Size 8, wmk 29	10.00	15.00
☐☐	Size 13, wmk 29	8.00	15.00
☐☐ U526 3¢	Mount Vernon, 6/16/32, DC, size 5, wmk 29	15.00	20.00
☐☐	Size 8, wmk 29	25.00	40.00
☐☐	Size 13, wmk 29	20.00	30.00
☐☐ U527 4¢	Mount Vernon, 1/1/32, DC, size 8, wmk 29	30.00	40.00
☐☐ U528 5¢	Mount Vernon, 1/1/32, DC, size 5, wmk 29	18.00	20.00
☐☐	Size 8, wmk 29	20.00	22.00
☐☐ U529 6¢	Washington, white paper, 8/18/32, Los Angeles, CA,		
	size 7, wmk 29	20.00	—
☐☐	Size 8, wmk 29	15.00	—
☐☐ U530 6¢	Washington, amber paper, 8/18/32, Los Angeles, CA,		
	size 7, wmk 29	20.00	—
☐☐	Size 8, wmk 29	15.00	—
	Size 8, wmk 29, with pair 723	25.00	—
☐☐ U531 6¢	Washington, blue paper, 8/19/32, DC, size 7, wmk 29	20.00	—
☐☐	Size 8, wmk 29	15.00	—
☐☐ U532 1¢	Franklin, 11/16/50, New York, NY, size 13, wmk 42	1.00	2.50
☐☐ U533a 2¢	Washington, 11/17/50, New York, NY, size 13, wmk 42	1.00	2.00
☐☐ U534a 3¢	Washington, die 1, 11/18/50, New York, NY, size 13, wmk 42	1.00	2.00
☐☐ U534b 3¢	Washington, die 2, 11/19/50, New York, NY, size 8, wmk 42	5.00	8.00
☐☐ U535 1½¢	Washington, 10/21/52, Dover & Kenvil, NJ, size 13, wmk 42	—	—
☐☐ U536 4¢	Franklin, 7/31/58, Montpelier, VT (163,746), size 6¾, wmk 46	1.00	2.00
☐☐	Size 8, wmk 46	60.00	—
☐☐	Size 13, window	60.00	—
☐☐	7/31/58, Wheeling, WV, size 6¾, wmk 46, with 1036a	35.00	—
☐☐	Size 13, window	25.00	—
☐☐ U540 3¢	+ 1¢ Rev.Washington (oval), eku 7/22/58, Kenvil, NJ,		
	size 8, wmk 46, die E	50.00	—
☐☐ U541 1¼¢	Franklin, 6/25/60, Birmingham, AL (211,500), size 6¾, wmk 46	.50	2.00
☐☐ U542 2½¢	Washington, 5/28/60, Chicago, IL (196,977), size 6¾, wmk 46	.50	2.00
☐☐ U543 4¢	Pony Express, 7/19/60, St. Joseph, MO (407,160),		
	size 6¾, wmk 46	.50	2.25
	7/19/60, Sacramento, CA, with 1154, size 6¾, wmk 46	3.50	5.00
☐☐ U544 5¢	Lincoln, 11/19/62, Springfield, IL (163,258), size 6¾, wmk 48	.50	2.00
☐☐ U546 5¢	World's Fair, 4/22/64, World's Fair, NY (466,422),		
	size 6¾, wmk 48	.50	1.50
☐☐ U547 1¼¢	Liberty Bell, 1/6/65, DC, size 6¾, wmk 49	.50	1.50
☐☐	1/8/65, DC, size 10, wmk 49	9.00	15.00
☐☐ U548 1.4¢	Liberty Bell, 3/26/68, Springfield, MA (134,832),		
	size 6¾, wmk 49	.50	1.50
☐☐	3/27/68, DC, size 10, wmk 48	5.00	8.00
☐☐ U548A 1.6¢	Liberty Bell, 6/16/69, DC, size 6¾, wmk 47	.50	1.50
☐☐	Size 10, wmk 49	1.25	1.75

Cacheted FDC prices in this period are for unaddressed covers. Addressed covers sell for much less.

U547, U548,
U548A, U556

U549, U552

U550, U553

U551, U561

U554

U555, U562

U557

Scott Number	Description	Uncach'd	Cach'd
☐☐ U549	4¢ **Old Ironsides,** 1/6/65, DC, size 6¾, wmk 49	.50	1.50
☐☐	1/8/65, DC, size 6¾, window, wmk 49	9.00	15.00
☐☐	Size 10, wmk 49	9.00	15.00
☐☐	Size 10, window, wmk 49	9.00	15.00
Total for Scott U547 and U549 is 451,960			
☐☐ U550	5¢ **Eagle,** 1/5/65, Williamsburg,PA (246,496), size 6¾, wmk 49	.50	2.00
☐☐	1/8/65, DC, size 6¾, window, wmk 49	9.00	15.00
☐☐	Size 10, wmk 49	9.00	15.00
☐☐	Size 10, window, wmk 49	9.00	15.00
☐☐ U550a	5¢ **Eagle,** luminescent, 8/15/67, DC & Dayton, OH, size 6¾, wmk 50	3.50	6.00
☐☐	Size 6¾, window, wmk 48	3.50	6.00
☐☐	Size 10, wmk 48	3.50	6.00
☐☐	Size 10, wmk 49, Dayton only	4.50	7.50
☐☐	Size 10, window, wmk 49	3.50	6.00
☐☐ U551	6¢ **Liberty,** 1/4/68, New York, NY (184,784), size 6¾, wmk 47 or 48	.50	1.75
☐☐	1/5/68, DC, size 6¾, window, wmk 48 or 49	2.50	4.00
☐☐	Size 10, wmk 47	2.50	4.00
☐☐	Size 10, window, wmk 49	2.50	4.00
☐☐	11/15/68, DC, new shiny plastic window, size 6¾, window, wmk 48	3.00	5.00
☐☐ U552	4¢ + 2¢ Rev. **Old Ironsides,** 2/5/68, DC, size 6¾, wmk 50	4.50	7.50
☐☐	Size 6¾, window, wmk 48	4.50	7.50
☐☐	Size 10, wmk 47	4.50	7.50
☐☐	Size 10, window, wmk 49	4.50	7.50
☐☐ U553	5¢ + 1¢ Rev. **Eagle,** 2/5/68, DC, Size 6¾, wmk 49	4.50	7.50
☐☐	Size 10, window, wmk 49	4.50	7.50
☐☐ U553a	5¢ + 1¢ Rev. **Eagle,** luminescent, 2/5/68, DC, size 6¾, wmk 48	4.50	7.50
☐☐	Size 10, wmk 47 or 49	4.50	7.50
☐☐	Size 10, window, wmk 49	4.50	7.50
☐☐ U554	6¢ **Moby Dick,** 3/7/70, New Bedford, MA (433,777), size 6¾, wmk 47	.50	1.75
☐☐ U555	6¢ **Youth Conf.,** 2/24/71, DC, (264,559), size 6¾, wmk 49	.50	1.50
☐☐ U556	1.7¢ **Liberty Bell,** 5/10/71, Baltimore, MD (150,767), size 6¾, wmk 48A	.50	1.50
☐☐	5/10/71, DC, size 6¾, wmk 49 with 1394	9.00	15.00
☐☐	5/10/71, Phoenix, AZ, size 6¾, wmk 48A with E23	18.00	30.00
☐☐	5/10/71, DC, size 6¾, combo with 1283	2.00	3.00

U563    U564    U565

 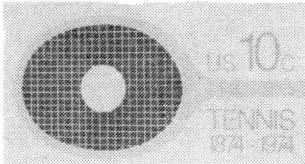

U567   U569

Scott Number	Description	Uncach'd	Cach'd
	5/11/71, DC, size 10, wmk 47 or 49	7.50	12.00
	5/11/71, DC, size 10, wmk 48A	3.50	6.00
U557	8¢ Eagle, 5/6/71, Williamsburg, PA (193,000), size 6¾, wmk 48A	.50	1.75
	Size 6¾, wmk 49	—	2.50
	5/7/71, DC, size 6¾, window, wmk 48A	2.00	3.50
	Size 10, wmk 49	2.00	3.50
	Size 10, window, wmk 47	2.00	3.50

Same size 10, wmk 47 were canceled without any authority at Williamsburg, PA on 5/6/71.

U561	6¢ + 2¢ Rev. Liberty, 5/16/71, DC, size 6¾, wmk 47	2.00	4.00
	Size 6¾, wmk 48A, (25 known)	—	17.50
	Size 6¾, wmk 49	2.50	4.00
	Size 6¾, window, wmk 47	2.00	3.00
	Size 10, wmk 48A	2.00	3.00
	Size 10, wmk 49	3.50	6.00
	Size 10, window, wmk 47	2.00	3.00
	Size 10, window, wmk 49	3.00	5.00
U562	6¢ + 2¢ Rev. Youth Conference, 5/16/71, DC, size 6¾, wmk 47	20.00	—
	Size 6¾, wmk 49	2.50	5.00
U563	8¢ Bowling, 8/21/71, Milwaukee, WI (281,342), size 6¾, wmk 49	.50	2.00
	Size 10, wmk 49	1.00	2.00
U564	8¢ Aging Conference, 11/15/71, DC (125,000), size 6¾, wmk 48A	.50	1.75
U565	8¢ Transpo '72, 5/2/72, DC, size 6¾, wmk 47	2.50	3.00
	Size 6¾, wmk 49	.50	1.00
U566	8¢ + 2¢ Rev. Eagle, 12/1/73, DC, size 6¾, wmk 47 or 49	.75	3.00
	Size 6¾, window, wmk 48A	7.50	
	Size 6¾, window, wmk 49	3.00	4.50
	Size 10, wmk 47	3.00	4.50
	Size 10, window, wmk 47	3.00	4.50
U567	10¢ Liberty Bell, 12/5/73, Phila., PA, size 6¾, wmk 47, old knife depth 58MM	.50	1.25
	Size 6¾, wmk 47, new knife depth 51MM	1.00	1.50
U568	1.8¢ Volunteer Non-Profit, 8/23/74, Cincinnati, OH, size 6¾, wmk 47	.50	1.25
	Size 10, wmk 47	.75	1.50
U569	10¢ Tennis, 8/31/74, Forest Hills, NY (245,000), size 6¾, wmk 49	.50	3.00
	Size 10, wmk 49	1.00	3.00
	9/3/74, DC, size 6¾, window, wmk 49	2.50	4.00
	Size 10, window, wmk 49	2.50	4.00

Note: Window envelopes were sold and canceled on the first day, contrary to regulations.

U568

U571-75

U576

U581

U584

Scott Number	Description	Uncach'd	Cach'd
☐☐ U571	**10¢ Seafaring,** 10/13/75, Minneapolis, MN (255,304), size 6¾	.50	1.50
☐☐	Size 10	.75	1.50
☐☐ U572	**13¢ Homemaker,** 2/2/76, Biloxi, MS (196,647), size 6¾	.50	1.00
☐☐	Size 10	.75	1.50
☐☐ U573	**13¢ Farmer,** 3/15/76, New Orleans, LA (214,563), size 6¾	.50	1.50
☐☐	Size 10	.75	1.50
☐☐ U574	**13¢ Doctor,** 6/30/76, Dallas, TX, size 6¾	.50	1.50
☐☐	Size 10	.75	1.50
☐☐ U575	**13¢ Craftsman,** 8/6/76, Hancock, TX, size 6¾	.50	1.50
☐☐	Size 10	.75	1.50
☐☐ U576	**13¢ Liberty Tree,** 11/8/75, Memphis, TN (226,824), size 6¾, wmk 48A	.50	1.00
☐☐	Size 10, wmk 47	.75	1.25
☐☐ U577	**2¢ Star and Pinwheel,** 9/10/76, Hempstead, NY (81,388), size 6¾, wmk 48A or 49	.50	1.00
☐☐	Size 10, wmk 48A	.75	1.25
☐☐ U578	**2.1¢ Non-Profit,** 6/3/77, Houston, TX (120,280), size 6¾, wmk 47	.50	1.00
☐☐	Size 10, wmk 47	.75	1.25
☐☐ U579	**2.7¢ Non-Profit,** 7/5/78, Raleigh, NC (92,687) size 6¾, wmk 47	.50	1.00
☐☐	Size 10, wmk 47	.75	1.25
☐☐ U580	**'A' (15¢) Eagle,** 5/22/78, Memphis, TN, size 6¾, wmk 47	1.00	1.50
☐☐	Size 6¾, wmk 48A	.50	1.00
☐☐	Size 6¾, window, wmk 47 or 48A	1.25	2.00
☐☐	Size 10, wmk 47 or 49	.75	1.25
☐☐	Size 10, window, wmk 47 or 49	1.25	2.00
☐☐	Size 6¾, wmk 48A with sheet, coil & booklet pane	5.00	10.00
☐☐ U581	**15¢ Uncle Sam,** 6/3/78, Williamsburg, PA (176,000), size 6¾, wmk 47 or 49	.50	1.00
☐☐	Size 6¾, window, wmk 47	1.25	2.00
☐☐	Size 10, wmk 47 or 48A	.75	1.25
☐☐	Size 10, window, wmk 48A or 49	1.25	2.00
☐☐	12/2/80, eku with luminescent bar, size 10, window, wmk 47 or 49	—	—
☐☐ U582	**13¢ Centennial Design,** 10/15/76, Los Angeles, CA (277,222), size 6¾, wmk 48A	2.00	3.00
☐☐	Size 6¾, wmk 49	.50	1.00
☐☐	Size 6¾, wmk 49, dark green	—	7.50
☐☐	Size 10, wmk 49	.75	1.25

Cacheted FDC prices in this period are for unaddressed covers. Addressed covers sell for much less.

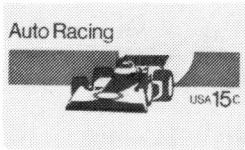

U587   U590   U593

Scott Number	Description	Uncach'd	Cach'd
□□ U583 13¢	**Golf,** 4/7/77, Augusta, GA (252,000), size 6¾, wmk 49	.50	1.10
□□	Size 10, wmk 49	.75	1.25
□□	4/8/77, DC, size 6¾, window, wmk 49	2.00	3.00
□□	Size 10, window, wmk 49	2.00	3.00
□□ U584 13¢	**Energy Conser.,** 10/20/77, Ridley Park, PA, size 6¾, wmk 49	.50	1.00
□□	Size 6¾, window, wmk 49	1.50	2.50
□□	Size 10, wmk 49	.75	1.25
□□	Size 10, window, wmk 49	1.50	2.50
□□	10/20/77, DC, with stamps, all sizes	3.50	4.00
□□ U585 13¢	**Energy Devel.,** 10/20/77, Ridley Park, PA, size 6¾, wmk 49	.50	1.00
□□	Size 6¾, window, wmk 49	1.50	2.50
□□	Size 10, wmk 49	.75	1.25
□□	Size 10, window, wmk 49	1.50	2.50
□□	10/20/77, DC, with stamps, all sizes	3.50	4.00
□□ U586 16¢	**Rev. to 15¢ USA,** 7/28/78, Williamsburg, PA (193,153), size 6¾, wmk 47	.50	1.00
□□	Size 10, wmk 47	.75	1.25
□□ U587 15¢	**Racing Car,** 9/2/78, Ontario, CA (209,147), size 6¾, wmk 49	.50	1.00
□□	Size 10, wmk 49	.75	1.25
□□ U588 13¢	**+ 2¢ Rev. Liberty Tree,** 11/22/78, Williamsburg, PA (137,500), size 6¾, wmk 47	.50	1.00
□□	Size 10, wmk 47	.75	1.25
□□	11/29/78, DC, size 6¾, window, wmk 47	1.25	2.00
□□	Size 10, window, wmk 48A	1.25	2.00
□□ U589 3.1¢	**Non-Profit,** 5/18/79, Denver, CO (117,575), size 6¾, wmk 48A	.50	1.00
□□	Size 6¾, window, wmk 48A	1.25	2.00
□□	Size 10, wmk 49	.75	1.25
□□	Size 10, window, wmk 49	1.25	2.00
□□ U590 3.5¢	**Non-Profit,** 6/23/80, Williamsburg, PA, size 6¾, wmk 48A or 49	.50	1.00
□□	Size 10, wmk 48A or 49	.75	1.25

Note: Window envelopes were sold and canceled contrary to regulations on the first day.

□□ U591 5.9¢	**Non-Profit,** 2/17/82, Wheeling, WV, size 6¾, wmk 47 or 49	.75	1.25
□□	Size 6¾, window, wmk 47	1.25	2.00
□□	Size 10, wmk 47 or 49	1.00	1.50
□□	Size 10, wmk 47	1.25	2.00
□□ U592 'B' (18¢)	**Eagle,** 3/15/81, Memphis, TN (179,171), size 6¾, wmk 47, 48A or 49	.50	1.00
□□	Size 6¾, window, wmk 47, 48A or 49	1.25	2.00
□□	Size 10, wmk 47, 48A or 49	.75	1.25
□□	Size 10, window, wmk 47	1.25	2.00
□□	3/15/81, San Francisco, CA, with 1818-1820 on any of the above	1.50	2.00
□□ U593 18¢	**Star,** 4/2/81, Star City, IN (160,439), size 6¾, wmk 47, 48A or 49	.50	1.00
□□	Size 10, wmk 47, 48 or 49	.75	1.25

Note: Window envelopes were sold and canceled contrary to regulations on the first day.

□□ U594 'C' (20¢)	**Eagle,** 10/11/81, Memphis, TN (304,404), all sizes, size 6¾, wmk 47 or 49	.75	1.25
□□	Size 10, wmk 47 or 49	1.00	1.50

Note: Window envelopes were sold and canceled contrary to regulations on the first day.

U595

U598

The Great Seal
of the United States
1782-1982

USA 20c

U602

Scott Number	Description	Uncach'd	Cach'd
☐☐ U595	15¢ **Veterinary Medicine,** 7/24/79, Seattle, WA (209,658),		
	size 6¾, wmk 49	.50	1.00
☐☐	Size 10, wmk 49	.75	1.25
☐☐	7/25/79, Seattle, WA, size 6¾, window, wmk 49	4.00	—
☐☐	Size 10, window, wmk 49	4.00	—
☐☐ U596	15¢ **Olympics 1980,** 12/10/79, E. Rutherford, NJ (179,336), size 6¾,		
	wmk 49	.50	1.00
☐☐	Size 10, wmk 49	.75	1.25
☐☐ U597	15¢ **Bicycling,** 5/16/80, Baltimore, MD (173,978), size 6¾, wmk 49	.50	1.00
☐☐	Size 10, wmk 49	.75	1.25
☐☐ U598	15¢ **America's Cup Yacht Races,** 9/15/80, Newport, RI,		
	size 6¾, wmk 49	.50	1.00
☐☐	Size 10, wmk 49	.75	1.25
☐☐ U599	15¢ **Honey Bee,** 10/10/80, Paris, IL, size 6¾, wmk 49	.50	1.00
☐☐	Size 10, wmk 49	.75	1.25
☐☐ U600	18¢ **Remember the Blinded,** 8/13/81, Arlington, VA (175,966),		
	size 6¾, wmk 49	.50	1.00
☐☐	Size 10, wmk 49	.75	1.25
☐☐ U601	20¢ **Capitol Dome,** 11/13/81, Los Angeles, CA, size 6¾,		
	wmk 48A or 49	.75	1.25
☐☐	Size 10, wmk 49	1.00	1.50
Note: Window envelopes were sold and canceled contrary to regulations on the first day.			
☐☐	1/26/82, eku with luminescent bar, size 10, wmk 47	—	—
☐☐ U602	20¢ **Great Seal,** 6/15/82, DC, (163,905), size 6¾, wmk 49	.75	1.25
☐☐	Size 10, wmk 49	1.00	1.50
☐☐ U603	20¢ **Purple Heart,** 8/6/82, DC (110,679), size 6¾, wmk 49	.75	1.25
☐☐	Size 10, wmk 49	1.00	1.50
☐☐ U604	5.2¢ **Non-Profit,** 3/21/83, Memphis, TN, size 6¾, wmk 47	.75	1.25
☐☐	Size 6¾, window, wmk 49	1.00	1.50
☐☐	Size 10, wmk 47	1.25	2.00
☐☐	Size 10, window, wmk 47	1.25	2.00
☐☐ U605	20¢ **Paralyzed Veterans,** 8/3/83, Portland, OR, size 6¾	.75	1.25
☐☐	Size 10	1.00	1.50
☐☐ U606	20¢ **Business,** 5/7/84, DC, size 6¾	.75	1.25
☐☐	Size 10	1.00	1.50

U607

U608

U609

Scott Number			Description	Uncach'd	Cach'd
☐☐	U607	"D" (22¢) Eagle, 2/1/85, Washington, DC, size 6¾		.75	1.25
☐☐		Size 6¾ window		1.00	1.50
☐☐		Size 10		1.25	2.00
☐☐		Size 10 window		1.25	2.00
☐☐	U608	22¢ Bison, 2/25/85, Washington, DC, size 6¾		.75	1.25
☐☐		Size 6¾ window		1.00	1.50
☐☐		Size 10		1.25	2.00
☐☐		Size 10 window		1.25	2.00
☐☐	U609	6¢ Old Ironsides, 5/3/85, Washington, DC, size 6¾		.75	1.25
☐☐		Size 10		1.25	2.00

AIRMAIL ENVELOPES & AIR LETTER SHEETS

UC1-7

UC14, UC18, UC26

UC16

UC25

UC17

UC32

UC33-34

UC36

UC35

UC37

UC38-39

	Scott Number		Description	Uncach'd	Cach'd
☐☐	UC1	5¢	**Blue,** 1/12/29, DC, size 13, wmk 28	45.00	—
☐☐			2/1/29, DC, size 5, wmk 28	50.00	—
☐☐			Size 8, wmk 28	75.00	—
☐☐	UC3	6¢	**Orange,** 7/1/34, DC, size 8, wmk 33	20.00	—
☐☐			Size 13, wmk 33	14.00	—
☐☐	UC7	8¢	**Olive green,** 9/26/32, DC, size 8, wmk 30a	25.00	—
☐☐			Size 13, wmk 30a	11.00	—
☐☐	UC10	5¢	**on 6¢ Orange,** 10/1/46, Aiea Heights, HI, size 13, die 2a, wmk 41	100.00	—
☐☐	UC11	5¢	**on 6¢ Orange,** 10/1/46, size 13, die 2b	150.00	—
☐☐	UC12	5¢	**on 6¢ Orange,** 10/1/46, Aiea Heights, HI, A.P.O. & New York, NY, size 13, die 2c, wmk 41	75.00	—
☐☐	UC13	5¢	**on 6¢ Orange,** 10/1/46, Aiea Heights, HI, size 13, die 3, wmk 41	75.00	—
☐☐	UC14	5¢	**Skymaster,** 9/25/46, DC, size 13, wmk 41	1.00	2.50
☐☐	UC16	10¢	**Skymaster Air Letter Sheet,** 4/29/47, DC (162,802), one size only, no wmk	2.50	7.50
☐☐	UC17	5¢	**Stamp Cent. - Type I,** 5/21/47, New York, NY, size 13, wmk 41	1.25	2.50
☐☐	UC17a	5¢	**Stamp Cent. - Type II,** 5/21/47, New York, NY, size 13, wmk 41	1.25	2.50
			There were 306,660 of Scott UC17 and UC17a canceled FD		
☐☐	UC18	6¢	**Skymaster,** 9/22/50, Phila., PA (74,006), size 13, wmk 43	.75	1.50
☐☐	UC22	6¢	**on 5¢ Carmine (UC15),** die 2, 8/29/52, Norfolk, VA, size 13, wmk 41	20.00	30.00
☐☐	UC25	6¢	**FIPEX,** 5/2/56, NY, NY (363,230), size 13, wmk 45, with short clouds	.75	1.25
☐☐			Size 13, wmk 45, with long clouds	.75	1.25
☐☐	UC26	7¢	**Skymaster,** 7/31/58, Dayton, OH (143,428), size 6¾, wmk 46, straight left wing	.50	3.00
☐☐			Size 6¾, wmk 46, crooked left wing	.50	3.00
☐☐			Size 8, wmk 46	35.00	—
☐☐	UC32a	10¢	**Jet Airliner** air letter sheet, 9/12/58, St. Louis, MO (92,400), one size only, no wmk, Type I	1.00	3.25
☐☐	UC33	7¢	**Jet,** Blue, 11/21/58, New York, NY (208,980), size 6¾, wmk 46	.50	2.00

UC42

UC40-45

UC43

UC44-44a

Scott Number		Description	Uncach'd	Cach'd
☐☐ UC34	7¢	**Jet**, Red, 8/18/60, Portland, OR (196,851), size 6¾, wmk 46	.50	2.00
☐☐ UC35	11¢	**Jet Airliner** air letter sheet, 6/16/61, Johnstown, PA (163,460), one size only, no wmk	1.00	2.50
☐☐ UC36	8¢	**Jet**, 11/17/62, Chantilly, VA (194,870), size 6¾, wmk 47	.50	1.00
☐☐ UC37	8¢	**Jet Triangle**, 1/7/65, Chicago, IL (230,600), size 6¾, wmk 49	.50	1.00
☐☐		1/8/65, DC, size 10, wmk 49	9.00	15.00
☐☐ UC37a	8¢	**Jet Triangle**, luminescent, 8/15/67, Dayton, OH & DC, size 6¾, wmk 48	3.50	6.00
☐☐		Size 10, wmk 49	4.50	7.50
☐☐ UC38	11¢	**Kennedy** air letter sheet, 5/29/65, Boston, MA (337,422), one size only, no wmk	.75	1.50
☐☐ UC39	13¢	**Kennedy** air letter sheet, 5/29/67, Chicago, IL (213,916), one size only, no wmk	.75	1.50
☐☐		5/29/67, Boston, MA, one size only, no wmk	5.00	7.50
☐☐		5/29/67, Brookline, MA, one size only, no wmk	5.00	7.50
☐☐ UC40	10¢	**Jet Triangle**, 1/8/68, Chicago, IL (157,553), size 6¾, wmk 48	.50	1.00
☐☐		1/9/68, DC, size 10, wmk 49	4.50	7.50
☐☐ UC41	8¢	**+ 2¢ Revalued UC37**, 2/5/68, DC, size 6¾, wmk 49	4.50	9.00
☐☐		Size 10, wmk 49	4.50	9.00
☐☐ UC42	13¢	**Human Rights** air letter sheet, 12/3/68, DC (195,898), one size only, no wmk	1.00	3.00
☐☐ UC43	11¢	**Jet**, 5/6/71, Williamsburg, PA (187,000), size 6¾, wmk 49	.50	1.00
☐☐		Size 10, wmk 49	3.50	6.00
☐☐ UC44	15¢	**Birds** air letter sheet, 5/28/71, Chicago, IL (130,669), one size only, no wmk	.75	1.50
☐☐ UC44a	15¢	**Birds** air letter sheet, 12/13/71, Phila., PA, one size only, no wmk	.75	1.50
☐☐ UC45	10¢	**+ 1¢ Revalued UC40**, 6/28/71, DC, size 6¾, wmk 47, 48A or 49	4.50	9.00
☐☐		Size 10, wmk 49	4.50	9.00
☐☐ UC46	15¢	**Ballooning** air letter sheet, 2/10/73, Albuquerque, NM (210,000), one size only, no wmk	.75	1.25

UC46

UC47

UC48

UC49

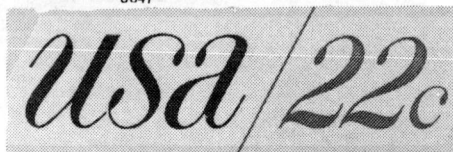
UC50

UC52

UC53-54

UC58

UC59

Scott Number	Description	Uncach'd	Cach'd
☐☐ UC47	13¢ **Bird in Flight,** 12/1/73, Memphis, TN (132,658), size 6¾, wmk 47	.50	1.00
☐☐	1/5/74, eku, size 10	3.00	5.00
☐☐ UC48	18¢ **USA** air letter sheet, 1/4/74, Atlanta, GA (119,615), one size only, no wmk	.75	1.25
☐☐ UC49	18¢ **NATO** air letter sheet, 4/4/74, DC, one size only, no wmk	.75	1.25
☐☐ UC50	22¢ **USA** air letter sheet, 1/16/76, Tempe, AZ (118,303), one size only, no wmk	.75	1.25
☐☐ UC51	22¢ **USA** air letter sheet, 11/3/78, St. Petersburg, FL (86,099), one size only, no wmk	.75	1.25
☐☐ UC52	22¢ **Olympic Games,** 1980 Letter Sheet, 12/5/79, Bay Shore, NY (129,221), one size only, no wmk	.75	1.25
☐☐ UC53	30¢ **USA** air letter sheet, 12/29/80, San Francisco, CA, one size only, no wmk	.75	1.25
☐☐ UC54	30¢ **USA** air letter sheet, 9/21/81, Honolulu, HI, one size only, no wmk	.75	1.25
☐☐ UC55	30¢ **USA & Globe** air letter sheet, 9/16/82, Seattle, WA, one size only, no wmk	.75	1.25
☐☐ UC56	30¢ **Communications** air letter sheet, 1/7/83, Anaheim, CA, one size only, no wmk	.75	1.25
☐☐ UC57	30¢ **Olympic Sports** air letter sheet, 10/14/85, Los Angeles, CA, one size only, no wmk	.75	1.25
☐☐ UC58	36¢ **Landsat,** air letter sheet, 2/14/85, Goddard Flight Center, MD	.80	1.35
☐☐ UC59	36¢ **Urban Skyline,** air letter sheet, 5/21/85, DC	.80	1.35
☐☐ UC60	36¢ **Comet Tail,** air letter sheet, 12/4/85, DC	.80	1.35

OFFICIAL MAIL

☐☐ UO73	20¢ **Eagle,** 1/12/83, DC, size 10, wmk 47	1.00	1.50
☐☐	Size 10, window, wmk 47	1.25	2.00
☐☐ UO74	22¢ **Eagle,** 2/26/85, DC, size 10	1.00	1.50
☐☐	Size 10 window	1.25	2.00

POSTAL CARDS

UX1, UX3, UX65

UX21

UX37

UX38

UX43

UX44

UX45, UY16

UX46, UY17

UX48

UX49, UX54, UY19, UY20

Scott Number		Description	Uncach'd	Cach'd
☐☐ UX1	1¢	**Liberty**, May 13, 1873, Boston, New York or DC, one size only	2250.00	—
☐☐ UX5	1¢	**Liberty**, Sept. 30, 1875, any city, one size only	1200.00	—
☐☐ UX21	1¢	**McKinley**, 2/13/10, any city, one size only	125.00	—
☐☐ UX37	3¢	**McKinley**, 2/1/26, DC, one size only	250.00	—
☐☐ UX38	2¢	**Franklin**, 11/16/51, New York, NY (170,000), one size only	1.00	4.00
☐☐ UX39	1¢	**Jefferson (UX27)**, revalued to 2¢, 1/1/52, DC	12.00	25.00
☐☐ UX40	1¢	**Lincoln**, (UX28) revalued to 2¢, 1/1/52	—	—
☐☐		3/22/52, DC	100.00	—

*These cards went on sale at the Philatelic Agency 3/22/52 & were canceled that day. It is
believed that the 1/1/52 cancels are not legitimate.*

☐☐ UX43	2¢	**Lincoln**, 7/31/52, DC (125,400), one size only	.75	2.50
☐☐ UX44	2¢	**FIPEX**, 5/4/56, New York, NY (537,474), one size only	.50	1.25
☐☐ UX45	4¢	**Liberty**, 11/16/56, New York, NY (129,841), one size only	.50	1.25
☐☐ UX46	3¢	**Liberty**, 8/1/58, Phila., PA (180,610), one size only	.50	1.25
☐☐ UX46a	3¢	**Liberty 'n God We Trust'**, 8/1/58, Phila., PA, one size only	175.00	200.00
☐☐ UX46c	3¢	**Liberty - Precanceled**, 9/15/61, Phila., PA, one size only	50.00	—
☐☐ UX48	4¢	**Lincoln**, 11/19/62, Springfield, IL (162,939), one size only	.50	1.50
☐☐ UX48a	4¢	**Lincoln**, luminescent, 6/25/66, Bellevue, OH	25.00	30.00
☐☐		7/6/66, DC	1.50	2.50
☐☐		Toledo, OH	7.50	12.50
☐☐		Overlook, OH	4.50	7.50
☐☐		Columbus, OH	7.50	12.50
☐☐		Bellevue, OH	15.00	25.00
☐☐		Cleveland, OH	6.00	10.00
☐☐		Cincinnati, OH	4.50	7.50
☐☐		Dayton, OH	3.50	6.00
☐☐		Indianapolis, IN	7.50	12.50
☐☐		Louisville, KY	7.50	12.50
☐☐ UX49	7¢	**Vacationland**, 8/30/63, New York, NY (148,000 est.), one size only	.50	1.00
☐☐ UX50	4¢	**Customs**, 2/22/64, DC (313,275)	.50	1.00
☐☐ UX51	4¢	**Social Security**, 9/26/64, DC (293,650)	.50	1.00
☐☐		with official government printed cachet	—	12.00
☐☐		with blue hand cancel & government cachet	—	20.00
☐☐ UX52	4¢	**Coast Guard**, 8/4/65, Newburyport, MA (338,225), one size only	.50	1.00

UX50

UX51

UX52

UX53

UX56

UX58, UY22

UX62

UX63

UX67

Scott Number		Description	Uncach'd	Cach'd
☐☐ UX53	4¢	Census Bureau, 10/21/65, Phila., PA (275,100), one size only	.50	1.00
☐☐ UX54	8¢	Vacationland, 12/4/67, DC (145,896)	.50	1.00
☐☐ UX55	5¢	Lincoln, 1/4/68, Hodgenville, KY (159,420), one size only	.50	1.00
☐☐ UX56	5¢	Women Marines, 7/26/68, San Fran., CA (203,714), one size only	.50	1.00
☐☐ UX57	5¢	Weathervane, 9/1/70, Fort Myer, VA (285,800), one size only	.50	1.00
☐☐ UX58	6¢	Paul Revere, 5/15/71, Boston, MA (197,000 est.)	.50	1.00
☐☐ UX59	10¢	Vacationland, 6/10/71, New York, NY (151,000 est.), one size only	.50	1.00
First Day cancels of Scott UX59 and UXC11 total 297,000				
☐☐ UX60	6¢	America's Hospitals, 9/16/71, NY, NY (218,200), one size only	.50	1.00
☐☐ UX61	6¢	U.S. Frigate Constellation, 6/29/72, any city	.50	1.00
☐☐ UX62	6¢	Monumental Valley, 6/29/72, any city	.50	1.00
☐☐ UX63	6¢	Gloucester, MA, 6/29/72, any city	.50	1.00
☐☐ UX64	6¢	John Hanson, 9/1/72, Baltimore, MD (156,000), one size only	.50	1.00
☐☐ UX65	6¢	Centenary of Postal Card, 9/15/73, DC (289,950)	.50	1.00
☐☐ UX66	8¢	Samuel Adams, 12/16/73, Boston, MA (147,522)	.50	1.00
☐☐ UX67	12¢	Ships Figurehead, 1/4/74, Miami, FL (138,500)	.50	1.00
☐☐ UX68	7¢	C. Thomson, 9/14/75, Bryn Mawr, PA (153,067 est.), one size only	.50	1.00
First Day cancels of Scott UX68 and UY25 total 321,910				
☐☐ UX69	9¢	J. Witherspoon, 11/10/75, Princeton, NJ (170,340 est.), one size only	.50	1.00
First Day cancels of Scott UX69 and UY26 total 254,239				
☐☐ UX70	9¢	Caesar Rodney, 7/1/76, Dover, DE (150,432 est.)	.50	1.00
First Day cancels of Scott UX70 and UY27 total 307,061				
☐☐ UX71	9¢	Federal Court House, Galveston, TX, 7/20/77, Galveston, TX (245,535)	.50	1.00

HISTORIC PRESERVATION USA 10c
UX73

US Coast Guard Eagle USA 14c
UX76

USA 10c
Casimir Pulaski, Savannah, 1779
UX79

USA 12c
Lewis and Clark Expedition, 1806
UX91

USA
Olympics 1980 14c
UX82

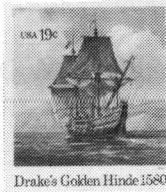
USA 19c
Drake's Golden Hinde 1580
UX86

US Domestic Rate
UX88, UY31

Scott Number		Description	Uncach'd	Cach'd
☐☐ UX72	9¢	Nathan Hale, 10/14/77, Coventry, CT (204,077 est.), one size only	.50	1.00
First day cancels of Scott UX72 and UY28 total 304,592				
☐☐ UX73	10¢	Cincinnati Music Hall, 5/12/78, Cincinnati, OH (300,000)	.50	1.00
☐☐ UX74 (10¢)		Domestic Rate J. Hancock, 5/19/78, Quincy, MA (299,623)	.50	1.00
☐☐ UX75	10¢	John Hancock, 6/20/78, Quincy, MA (187,120)	.50	1.00
☐☐ UX76	14¢	Coast Guard Eagle, 8/4/78, Seattle, WA (196,400)	.50	1.00
☐☐ UX77	10¢	Molly Pitcher, 9/8/78, Freehold, NJ (180,280), one size only	.50	1.00
☐☐ UX78	10¢	George R. Clark, 2/23/79, Vincennes, IN (260,110), one size only	.50	1.00
☐☐ UX79	10¢	Casimir Pulaski, 10/11/79, Savannah, GA (210,000), one size only	.50	1.00
☐☐ UX80	10¢	Olympic Games, 9/17/79, Eugene, OR (206,000), one size only	.50	1.00
☐☐ UX81	10¢	Iolani Palace, 10/1/79, Honolulu, HI (242,804)	.50	1.00
☐☐ UX82	14¢	Olympic Games - Skater, 1/15/80, Atlanta, GA (160,977)	.50	1.00
☐☐ UX83	10¢	Salt Lake Temple, 4/5/80, Salt Lake City, UT (325,260), one size only	.50	1.00
☐☐ UX84	10¢	Count Rochambeau, 7/11/80, Newport, RI	.50	1.00
☐☐ UX85	10¢	Battle of Kings Mountain, 10/7/80, Kings Mountain, NC	.50	1.00
☐☐ UX86	19¢	Drake's Golden Hinde, 9/26/80, San Rafael, CA	.75	1.25
☐☐ UX87	10¢	Battle of Cowpens, 1/17/81, Cowpens, SC (160,000)	.50	1.00
☐☐ UX88 (12¢)		Domestic Rate Eagle, 3/15/81, Memphis, TN	.50	1.00
☐☐ UX89	12¢	Isaiah Thomas, 5/5/81, Worcester, MA (185,601)	.50	1.00
☐☐ UX90	12¢	Nat. Greene, 9/8/81, Eutaw Springs, SC (115,755), one size only	.50	1.00

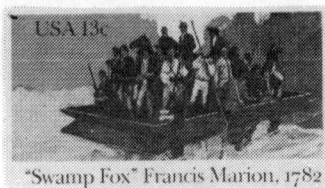

USA 13c

"Swamp Fox" Francis Marion, 1782

UX94

UX95, UY21

PHILADELPHIA

ACADEMY OF MUSIC
USA 13¢

UX96

HISTORIC PRESERVATION

UX97

Clipper *Flying Cloud* 1852   USA 25

UX107

Scott Number		Description	Uncach'd	Cach'd
☐☐ UX91	12¢	Lewis & Clark Expedition, 9/23/81, St. Louis, MO	.50	1.00
☐☐ UX92	(13¢)	Domestic Rate Robert Morris, 10/11/81, Memphis, TN	.50	1.00
☐☐ UX93	13¢	Robert Morris, 11/10/81, Phila., PA	.50	1.00
☐☐ UX94	13¢	Francis Marion, 4/3/82, Marion, SC (141,162)	.50	1.00
☐☐ UX95	13¢	LaSalle Claims Louisiana, 4/7/82, New Orleans, LA (157,691), one size only	.50	1.00
☐☐ UX96	13¢	Phila. Academy of Music, 6/18/82, Phila., PA (193,089), one size only	.50	1.00
☐☐ UX97	13¢	Old Post Office, St. Louis, MO, 10/14/82, St. Louis, MO	.50	1.00
☐☐ UX98	13¢	Oglethorpe, 2/12/83, Savannah, GA	.50	1.00
☐☐ UX99	13¢	Old Washington Post Office, 4/19/83, DC	.50	1.00
☐☐ UX100	13¢	Olympics - Yachting, 8/5/83, Long Beach, CA	.50	1.00
☐☐ UX101	13¢	Maryland 350th Anniv., 3/25/84, St. Clement's Island, MD	.50	1.00
☐☐ UX102	13¢	Olympic Torch, 4/30/84, Los Angeles, CA	.50	1.00
☐☐ UX103	13¢	Baraga, 6/29/84, Marquette, MI	.50	1.00
☐☐ UX104	13¢	Historic Preservation, 9/17/84, Compton, CA	.50	1.00
☐☐ UX105	14¢	Charles Carroll, 2/1/85, New Carrollton, MD	.50	1.00
☐☐ UX106	14¢	Charles Carroll, 3/6/85, Annapolis, MD	.50	1.00
☐☐ UX107	25¢	Clipper Flying Cloud, 2/27/85, Salem, MA	.50	1.00
☐☐ UX108	14¢	George Wythe, 6/20/85, Williamsburg, VA	.50	1.00
☐☐ UX109	14¢	Connecticut, 4/18/86, Hartford, CT	.50	1.00
☐☐ UX110	14¢	Stamps, 5/23/86, Chicago, IL	.50	1.00
☐☐ UX111	14¢	Vigo, 5/24/86, Vincennes, IN	.50	1.00
☐☐ UX112	14¢	Rhode Island, 6/26/86, Providence, RI	.50	1.00
☐☐ UX113	14¢	Wisconsin, 7/3/86, Mineral Point, WI	.50	1.00

Scott Number	Description	Uncach'd	Cach'd
☐☐ UX114 14¢	National Guard Heritage, 12/12/86, Boston, MA	.50	1.00
☐☐ UX115 14¢	Self-Scouring Steel Plow, 5/22/87, Moline, IL	.50	1.00
☐☐ UX116 14¢	Convening of the Constitutional Convention, 5/25/87, Philadelphia, PA	.50	1.00
☐☐ UX117 14¢	Flag, 6/14/87, Baltimore, MD	.50	1.00
☐☐ UX118 14¢	Take Pride in America, 9/22/87, Jackson, WY	.50	1.00
☐☐ UX119 14¢	Timberline Lodge, 9/28/87, Timberline Lodge, OR	.50	1.00

REPLY POSTAL CARDS

☐☐ UY1	1¢	+ 1¢ Grant, Oct. 25, 1892	350.00	—
☐☐ UY12	3¢	+ 3¢ McKinley, 2/1/26, any city	250.00	—
☐☐ UY13	2¢	+ 2¢ Washington, 12/29/51, DC (49,294)	.75	3.00
☐☐ UY14	2¢	on 1¢ + 2¢ on 1¢ Washington, 1/1/52, any city	35.00	50.00
☐☐ UY16	4¢	+ 4¢ Liberty, Intern'l, 11/16/56, New York, NY (127,874), one size only	.50	1.50
☐☐ UY16a	4¢	+ 4¢ Liberty, International, message card printed on both halves, 11/16/56, New York, NY	75.00	100.00
☐☐ UY16b	4¢	+ 4¢ Liberty, International, reply card printed on both halves, 11/16/56, New York, NY	50.00	75.00
☐☐ UY17	3¢	+ 3¢ Liberty, 7/31/58, Boise, ID (136,768)	.50	1.00
☐☐ UY18	4¢	+ 4¢ Lincoln, 11/19/62, Springfield, IL (107,746), one size only	.50	2.25
☐☐ UY18a 34¢		+ 4¢ Lincoln, luminescent, 3/7/67, eku, Dayton, OH, about 7 known, one size only	500.00	—
☐☐ UY19	7¢	+ 7¢ Map, Intern'l, 8/30/63, New York, NY (122,000 est.), only size only	.50	1.50
☐☐ UY20	8¢	+ 8¢ Map, International, 12/4/67, DC (122,181)	.50	1.50
☐☐ UY21	5¢	+ 5¢ Lincoln, 1/4/68, Hodgenville, KY (114,580), one size only	.50	1.50
☐☐ UY22	6¢	+ 6¢ Paul Revere, 5/15/71, Boston, MA (143,000)	.50	1.25
☐☐ UY23	6¢	+ 6¢ John Hanson, 9/1/72, Baltimore, MD (105,708), one size only	.50	1.00
☐☐ UY24	8¢	+ 8¢ Samuel Adams, 12/16/73, Boston, MA (105,369)	.50	1.00
☐☐ UY25	7¢	+ 7¢ Charles Thomson, 9/14/75, Bryn Mawr, PA (76,533 est.), one size only	.50	1.00
☐☐ UY26	9¢	+ 9¢ John Witherspoon, 11/10/75, Princeton, NJ (83,899 est.), one size only	.50	1.25
☐☐ UY27	9¢	+ 9¢ Caesar Rodney, 7/1/76, Dover, DE (100,340 est.)	.50	1.00
☐☐ UY28	9¢	+ 9¢ Nathan Hale, 10/14/77, Coventry, CT (100,515 est.), one size only	.50	1.25
☐☐ UY29	(10¢	+ 10¢) John Hancock, 5/19/78, Quincy, MA (71,000 est.)	1.75	3.50
☐☐ UY30	10¢	+ 10¢ John Hancock, 6/20/78, Quincy, MA (61,750 est.)	.75	1.50
☐☐ UY31	(12¢	+ 12¢) Domestic Rate Eagle, 3/15/81, Memphis, TN	.75	1.25
☐☐ UY32	12¢	+ 12¢ Isaiah Thomas, 5/5/81, Worcester, MA	.75	1.25
☐☐ UY32a		Small die	3.00	5.00
☐☐ UY33	(13¢	+ 13¢) Domestic Rate Robert Morris, 10/11/81, Memphis, TN	.75	1.25
☐☐ UY34 13¢		+ 13¢ Robert Morris, 11/10/81, Phila., PA	.75	1.25
☐☐ UY35 14¢		+ 14¢ Charles Carroll, 2/1/85, New Carrollton, MD	.75	1.25
☐☐ UY36 14¢		+ 14¢ Charles Carroll, 3/6/85, Annapolis, MD	.75	1.25
☐☐ UY37 14¢		+ 14¢ George Wythe, 6/20/85, Williamsburg, VA	.75	1.25
☐☐ UY38 14¢		+ 14¢ Flag, 9/1/87, DC	.75	1.25

Cacheted FDC prices in this period are for unaddressed covers. Addressed covers sell for much less.

AIR MAIL POSTAL CARDS

UXC1 · UXC4 · UXC5, UXC8, UXC11 · UXC9-10

UXC6 · UXC7

UXC14 · UXC16 · UXC18

UXC20 · UXC22

Scott Number		Description	Uncach'd	Cach'd
☐☐ UXC1	4¢	**Eagle,** 1/10/49, DC (236,620) with round 'O' in January 10	.50	4.00
☐☐		with oval 'O' in January 10	1.00	4.75
☐☐ UXC2	5¢	**Eagle,** 7/31/58, Wichita, KS (156,474)	.50	3.00
☐☐ UXC3	5¢	**Eagle,** 6/18/60, Minneapolis, MN (228,500)	.75	2.75
☐☐		with thin dividing line at top	2.25	4.50
☐☐ UXC4	6¢	**Bald Eagle,** 2/15/63, Maitland, FL (216,203), one size only	.50	2.25
☐☐ UXC5	11¢	**Visit USA,** 5/27/66, DC (272,813)	.50	2.00
☐☐ UXC6	6¢	**Virgin Islands,** 3/31/67, Charlotte Amalie, VI (346,906), one size only	.50	1.75
☐☐ UXC7	6¢	**Boy Scouts,** 8/4/67, Farragut State Park, ID (471,585), one size only	.50	1.50
☐☐ UXC8	13¢	**Visit the USA,** 9/8/67, Detroit, MI (178,189)	.50	1.75
☐☐ UXC9	8¢	**Eagle,** 3/1/68, New York, NY (179,923)	.50	1.50
☐☐ UXC9a	8¢	**Eagle,** luminescent, 3/19/69, DC	10.00	15.00
☐☐ UXC10	9¢	**Eagle,** 5/15/71, Kitty Hawk, NC (167,000 est.), one size only	.50	2.00
☐☐ UXC11	15¢	**Visit the USA,** 6/10/71, New York, NY (146,000)	.50	1.75
☐☐ UXC12	9¢	**Grand Canyon,** 6/29/72, any city	.50	1.50
☐☐ UXC13	15¢	**Niagara Falls,** 6/29/72, any city	.50	1.50
☐☐ UXC13a	15¢	**Niagara Falls,** without stamp, 6/29/72, any city	600.00	—

Scott Number	Description	Uncach'd	Cach'd
☐☐ UXC14 11¢ Modern Eagle, 1/4/74, State College, PA (160,500),			
one size only		.50	1.25
☐☐ UXC15 18¢ Eagle Weathervane, 1/4/74, Miami, FL (132,114)		.50	1.50
☐☐ UXC16 21¢ Angel Weathervane, 12/17/75, Kitty Hawk, NC (113,191),			
one size only		.75	1.50
☐☐ UXC17 21¢ Jenny, 9/16/78, San Diego, CA (174,886), one size only		.75	1.75
☐☐ UXC18 21¢ Olympics - Gymnast, 12/1/79, Fort Worth, TX (150,124),			
one size only		.75	1.25
☐☐ UXC19 28¢ First Transpacific Flight, 1/2/81, Wenatchee, WA		.75	1.25
☐☐ UXC20 28¢ Soaring, 3/5/82, Houston, TX (106,932)		.75	1.25
☐☐ UXC21 28¢ Olympics - Speedskating, 12/29/83, Milwaukee, WI		.75	1.25
☐☐ UXC22 33¢ China Clipper Seaplane, 2/15/85, San Francisco, CA		.75	1.25
☐☐ UXC23 33¢ Chicago Skyline, 2/1/86, Chicago, IL		.75	1.25

OFFICIAL POSTAL CARD

☐☐ UZ2 13¢ Eagle, 1/12/83, DC		.75	1.25
☐☐ UZ3 14¢ Eagle, 2/26/85, DC		.75	1.25

3 x 5 FDC Inventory Index Cards

These 3 x 5 FDC Inventory Index Cards let you keep a detailed history of your first day cover collection. They also contain a special section for keeping a 10-year history of price trends.

100 for $5.00   500 for $14.75   1000 for $21.75
(postpaid)

FDC Publishing Co.
Stewartsville, NJ 08886

- [ ] _____
- [ ] _____
- [ ] _____
- [ ] _____
- [ ] _____
- [ ] _____
- [ ] _____
- [ ] _____
- [ ] _____
- [ ] _____
- [ ] _____
- [ ] _____
- [ ] _____
- [ ] _____
- [ ] _____
- [ ] _____
- [ ] _____
- [ ] _____
- [ ] _____
- [ ] _____
- [ ] _____
- [ ] _____
- [ ] _____
- [ ] _____
- [ ] _____
- [ ] _____
- [ ] _____
- [ ] _____
- [ ] _____
- [ ] _____
- [ ] _____
- [ ] _____
- [ ] _____
- [ ] _____
- [ ] _____
- [ ] _____
- [ ] _____

- [ ] _____
- [ ] _____
- [ ] _____
- [ ] _____
- [ ] _____
- [ ] _____
- [ ] _____
- [ ] _____
- [ ] _____
- [ ] _____
- [ ] _____
- [ ] _____
- [ ] _____
- [ ] _____
- [ ] _____
- [ ] _____
- [ ] _____
- [ ] _____
- [ ] _____
- [ ] _____
- [ ] _____
- [ ] _____
- [ ] _____
- [ ] _____
- [ ] _____
- [ ] _____
- [ ] _____
- [ ] _____
- [ ] _____
- [ ] _____
- [ ] _____
- [ ] _____
- [ ] _____
- [ ] _____
- [ ] _____
- [ ] _____
- [ ] _____
- [ ] _____
- [ ] _____
- [ ] _____

☐☐ _____
☐☐ _____
☐☐ _____
☐☐ _____
☐☐ _____
☐☐ _____
☐☐ _____
☐☐ _____
☐☐ _____
☐☐ _____
☐☐ _____
☐☐ _____
☐☐ _____
☐☐ _____
☐☐ _____
☐☐ _____
☐☐ _____
☐☐ _____
☐☐ _____
☐☐ _____
☐☐ _____
☐☐ _____
☐☐ _____
☐☐ _____
☐☐ _____
☐☐ _____
☐☐ _____
☐☐ _____
☐☐ _____
☐☐ _____
☐☐ _____
☐☐ _____
☐☐ _____
☐☐ _____
☐☐ _____
☐☐ _____
☐☐ _____

FIRST DAY CEREMONY PROGRAMS

First Day Ceremony Programs are produced and distributed at ceremonies dedicating a new stamp. In most cases the programs are produced by either the U.S. Postal Service or local sponsoring groups.

The formats of the programs vary greatly. They can be as simple as a single sheet of paper, to a very elaborate work of graphic art. However, most programs contain the words "First Day Ceremony Program" and contain a listing of the ceremony order of events.

Collectors interested in obtaining more information regarding ceremony programs are urged to join the American Ceremony Program Society. This organization publishes a newsletter, The Ceremonial, the purpose of which is to share information among its hundreds of members. Applications for membership are available from Steve Bondarenko; 261 Ridge St.; New Milford, NJ 07646.

The following is a list of all known First Day Ceremony Programs. Prices are for the most common type of programs for each issue.

Prices from 1940-1957, unless otherwise stated, are for programs without stamps and first-day cancels. Programs containing stamps and first-day cancels usually sell for twice the stated price.

Prices from 1958 to date, unless otherwise stated, are for programs with stamps and first-day cancels. Programs without stamps and first-day cancels usually sell for half the stated price.

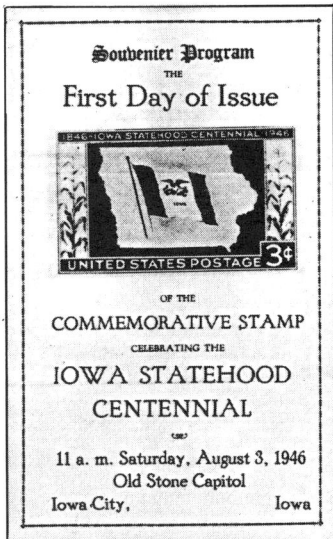

1940
☐ 873	10¢ **Booker T. Washington,** 4/7/40, Tuskeege Inst, AL	50.00
☐ 890	2¢ **Samuel F.B. Morse,** 10/7/40, New York, NY	50.00

1945
☐ 936	3¢ **Coast Guard,** 11/19/45, New York, NY	65.00
☐ 937	3¢ **Alfred E. Smith,** 11/26/45, New York, NY	50.00
☐ 942	3¢ **Iowa,** 8/3/46, Iowa City, IO	50.00

1947
☐ 946	3¢ **Joseph Pulitzer,** 4/10/47, New York, NY	50.00
☐ 951	3¢ **Constitution,** 10/21/47, Boston, MA	50.00

1948
☐ 952	3¢ **Everglades Park,** 12/5/47, Florida City, FL	50.00
☐ 953	3¢ **George Washington Carver,** 1/5/48, Tuskeege Inst., AL	50.00
☐ 954	3¢ **California Gold,** 1/24/48, Coloma, CA	50.00
☐ 957	3¢ **Wisconsin Centennial,** 5/29/48, Madison, WI	50.00
☐ 958	5¢ **Swedish Pioneers,** 6/4/48, Chicago, IL	50.00
☐ 964	3¢ **Oregon Territory Establishment,** 8/14/48, Oregon City, OR	50.00
☐ 966	3¢ **Palomar Observatory,** 8/30/48, Palomar Mountain, CA	50.00
☐ 967	3¢ **Clara Barton,** 9/7/48, Oxford, MA	50.00
☐ 970	3¢ **Fort Kearny,** 9/22/48, Minden, NE	35.00

1949
☐ 981	3¢ **Minnesota Territory,** 3/3/49, St. Paul, MN	50.00
☐ 982	3¢ **Washington & Lee Univ.,** 4/12/49, Lexington, VA	50.00
☐ 982	3¢ **Annapolis,** 5/23/49, Annapolis, MD	50.00
☐ 985	3¢ **G.A.R.,** 8/29/49, Indianapolis, IN	50.00
☐ 986	3¢ **Edgar Allen Poe,** 10/7/49, Richmond, VA	50.00

1950
☐ 990	3¢ **Nat. Capital Sesqui. (Executive),** 6/12/50, DC	50.00
☐ 993	3¢ **Railroad Engineers,** 4/29/50, Jackson, TN	50.00
☐ 994	3¢ **Kansas City Centenary,** 6/3/50, Kansas City, MO	40.00
☐ 995	3¢ **Boy Scouts,** 6/30/50, Valley Forge, PA	50.00

1951
☐ 998	3¢ **United Confederate Veterans,** 5/30/51, Norfolk, VA	40.00
☐ 999	3¢ **Nevada Centennial,** 7/14/51, Genoa, NV w/stamp & cancel	30.00
☐ 1000	3¢ **Landing of Cadillac,** 7/24/51, Detroit, MI	30.00
☐ 1001	3¢ **Colorado Statehood,** 8/1/51, Minturn, CO	30.00
☐ 1002	3¢ **Am. Chemical Soc.,** 9/4/51, New York, NY	30.00
☐ 1003	3¢ **Battle of Brooklyn,** 12/10/51, Brooklyn, NY	20.00

1952
☐ 1004	3¢ **Betsy Ross,** 1/2/52, Philadelphia, PA	30.00
☐ 1005	3¢ **4-H Clubs,** 1/15/52, Springfield, OH w/stamp & cancel	35.00
☐ 1006	3¢ **B. & O. Railroad,** 2/28/52, Baltimore, MD	30.00
☐ 1007	3¢ **Am. Automobile Assoc.,** 3/04/52, Chicago, IL	30.00
☐ 1009	3¢ **Grand Coulee Dam,** 5/15/52, Grand Coulee, WA	30.00
☐ 1011	3¢ **Mt. Rushmore Mem.,** 8/11/52, Keystone, SD	30.00
☐ 1012	3¢ **Civil Engineers,** 9/6/52, Chicago, IL	30.00
☐ 1015	3¢ **Newspaper Boys,** 10/4/52, Philadelpohia, PA	30.00

1953
☐ 1017	3¢ **National Guard,** 2/23/53, DC	30.00
☐ 1018	3¢ **Ohio Sesquicentennial,** 3/2/53, Chillicothe, OH	30.00
☐ 1019	3¢ **Washington Territory,** 3/2/53, Olympia, WA	30.00

☐ 1020	3¢ **Louisiana Purchase,** 4/30/53, St. Louis, MO	30.00
☐ 1021	5¢ **Opening of Japan,** 7/14/53, DC	30.00
☐ 1022	3¢ **American Bar Assoc.,** 8/24/53, Boston, MA	30.00
☐ 1023	3¢ **Sagamore Hill,** 9/14/53, Oyster Bay, NY	30.00
☐ 1024	3¢ **Future Farmers,** 10/13/53, Kansas City, MO	30.00
☐ 1025	3¢ **Trucking Industry,** 10/27/53, Los Angeles, CA	30.00
☐ 1026	3¢ **General G.S. Patton, Jr.,** 11/11/53, Fort Knox, KY	50.00
☐ 1027	3¢ **New York City,** 11/20/53, New York, NY	30.00
☐ 1028	3¢ **Gadsden Purchase,** 12/30/53, Tucson, AZ	30.00

1954
☐ 1029	3¢ **Columbia University,** 1/4/54, New York, NY	35.00

1954-68
☐ 1030	½¢ **Franklin,** 10/20/55, DC	30.00
☐ 1031	1¢ **Washington,** 8/26/54, Chicago, IL	30.00
☐ 1031A	1¼¢ **Palace,** 6/17/60, Santa, Fe, NM with stamp & cancel	15.00
☐ 1033	2¢ **Jefferson,** 9/15/54, San Francisco, CA	30.00
☐ 1034	2½¢ **Bunker Hill,** 6/17/59, Boston, MA w/stamp & cancel	20.00
☐ 1035	3¢ **Statue of Liberty,** 6/24/54, Albany, NY	35.00
☐ 1036	3¢ **Lincoln,** 11/19/54, New York, NY	35.00
☐ 1037	4½¢ **Hermitage,** 3/16/59, Hermitage, TN	35.00
☐ 1038	5¢ **Monroe,** 12/2/54, Fredericksburg, VA	25.00
☐ 1039	6¢ **Roosevelt,** 11/18/55, New York, NY	25.00
☐ 1040	7¢ **Wilson,** 1/10/56, Staunton, V	20.00
☐ 1041	8¢ **Statue of Liberty,** 4/9/54, DC	20.00
☐ 1042	8¢ **Statue of Liberty,** 3/22/58, Cleveland, OH	15.00
☐ 42A	8¢ **Pershing,** 11/17/61, New York, NY	15.00
☐ 1043	9¢ **The Alamo,** 6/14/56, Cleveland, OH	25.00
☐ 1044	10¢ **Independence Hall,** 7/4/56, Philadelphia, PA	25.00
☐ 1044A	11¢ **Statue of Liberty,** 6/15/61, Washington, DC	18.00
☐ 1045	12¢ **Harrison,** 6/6/59, Oxford, OH	10.00
☐ 1047	20¢ **Monticello,** 4/13/56, Charlottesville, VA	20.00
☐ 1048	25¢ **Paul Revere,** 4/18/58, Boston, MA	50.00
☐ 1049	30¢ **Robert Lee,** 9/21/55, Norfolk, VA, with stamp & cancel¢	50.00
☐ 1051	50¢ **Susan Anthony,** 8/25/55, Louisville, KY with stamp	50.00
☐ 1052	$1 **Patrick Henry,** 10/7/55, Joplin, MO	70.00

1954-73
☐ 1054	1¢ **Washington,** coil, 10/8/54, Baltimore, MD	25.00
☐ 1054A	1¼¢ **Palace,** coil, 6/17/60, Santa, Fe, NM	15.00
☐ 1056	2½¢ **Bunker Hill,** coil, 9/9/59, Los Angeles, CA	35.00

1954
☐ 1960	3¢ **Nebraska Territory,** 5/7/54, Nebraska City, NE	25.00
☐ 1061	3¢ **Kansas Territory,** 5/31/54, Ft. Leavenworth, KS	25.00
☐ 1062	3¢ **George Eastman,** 7/12/54, Rochester, N.Y.	30.00
☐ 1063	3¢ **Lewis & Clark Expedition,** 7/28/54, Sioux City, IA	20.00

1955
☐ 1064	3¢ **Pennsylvania Academy of Fine Arts,** 1/15/55, Philadelphia, PA	20.00
☐ 1065	3¢ **Land Grant Colleges,** 2/12/55, East Lansing, MI	15.00
☐ 1066	8¢ **Rotary International,** 2/23/55, Chicago, IL	25.00
☐ 1067	3¢ **Armed Forces Reserve,** 5/21/55, DC	20.00
☐ 1068	3¢ **New Hampshire,** 6/21/55, Franconia, NH	18.00
☐ 1071	3¢ **Fort Ticonderoga,** 9/18/55, Ticonderoga, NY	18.00
☐ 1072	3¢ **Andrew W. Mellon,** 12/20/55, DC	18.00

1956

☐ 1073	3¢ **Benjamin Franklin,** 1/17/56, Philadelphia, PA	30.00
☐ 1074	3¢ **Booker T. Washington,** 4/5/56, BTW Birthplace, V	30.00
☐ 1078	3¢ **Wildlife (Antelope),** 6/22/56, Gunnison, CO	18.00
☐ 1080	3¢ **Pure Food & Drug Laws,** 6/27/56, DC	18.00
☐ 1081	3¢ **Wheatland,** 7/5/56, Lancaster, PA	18.00
☐ 1082	3¢ **Labor Day,** 9/3/56, Camden, NJ	25.00
☐ 1083	3¢ **Nassau Hall,** 9/22/56, Princeton, NJ	20.00
☐ 1084	3¢ **Devil's Tower,** 9/24/56, Devil's Tower, WY	18.00
☐ 1085	3¢ **Children,** 12/15/56, DC	18.00

1957

☐ 1087	3¢ **Polio,** 1/15/57, DC (without stamp)	18.00
☐ 1088	3¢ **Coast & Geodetic Survey,** 2/11/57, Seattle, WA	15.00
☐ 1089	3¢ **Architects,** 2/23/57, New York, NY	15.00
☐ 1091	3¢ **Naval Review,** 6/10/57, Norfolk, Va	15.00
☐ 1092	3¢ **Oklahoma Statehood,** 6/14/57, Oklahoma City, OK	15.00
☐ 1095	3¢ **Shipbuilding,** 8/15/57, Bath, ME	10.00
☐ 1096	8¢ **Ramon Magsayay,** 8/31/57, DC	18.00
☐ 1098	3¢ **Wildlife (Whooping Cranes),** 11/22/57, Corpus Christi, TX or New York	18.00
☐ 1099	3¢ **Religious Freedom,** 12/27/57, Flushing, NY	12.00

1958

☐ 1100	3¢ **Gardening - Horticulture,** 3/15/58, Ithaca, NY	25.00
☐ 1104	3¢ **Brussels Exhibition,** 4/17/58, Detroit, MI	20.00
☐ 1105	3¢ **James Monroe,** 4/28/58, Montrose, VA	20.00
☐ 1106	3¢ **Minnesota Statehood,** 4/11/58, St. Paul, MN	20.00
☐ 1107	3¢ **Int'l. Geohysical Year,** 4/31/58, Chicago, IL	18.00
☐ 1110-1011	4¢ & 8¢ **Simon Bolivar,** 7/24/58, DC	25.00
☐ 1112	4¢ **Atlantic Cable,** 8/15/58, New York, NY	25.00

1958-59

☐ 1113	1¢ **Lincoln Sesqui.,** 2/12/59, Hodgenville, KY	20.00
☐ 1114	3¢ **Lincoln Sesqui.,** 2/27/59, New York, NY	20.00
☐ 1115	4¢ **Lincoln-Douglas Debates,** 8/27/58, Freeport, IL	20.00
☐ 1116	4¢ **Lincoln Sesqui.,** 5/30/59, DC	**20.00**

1958

☐ 1117-1118	4¢ & 8¢ **Lajos Kossuth,** 9/49/58, DC (with stamp & without cancel)	20.00
☐ 1119	4¢ **Freedom of Press,** 9/22/58, Columbia, MO	20.00
☐ 1120	4¢ **Overland Mail,** 10/10/58, San Francisco, CA	40.00
☐ 1121	4¢ **Noah Webster,** 10/16/58, West Hartford, CT	30.00
☐ 1122	4¢ **Forest Conservation,** 10/27/58, Tucson, AZ	25.00

1959

☐ 1124	4¢ **Oregon Statehood,** 2/14/59, Astoria, OR	20.00
☐ 1125-1126	4¢ & 8¢ **San Martin,** 2/25/59, DC	18.00
☐ 1127	4¢ **NATO,** 4/1/59, DC	20.00
☐ 1128	4¢ **Arctic Explorations,** 4/6/59, Cresson, PA	20.00
☐ 1131	4¢ **St. Lawrence Seaway,** 6/26/59 2nd day, Massena, NY	30.00
☐ 1133	4¢ **Soil Conservation,** 8/26/59, Rapid City, SD	25.00
☐ 1134	4¢ **Petroleum Industry,** 8/27/59, Titusville, PA	25.00
☐ 1135	4¢ **Dental Health,** 9/14/59, New York, NY	20.00
☐ 1136-1137	4¢ & 8¢ **Reuter,** /9/29/59, DC	**20.00**
☐ 1138	4¢ **Dr. Ephraim McDowell,** 12/3/59, Danville, KY	25.00

1960-61

☐ 1139	4¢ **Washington,** "Credo," 1/20/60, Mt. Vernon, VA	20.00
☐ 1140	4¢ **Franklin,** "Credo," 3/31/59, Philadelphia, PA	12.00

☐ 1141	4¢	Jefferson, "Credo," 5/18/60, Charlottesville, VA	15.00
☐ 1142	3¢	Francis scott Key, "Credo," 9/14/60, Baltimore, MD	15.00
☐ 1143	4¢	Lincoln, "Credo," 11/19/60, New York, NY	15.00
☐ 1144	4¢	Patrick Henry, "Credo," 1/11/61, Richmond, VA	15.00

1960

☐ 1145	4¢	Boy Scouts, 2/8/60, DC	25.00
☐ 1147-1148	4¢ & 8¢	Masaryk, 3/7/60, DC	15.00
☐¼149	4¢	World Refugee Year, 4/7/60, DC	20.00
☐ 1150	4¢	Water Conservation, 4/18/60, DC	20.00
☐ 1151	4¢	SEATO, 4/31/60, DC	20.00
☐ 1152	4¢	American Woman, 6/2/60, DC	20.00
☐ 1153	4¢	50-Star Flag, 7/4/60, Honolulu, HI	20.00
☐ 1154	4¢	Pony Express Cent., 7/19/60, Sacramento, CA	20.00
☐ 1155	4¢	Employ the Handicapped, 8/28/60, New York, NY	15.00
☐ 1156	4¢	World Forestry Congress, 8/29/60, Seattle, WA	20.00
☐ 1157	4¢	Mexican Indepen., 9/16/60, Los Angeles, CA	20.00
☐ 1158	4¢	U.S.-Japan Traty, 9/28/60, DC	20.00
☐ 1159-1160	4¢& 8¢	Paderewski, 10/8/60, DC	15.00
☐ 1116	4¢	Robert A. Taft, 10/10/60, Cincinnati, OH	20.00
☐ 1162	4¢	Wheels of Freedom, 10/15/60, Detroit, MI	18.00
☐ 1164	3¢	Automated P.O., 10/20/60, Providence, RI	12.00
☐ 1165-1166	4¢ & 8¢	Mannerheim, 10/26/60, DC	15.00
☐ 1168-1169	4¢ & 8¢	Garibaldi, 11/2/60, DC	15.00
☐ 1170	4¢	Senator George, 11/5/60, Vienna, GA	12.00
☐ 1171	4¢	Andrew Carnegie, 11/25/60, New York, NY	25.00
☐ 1172	4¢	John Foster Dulles, 12/6/60, DC	15.00
☐ 1173	4¢	Echo I, 12/15/60, DC	25.00

1961

☐ 1174-1175	4¢ & 8¢	Gandhi, 1/26/61, DC	15.00
☐ 1176	4¢	Range Conservation, 2/2/61, Salt Lake City, UT	20.00
☐ 1177	4¢	Horace Greeley, 2/3/61, Chappaqua, NY	20.00

1961-65

☐ 1178	4¢	Fort Sumter, 4/12/61, Charleston, SC	20.00
☐ 1179	4¢	Battle of Shiloh, 4/7/62, Shiloh, TN	20.00
☐ 1180	5¢	Battle of Gettysburg, 7/1/63, Gettysburg, PA	20.00
☐ 1181	5¢	Battle of Wilderness, 5/5/64, Fredericksburg, VA	20.00
☐ 1182	5¢	Appomattox, 4/9/65, Appomatox, VA	20.00

1961

☐ 1183	4¢	Kansas Statehood, 5/10/61, Council Grove, KS	15.00
☐ 1184	4¢	Senator Norris, 7/11/61, DC	15.00
☐ 1185	4¢	Naval Aviation, 8/20/61, San Diego, CA	30.00
☐ 1186	4¢	Workmen's Comp., 9/4/61, Milwaukee, WI	15.00
☐ 1187	4¢	Frederic Remington, 10/4/61, DC	15.00
☐ 1188	4¢	China Republic, 10/10/61, DC	18.00
☐ 1189	4¢	Naismith, 11/6/61, DC	60.00
☐ 1190	4¢	Nursing, 12/28/61, DC	15.00

1962

☐ 1191	4¢	New Mexico Statehood, 1/6/62, Santa Fe, NM	15.00
☐ 1192	4¢	Arizona Statehood, 2/14/62, Phoenix, AZ	15.00
☐ 1194	4¢	Malaria Eradication, 3/30/62, DC	15.00
☐ 1195	4¢	Charles Evans Hughes, 4/11/62, DC	15.00
☐ 1196	4¢	Seattle World's Fair, 4/25/62, Seattle, WA	15.00
☐ 1197	4¢	Louisiana Statehood, 4/30/62, New Orleans, LA	15.00

☐ 1198	4¢ **Homestead Act,** 5/20/62, Beatrice, NE	15.00
☐ 1199	4¢ **Girl Scouts,** 7/24/62, Burlington, VT	15.00
☐ 1200	4¢ **Brian McMahon,** 7/28/62, Norwalk, CT	18.00
☐ 1201	4¢ **Apprenticeship,** 8/31/62, DC	15.00
☐ 1202	4¢ **Sam Rayburn,** 9/16/62, Bonham, TX	15.00
☐ 1203	4¢ **Dag Hammarskjold,** 10/23/62, New York, NY	18.00
☐ 1205	4¢ **Christmas,** 11/1/62, Pittsburgh, PA	15.00
☐ 1206	4¢ **Higher Education,** 11/14/62, DC	15.00
☐ 1207	4¢ **Winslow Homer,** 12/15/62, Gloucester, MA	18.00

1963-66
☐ 1208	5¢ **Flag,** 1/9/63, DC	12.00

1962-66
☐ 1209	1¢ **Jackson,** 3/22/63, New York, NY	15.00
☐ 1213	5¢ **Washington,** 11/23/62, New York, NY	15.00
☐ 1225	1¢ **Coil,** 5/31/63, Chicago, IL	15.00

1963
☐ 1230	5¢ **Carolina Charter,** 4/6/63, Edenton, NC	15.00
☐ 1231	5¢ **Food for Peace,** 6/4/63, DC	15.00
☐ 1232	5¢ **W. Virginia Statehood,** 6/20/63, Wheeling, WV	20.00
☐ 1233	5¢ **Emancipation Procl.,** 8/16/63, Chicago, IL	15.00
☐ 1234	5¢ **Alliance for Progress,** 8/17/63, DC	15.00
☐ 1235	5¢ **Cordell Hull,** 10/5/63, Carthage, TN	15.00
☐ 1236	5¢ **Eleanor Roosevelt,** 10/11/63, DC	15.00
☐ 1237	5¢ **Science,** 10/14/63, DC	15.00
☐ 1238	5¢ **City Mail Delivery,** 10/26/63, DC	20.00
☐ 1239	5¢ **Red Cross,** 10/29/63, DC	15.00
☐ 1240	5¢ **Christmas,** 11/1/63, Santa Claus, IN	15.00
☐ 1241	5¢ **Audubon,** 12/7/63, Henderson, KY	15.00

1964
☐ 1242	5¢ **Sam Houston,** 1/10/64, Houston, TX	20.00
☐ 1244 & U546	5¢ **N.Y. World's Fair,** 4/22/64, World's Fair, NY	18.00
☐ 1245	5¢ **John Muir,** 4/29/64, Martinez, CA	15.00
☐ 1246	5¢ **John F. Kennedy,** 5/29/64, Boston, MA	20.00
☐ 1247	5¢ **New Jersey Tercent.,** 6/15/64, Elizabeth, NJ	12.00
☐ 1248	5¢ **Nevada Statehood,** 7/22/64, Carson City, NV	15.00
☐ 1249	5¢ **Register & Vote,** 8/1/64, DC	15.00
☐ 1250	5¢ **Shakespeare,** 8/14/64, Stratford, CT	45.00
☐ 1251	5¢ **Drs. Mayo,** 9/11/64, Rochester, MN	20.00
☐ 1252	5¢ **American Music,** 10/15/64, New York, NY	15.00
☐ 1253	5¢ **Homemakers,** 10/26/64, Honolulu, HI	15.00
☐ 1254-1257	5¢ **Christmas,** 11/9/64, Bethlehem, PA	40.00
☐ 1258	5¢ **Verrazano-Narrows Bridge,** 11/21/64, Staten Island, NY	15.00
☐ 1259	5¢ **Fine Arts,** 12/2/64, Washington, DC	15.00
☐ 1260	5¢ **Amateur Radio,** 12/15/64, Anchorage, AK	20.00

1965
☐ 1261	5¢ **Battle of New Orleans,** 1/8/65, New Orleans, LA	25.00
☐ 1262	5¢ **Physical Fitness - Sokol,** 2/15/65, DC	10.00
☐ 1263	5¢ **Cancer,** 4/1/65, DC	15.00
☐ 1264	5¢ **Churchill,** 5/13/65, Fulton, MO	12.00
☐ 1265	5¢ **Magna Carta,** 6/15/65, Jamestown, VA	35.00
☐ 1266	5¢ **Int. Cooperation Year,** 6/26/65, San Francisco, CA	35.00
☐ 1267	5¢ **Salvation Army,** 7/2/65, New York, NY	15.00
☐ 1268	5¢ **Dante,** 7/17/65, San Francisco, CA	15.00

☐	1269	5¢ Herbert Hoover, 8/10/65, West Branch, IA	15.00
☐	1270	5¢ Robert Fulton, 8/19/65, Clermont, NY	15.00
☐	1271	5¢ Florida Settlement, 8/28/65, St. Augustine, FL	15.00
☐	1272	5¢ Traffic Safety, 9/3/65, Baltimore, MD	15.00
☐	1273	5¢ Copley, 9/17/65, DC	15.00
☐	1274	11¢ Int'l. Telecommunications Union, 10/6/65, DC	15.00
☐	1275	5¢ Adlai Stevenson, 10/23/65, Bloomington, IL	15.00
☐	1276	5¢ Christmas, 11/2/65, Silver Bell, AZ	15.00

1965-78

☐	1278	1¢ Jefferson, 1/12/68, Jefferson, IN	25.00
☐	1278a	1¢ Jefferson, Booklet Pane, 1/12/68, Jeffersonville, IN	25.00
☐	1279	1¼¢ Gallatin, 1/30/67, Gallatin, MO	20.00
☐	1280	2¢ Wright, 6/8/66, Spring, Green, WI	18.00
☐	1280a	2¢ Wright, Booklet Pane of 5, 1/8/68, Buffalo, NY	20.00
☐	1281	3¢ Parkman, 9/16/67, Boston, MA	15.00
☐	1282	4¢ Lincoln, 11/19/65, New York, NY	15.00
☐	1283	5¢ Washington, 2/22/66, DC	20.00
☐	1283B	5¢ Washington, Redrawn, 11/17/67, New York, NY	15.00
☐	1284	6¢ Roosevelt, 1/29/66, Hyde Park, NY	15.00
☐	1285	8¢ Einstein, 3/14/66, Princeton, NJ	20.00
☐	1286	10¢ Jackson, 3/15/67, Hermitage, TN	20.00
☐	1286A	12¢ Ford, 7/30/68, Greenfield Vill., MI	20.00
☐	1287	13¢ Kennedy, 5/29/67, Brookline, MA	25.00
☐	1288	15¢ Holmes, 3/8/68, DC	25.00
☐	1289	20¢ Marshall, 10/24/67, Lexington, VA	20.00
☐	1290	25¢ Douglass, 2/14/67, DC	20.00
☐	1291	30¢ Dewey, 10/21/68, Burlington, VT	25.00
☐	1292	40¢ Paine, 1/29/69, Philadelphia, PA	25.00
☐	1293	50¢ Stone, 8/13/68, Dorchester, MA	25.00
☐	1294	$1 O'Neill, 10/16/67, New London, CT	50.00
☐	1295	$5 Moore, 12/3/66, Smyrna, DL	100.00

1966-81

☐	1297	3¢ Parkman, coil, 11/4/75, Pendleton, OR	15.00
☐	1299	1¢ Jefferson, coil, 1/12/68, Jefferson, IN	25.00
☐	1303	4¢ Lincoln, coil, 5/28/66, Springfield, IL	25.00
☐	1304	5¢ Washington, coil, 9/8/66, Cincinnati, OH	15.00
☐	1305C	$1 O'Neill, coil, 1/12/73, Hempstead, NY	50.00

1966

☐	1306	5¢ Migratory Bird Treaty, 3/16/66, Pittsburgh, PA	18.00
☐	1307	5¢ Humane Treatment of Animals, 4/9/66, New York, NY	12.00
☐	1308	5¢ Indiana Statehood, 4/16/66, Corydon, IN	15.00
☐	1309	5¢ Circus, 5/2/66, Delavan, WI	15.00
☐	1310	5¢ SIPEX, 5/21/66, DC	18.00
☐	1311	5¢ SIPEX, Souvenir Sheet, 5/23/66, DC	18.00
☐	1312	5¢ Bill of Rights, 7/1/66, Miami Beach, FL	15.00
☐	1313	5¢ Polish Millennium, 7/30/66, DC	15.00
☐	1314	5¢ Nat'l. Park Serv., 8/25/66, Yellowstone, WY	15.00
☐	1315	5¢ Marine Corps Reserve, 8/29/66, DC	20.00
☐	1316	5¢ Gen'l. Fed. of Women's Clubs, 9/12/66, New York, NY	20.00
☐	1317	5¢ Johnny Appleseed, 9/24/66, Leominster, MA	20.00
☐	1318	5¢ Beautification of America, 10/5/66, DC	20.00
☐	1319	5¢ Great River Road, 10/21/66, Baton Rouge, LA	18.00
☐	1320	5¢ Savings Bonds-Servicemen, 10/26/66, Sioux City, IA	15.00
☐	1321	5¢ Christmas, 11/1/66, Christmas, MI	18.00
☐	1322	5¢ Mary Cassatt, 11/17/66, DC	20.00

1967

☐ 1323	5¢ National Grange, 4/17/67, DC	20.00
☐ 1324	5¢ Canada Centenary, 5/25/67, Montreal, PQ	18.00
☐ 1325	5¢ Erie Canal, 7/4/67, Rome, NY	18.00
☐ 1326	5¢ Search for Peace, 7/5/67, Chicago, IL	15.00
☐ 1327	5¢ Thoreau, 7/12/67, Concord, MA	15.00
☐ 1328	5¢ Nebraska Statehood, 7/29/67, Lincoln, NE	15.00
☐ 1329	5¢ Voice of America, 8/1/67, DC	20.00
☐ 1330	5¢ Davy Crockett, 8/17/67, San Antonio, TX	15.00
☐ 1331-1332	5¢ Space Accomplishments, 9/29/67, Kennedy Space Center, FL	25.00
☐ 1333	5¢ Urban Planning, 10/2/67, DC	20.00
☐ 1334	5¢ Finland Independence, 10/6/67, Finland, MN	18.00
☐ 1335	5¢ Thomas Eakins, 11/2/67, DC	18.00
☐ 1336	5¢ Christmas, 11/6/67, Bethlehem, GA	18.00
☐ 1337	5¢ Mississippi Statehood, 12/11/67, Natchez, MS	18.00

1968-71

☐ 1338	6¢ Flag, 1/24/68, DC	15.00

1969-71

☐ 1338A	6¢ Flag, coil, 5/30/69, Chicago, IL	15.00

1968

☐ 1339	6¢ Illinois Statehood, 2/12/68, Shawneetown, Il	18.00
☐ 1340	6¢ Hemis Fair '68, 3/30/68, Seattle, WA	18.00
☐ 1341	$1 Airlift, 4/4/68, Seattle, WA	30.00
☐ 1342	6¢ Youth - Elks, 5/1/68, Chicago, IL	15.00
☐ 1343	6¢ Law and Order, 5/17/68, DC	20.00
☐ 1344	6¢ Register and Vote, 6/27/68, DC	15.00
☐ 1345-1354	6¢ Historic Flags, 7/4/68, Pittsburgh, PA	25.00
☐ 1355	6¢ Disney, 9/11/68, Marceline, MO	30.00
☐ 1356	6¢ Marquette, 9/20/68, Sault Ste Marie, MI	15.00
☐ 1357	6¢ Daniel Boone, 9/26/68, Frankfort, KY	15.00
☐ 1359	6¢ Leif Erikson, 10/9/68, Seattle, WA	18.00
☐ 1360	6¢ Cherokee Strip, 10/15/68, Ponca City, OK	18.00
☐ 1361	6¢ John Trumbull, 10/18/68, New Haven, CT	20.00
☐ 1362	6¢ Waterfowl Conser., 10/24/68, Cleveland, OH	20.00
☐ 1363	6¢ Christmas, 11/1/68, DC	18.00
☐ 1364	6¢ American Indian, 11/4/68, DC	18.00

1969

☐ 1365-1368	6¢ Beautification of America, 1/16/69, DC	20.00
☐ 1369	6¢ American Legion, 3/15/69, DC	15.00
☐ 1370	6¢ Grandma Moses, 5/1/69, DC	18.00
☐ 1371	6¢ Apollo 8, 5/5/69, Houston, TX	25.00
☐ 1372	6¢ W.C. Handy, 5/17/69, Memphis, TN	15.00
☐ 1373	6¢ California Bicentenary, 7/16/69, San Diego, CA	15.00
☐ 1374	6¢ J.W. Powell, 8/1/69, Page, AZ	18.00
☐ 1375	6¢ Alabama Statehood, 8/2/69, Huntsville, AL	18.00
☐ 1376-1379	6¢ Botanical Congress, 8/23/69, Seattle, WA	25.00
☐ 1380	6¢ Dartmouth Case, 9/22/69, Hanover, NH	18.00
☐ 1381	6¢ Professional Baseball, 9/24/69, Cincinnati, OH	60.00
☐ 1382	6¢ Intercollegiate Football, 9/26/69, New Brunswick, NJ	50.00
☐ 1383	6¢ Dwight D. Eisenhower, 10/14/69, Abilene, KS	15.00
☐ 1384	6¢ Christmas, 11/3/69, Christmas, FL	18.00
☐ 1385	6¢ Hope For Crippled, 11/20/69, Columbus, OH	15.00
☐ 1386	6¢ William M. Harnett, 12/3/69, Boston, MA	15.00

1970

☐ 1387-1390	6¢ Natural History, 5/6/70, New York, NY	20.00
☐ 1391	6¢ Maine Statehood, 7/9/70, Portland, ME	18.00
☐ 1392	6¢ Wildlife Conservation, 7/20/70, Custer, SD	15.00

1970-74

☐ 1393	6¢ Eisenhower, 8/6/70, DC	15.00
☐ 1393D	7¢ Franklin, 10/20/72, Philadelphia, PA	18.00
☐ 1395c	8¢ Eisenhower, Booklet Pane of 4, 1/28/72, Casa Grande, AZ	20.00
☐ 1395d	8¢ Eisenhower, Booklet Pane of 7, 1/28/72, Casa Grande, AZ	25.00
☐ 1396	8¢ Postal Service Emblem, 7/1/71, DC	8.00
☐ 1397	14¢ Fiorella H. LaGuardia, 4/24/72, New York, NY	18.00
☐ 1398	16¢ Ernie Pyle, 5/7/71, DC	10.00
☐ 1399	18¢ Elizabeth Blackwell, 1/23/74, Geneva, NY	8.00
☐ 1400	21¢ Amadeo Giannini, 6/27/73, San Mateo, CA	12.00

1970

☐ 1405	6¢ Edgar Lee Masters, 8/22/70, Petersburg, IL	18.00
☐ 1406	6¢ Woman Suffrage, 8/26/70, Adams, MA	18.00
☐ 1407	6¢ South Carolina, 9/12/70, Charleston, SC	18.00
☐ 1408	6¢ Stone Mt. Memorial, 9/19/70, Stone Mountain, GA	10.00
☐ 1409	6¢ Fort Snelling, 10/17/70, Fort Snelling, MN	12.00
☐ 1410-1413	6¢ Anti-Pollution, 10/28/70, San Clemente, CA	25.00
☐ 1414-1418	6¢ Christmas, 11/5/70, DC (without insert)	12.00
☐ 1419	6¢ United Nations, 11/20/70, New York, NY	12.00
☐ 1420	6¢ Pilgrims' Landing, 11/21/70, Plymouth, MA	12.00
☐ 1421	6¢ Disabled Veterans, 11/24/70, Cincinnati, OH	12.00
☐ 1422	6¢ U.S. Serviceman, 11/24/70, Montgomery, AL	12.00

1971

☐ 1423	6¢ Wool Industry, 1/19/71, Las Vegas, NV	12.00
☐ 1424	6¢ MacArthur, 1/26/71, Norfolk, VA	12.00
☐ 1425	6¢ Blood Donor, 3/12/71, New York, NY	12.00
☐ 1426	8¢ Missouri Sesqui., 5/8/71, Independence, MO	12.00
☐ 1427-1430	8¢ Wildlife Conservation, 6/12/71, Avery Island, LA	25.00
☐ 1431	8¢ Antarctic Treaty, 6/23/71, DC	12.00
☐ 1433	8¢ John Sloan, 8/2/71, Lock Haven, PA	12.00
☐ 1434-1435	8¢ Space Achievement Decade, 8/2/71, Huntsville, AL	20.00
☐ 1436	8¢ Emily Dickinson, 8/28/71, Amherst, MA	12.00
☐ 1437	8¢ San Juan, 9/12/71, San Juan, PR	12.00
☐ 1438	8¢ Drug Abuse, 10/4/71, Dallas, TX	12.00
☐ 1439	8¢ CARE, 10/27/71, New York, NY	18.00
☐ 1444-45	8¢ Christmas, 11/10/71, DC (without insert)	10.00

1972

☐ 1446	8¢ Sidney Lanier, 2/3/72, Macon, GA	12.00
☐ 1447	8¢ Peace Corps, 2/11/72, DC	12.00
☐ 1448-1451	2¢ National Parks Centennial, 4/5/72, Hatteras, NC (without insert)	15.00
☐ 1452	6¢ National Parks, 6/26/72, Vienna, VA	20.00
☐ 1453	8¢ National Parks, 3/1/72, DC or Yellowstone	20.00
☐ 1454	15¢ National Parks, 7/28/72, McKinley Park, AK	25.00
☐ 1455	8¢ Family Planning, 3/18/72, New York, NY	15.00
☐ 1456-1459	8¢ Colonial Craftsmen, 7/4/72, Williamsburg, VA	15.00
☐ 1460-1462,	C85 Olympics, 8/17/72, Washington, DC	8.00
☐ 1463	8¢ P.T.A., 9/15/72, San Francisco, CA	8.00
☐ 1464-1467	8¢ Wildlife, 9/20/72, Warm Springs, OR	12.00
☐ 1468	8¢ Mail Order, 9/27/72, Chicago, IL	25.00
☐ 1469	8¢ Osteopathy, 10/9/72, Miami, FL	8.00

☐ 1470	8¢ **Tom Sawyer,** 10/13/72, Hannibal, MO	12.00
☐ 1471-1472	8¢ **Christmas,** 11/9/72, DC (without insert)	12.00
☐ 1473	8¢ **Pharmacy,** 11/10/72, Cincinnati, OH	8.00
☐ 1474	8¢ **Stamp Collecting,** 11/17/72, New York, NY	12.00

1973

☐ 1475	8¢ **Love,** 1/26/73, Philadelphia, PA	12.00
☐ 1476	8¢ **Pamphleteer,** 2/16/73, Portland, OR	12.00
☐ 1477	8¢ **Broadside,** 4/13/73, Atlantic City, NJ	12.00
☐ 1478	8¢ **Post Rider,** 6/22/73, Rochester, NY	12.00
☐ 1479	8¢ **Drummer,** 9/28/73, New Orleans, LA	12.00
☐ 1480-1483	8¢ **Boston Tea Party,** 7/4/73, Boston, MA	15.00
☐ 1484	8¢ **George Gershwin,** 2/28/73, Beverly Hills, CA	25.00
☐ 1485	8¢ **Robinson Jefferson,** 8/13/73, Carmel, CA	12.00
☐ 1486	8¢ **Henry O. Tanner,** 9/10/73, Pittsburgh, PA	12.00
☐ 1487	8¢ **Willa Cather,** 9/20/73, Red Cloud, NE	8.00
☐ 1488	8¢ **Nicolaus Copernicus,** 4/23/73, DC	10.00
☐ 1489-98	8¢ **Postal People,** 4/30/73, DC	15.00
☐ 1499	8¢ **Harry S. Truman,** 5/8/73, Independence, MO	15.00
☐ 1500-1502	6¢ - 15¢ **Electronics,** 7/10/73, New York, NY	25.00
☐ 1503	8¢ **Lyndon B. Johnson,** 8/27/73, Austin, TX	15.00

1973-74

☐ 1504	8¢ **Angus Cattle,** 10/5/73, St. Joseph, MO	15.00
☐ 1505	10¢ **Chautauqua,** 8/6/74, Chautauqua, NY	15.00
☐ 1506	10¢ **Wheat,** 8/16/74, Hillsboro, KS	15.00

1973

☐ 1507-1508	8¢ **Christmas,** 11/7/73, DC (without insert)	15.00

1973-74

☐ 1509	10¢ **Crossed Flags,** 12/8/73, San Francisco, CA	18.00
☐ 1510d	10¢ **Jefferson Memorial,** Booklet Pane of 6, 8/5/74, Oakland, CA	18.00
☐ 1518	6.3¢ **Bell Coil,** 10/1/74, DC	8.00

1974

☐ 1525	10¢ **Veterans of Foreign Wars,** 3/11/74, DC	15.00
☐ 1526	10¢ **Robert Frost,** 3/26/74, Derry, NH	12.00
☐ 1527	10¢ **EXPO '74,** 4/18/74, Spokane, WA	15.00
☐ 1528	10¢ **Horse Racing,** 5/4/74, Louisville, KY (with insert)	18.00
☐ 1529	10¢ **Skylab,** 5/14/74, Houston, TX	20.00
☐ 1530-1537	10¢ **UPU Centenary,** 6/6/74, DC	20.00
☐ 1538-1541	10¢ **Mineral Heritage,** 6/13/74, Lincoln, NE	20.00
☐ 1542	10¢ **Kentucky Settlement,** 6/15/74, Harrodsville, KY	10.00
☐ 1543-1546	10¢ **Continental Congress,** 7/4/74, Philadelphia, PA	20.00
☐ 1547	10¢ **Energy Conservation,** 9/23/74, Detroit, MI	8.00
☐ 1548	10¢ **Sleepy Hollow,** 10/10/74, North Tarrytown, NY	15.00
☐ 1549	10¢ **Retarded Children,** 10/12/74, Arlington, TX	12.00
☐ 1550-1551	10¢ **1974 Christmas,** 10/23/74, New York, NY	20.00
☐ 1550-1552	10¢ **1974 Christmas,** 10/23/74, New York, NY (less than 10 known)	100.00

1975

☐ 1553	10¢ **Benjamin West,** 2/10/75, Swarthmore, PA	20.00
☐ 1554	10¢ **Paul L. Dunbar,** 5/1/75, Dayton, OH	12.00
☐ 1555	10¢ **D.W. Griffith,** 5/27/75, Beverly Hills, CA	12.00
☐ 1556	10¢ **Pioneer-Jupiter,** 2/28/75, Mountain View, CA	20.00
☐ 1557	10¢ **Mariner 10,** 4/4/75, Pasadena, CA	20.00
☐ 1558	10¢ **Collective Bargaining,** 3/13/75, DC	15.00
☐ 1559	8¢ **Sybil Ludington,** 3/25/75, Carmel, NY	10.00

☐ 1560	10¢ Salem Poor, 3/25/75, Cambridge, MA	12.00
☐ 1561	10¢ Haym Salomon, 3/25/75, Chicago, IL	15.00
☐ 1562	18¢ Peter Francisco, 3/25/75, Greensboro, NC	12.00
☐ 1563	10¢ Lexington-Concord, 4/19/75, Concord, MA	10.00
☐ 1563	10¢ Lexington-Concord, 4/19/75, Lexington, MA	15.00
☐ 1564	10¢ Bunker Hill, 6/17/75, Charlestown, MA	12.00
☐ 1565-1568	10¢ Military Service, 7/4/75, DC	15.00
☐ 1571	10¢ Int'l. Women's Year, 8/26/75, Seneca Falls, NY	15.00
☐ 1572-1575	10¢ Postal Service Bicentennial, 9/3/75, Philadelphia, PA	15.00
☐ 1577-1578	10¢ Banking - Commerce, 10/6/75, New York, NY	12.00
☐ 1579-1580	10¢ Christmas, 10/14/75, DC (with insert)	15.00

1973-81

☐ 1581-1585	1¢ - 4¢ Americana Series, 12/8/77, St. Louis, MO	12.00
☐ 1592	10¢ Contemplation of Justice, 11/17/77, New York, NY	10.00
☐ 1593	11¢ Early Am. Printing Press, 11/13/75, Philadelphia, PA	12.00
☐ 1594 & 1816	12¢ Liberty's Torch, Sheet Coil, 4/8/81, Dallas, TX	12.00
☐ 1595a-c	13¢ Liberty Bell, Booklet, 10/31/75, Cleveland, OH	20.00
☐ 1595d	13¢ Liberty Bell, Booklet Pane of 5, 4/2/76, Liberty, MO	15.00
☐ 1596	13¢ Eagle & Shield, 12/1/75, Juneau, AK	12.00
☐ 1597	15¢ Ft. McHenry Flag, 6/30/78, Baltimore, MD	12.00
☐ 1603	24¢ Old North Church, 11/14/75, Boston, MA	12.00
☐ 1604	28¢ Ft. Nisqually, 8/11/78, Tacoma, WA	10.00
☐ 1605	29¢ Sandy Hook Lighthouse, 4/14/78, Atlantic City, NJ	12.00
☐ 1606	30¢ Morris Township School No. 2, 8/27/79, Devils Lake, ND	15.00
☐ 1608	50¢ Iron "Betty" Lamp, 9/11/79, San Juan, PR	20.00
☐ 1611	$2 Kerosene Table Lamp, 11/16/78, New York, NY	15.00
☐ 1612	$5 Railroad Lantern, 8/23/79, Boston, MA	30.00
☐ 1614	7.7¢ Saxhorns, 11/20/76, New York, NY	12.00
☐ 1615	7.9¢ Drum, 4/23/76, Miami, FL	12.00
☐ 1615C	8.4¢ Grand Piano, 7/13/78, Interlochen, MI	30.00
☐ 1616	9¢ Dome of the Capitol, 3/5/76, Milwaukee, WI	15.00
☐ 1617	10¢ Contemplation of Justice, 11/4/77, Tampa, FL	12.00
☐ 1618	13¢ Liberty Bell, 11/25/75, Allentown, PA	12.00
☐ 1622	13¢ Flag Over Independence Hall, 11/15/75, Philadelphia, PA	12.00

1975-77

☐ 1623c	13¢ Flag Over Capitol, Perf 10, 3/11/77, New York, NY	25.00
☐ 1623d	13¢ Flag & 9¢ Capitol, Booklet Perf 10½x11, 3/11/77, New York, NY	100.00

1976

☐ 1632	13¢ Interphil '76, 1/17/76, Philadelphia, PA	15.00
☐ 1633-1682	13¢ State Flags, 2/23/76, DC	30.00
☐ 1683	13¢ Telephone, 3/10/76, Boston, MA	15.00
☐ 1684	13¢ Commercial Aviation, 3/19/76, Chicago, IL	15.00
☐ 1685	13¢ Chemistry, 4/6/76, New York, NY	15.00
☐ 1686-1689	13¢-31¢ Bicentennial Souvenir Sheets, 5/29/76, Phila., PA (any single stamp)	20.00
☐ 1690	13¢ Franklin, /6/1/76, Philadelphia, PA	15.00
☐ 1691-1694	13¢ Declaration of Independence, 7/4/76, Philadelphia, PA	50.00
☐ 1695-1698	13¢ Olympic Games, 7/16/76, Lake Placid, NY	20.00
☐ 1699	13¢ Clara Maass, 8/18/76, Belleville, NJ	15.00
☐ 1701-1702	13¢ Christmas, 10/27/76, Boston, MA	12.00

1977

☐ 1704	13¢ Washington, 1/3/77, Princeton, NJ	15.00
☐ 1705	13¢ Sound Recording, 3/23/77, DC	15.00
☐ 1706-1709	13¢ Pueblo Pottery, 4/13/77, Sante Fe, NM	12.00
☐ 1710	13¢ Solo Flight, 5/20/77, Garden City, NY	15.00

☐ 1711	13¢ **Colorado**, 5/21/77, Denver, CO	12.00
☐ 1712-1715	13¢ **Butterflies**, 6/6/77, Indianapolis, In	18.00
☐ 1716	13¢ **Lafayette**, 6/13/77, Charlestown, SC	15.00
☐ 1717-1720	13¢ **Skilled Hands**, 7/4/77, Cincinnati, OH	18.00
☐ 1721	13¢ **Peace Bridge**, 8/4/77, Buffalo, NY	15.00
☐ 1722	13¢ **Herkimer**, 8/6/77, Herkimer, NY	20.00
☐ 1725	13¢ **Alta CA.**, 9/9/77, San Jose, CA	10.00
☐ 1726	13¢ **Articles Of Confederation**, 9/30/77, York, PA	12.00
☐ 1727	13¢ **Talking Pictures**, 10/6/77, Hollywood, CA	30.00
☐ 1728	13¢ **Surrender at Saratoga**, 10/7/77, Schuylerville, PA	12.00
☐ 1729	13¢ **Christmas (Valley Forge)**, 10/21/77, Valley Forge, PA	20.00
☐ 1730	13¢ **Christmas (mailbox)**, 10/21/77, Omaha, NE	18.00

1978

☐ 1731	13¢ **Carl Sandburg**, 1/6/78, Galesburg, IL	15.00
☐ 1732-1733	13¢ **Captain Cook**, 1/20/78, Anchorage, AK or Honolulu, HI	15.00

1978-80

☐ 1734	13¢ **Indian Head Penny**, 1/11/78, Kansas City, MO	12.00
☐ 1737a	13¢ **Roses, Booklet**, 7/11/78, Shreveport, LA	20.00
☐ 1738-1742	15¢ **Windmills Booklet**, 2/7/80, Lubbock, TX	40.00

1978

☐ 1744	13¢ **Harriet Tubman**, 2/1/78, DC	15.00
☐ 1745-1748	13¢ **American Quilts**, 3/8/78, Charleston, WV	20.00
☐ 1749-1752	13¢ **American Dance**, 4/26/78, New York, NY	10.00
☐ 1753	13¢ **French Alliance**, 5/4/78, York, PA	12.00
☐ 1754	13¢ **Papanicolaou**, 5/18/78, Miami, FL	25.00
☐ 1755	13¢ **Jimmie Rodgers**, 5/24/78, Meridian, MS	20.00
☐ 1756	15¢ **Geo. M. Cohan**, 7/3/78, Providence, RI	18.00
☐ 1758	15¢ **Photography**, 6/26/78, Las Vegas, NV	15.00
☐ 1759	15¢ **Viking Missions**, 7/20/78, Hampton, VA	20.00
☐ 1760-1763	15¢ **American Owls**, 8/26/78, Fairbanks, AK	18.00
☐ 1764-1767	15¢ **American Trees**, 10/9/78, Hot Springs National Park, AR	18.00
☐ 1768	15¢ **Christmas Madonna**, 10/18/78, DC	8.00
☐ 1769	15¢ **Christmas (Hobby Horse)**, 10/18/78, Holly, MI	15.00

1979

☐ 1770	15¢ **Robert F. Kennedy**, 1/12/79, DC	25.00
☐ 1771	15¢ **Martin Luther King, Jr.**, 1/13/79, Atlanta, GA	20.00
☐ 1772	15¢ **Int'l. Year of the Child**, 2/5/79, Philadelphia, PA	18.00
☐ 1773	15¢ **John Steinbeck**, 2/27/79, Salinas, CA	20.00
☐ 1774	15¢ **Albert Einstein**, 3/4/79, Princeton, NJ	18.00
☐ 1775-1778	15¢ **Penn. Toleware**, 4/19/79, Lancaster, PA	12.00
☐ 1779-1782	15¢ **Am. Architecture**, 6/4/79, Kansas City, MO	10.00
☐ 1783-1786	15¢ **Endangered Flora**, 6/7/79, Milwaukee, WI	15.00
☐ 1787	15¢ **Seeing Eye Dogs**, 6/15/79, Morristown, NJ	25.00
☐ 1788	15¢ **Special Olympics**, 8/9/79, Brockport, NY	18.00
☐ 1789	15¢ **John Paul Jones**, 9/23/79, Annapolis, MD	15.00

1979-80

☐ 1790	10¢ **Olympic Javelin**, 9/5/79, Olympia, WA	12.00
☐ 1791-1794	15¢ **Summer Olympics**, 9/28/79, Los Angeles, CA	12.00
☐ 1795-1798	15¢ **Winter Olympics**, 2/1/80, Lake Placid, NY	12.00

1979

☐ 1799	15¢ **Christmas-Virgin and Child**, 10/18/79, DC	10.00
☐ 1800	15¢ **Christmas - Santa Claus**, 10/18/79, North Pole, AK	12.00

☐	1801	15¢ Will Rogers, 11/4/79, Claremore, OK	10.00
☐	1802	15¢ Vietnam Veterans, 11/11/79, Arlington, VA	10.00

1980

☐	1803	15¢ W.C. Fields, 1/29/80, Beverly Hills, CA	12.00
☐	1804	15¢ Benjamin Banneker, 2/15/80, Annapolis, MD	8.00
☐	1805-1810	15¢ Nat'l. Letter Writing Week, 2/25/80, DC	12.00
☐	1821	15¢ Frances Perkins, 4/10/80, DC	8.00
☐	1822	15¢ Dolley Madison, 5/10/80, DC	10.00
☐	1823	15¢ Emily Bissell, 5/31/80, Wilmington, DE	10.00
☐	1824	15¢ Helen Keller & Anne Sullivan, 6/27/80, Tuscumbia, AL	18.00
☐	1825	15¢ Veterans Administration, 7/21/80, DC	10.00
☐	1826	15¢ Bernardode Galvez, 7/23/80, New Orleans, LA	10.00
☐	1827-1830	15¢ Coral Reefs, 8/26/80, Charlotte Amalie, VI	25.00
☐	1831	15¢ Organized Labor, 9/1/80, DC	20.00
☐	1832	15¢ Edith Wharton, 9/5/80, New Haven, CT	12.00
☐	1833	15¢ Education, 9/12/80, Franklin, MA	10.00
☐	1834-37	15¢ Pacific N/W Indian Masks, 9/25/80, Spokane, WA	12.00
☐	1838-41	15¢ Am. Architecture, /10/9/80, New York, NY	10.00
☐	1842	15¢ Christmas Madonna & Child, 10/31/80, DC	8.00
☐	1843	15¢ Christmas - Wreath & Roys, 10/31/80, Munising, MI	10.00

1980-85

☐	1844	1¢ Dorthea Dix, 9/23/83, Hampden, ME	8.00
☐	1845	2¢ Igor Stravinsky, 11/18/82, New York, NY	6.00
☐	1846	3¢ Henry Clay, 7/13/83, DC	6.00
☐	1847	4¢ Carl Schurz, 6/3/83, Watertown, WI	6.00
☐	1848	5¢ Pearl Buck, 6/25/83, Hillsboro, WV	20.00
☐	1849	6¢ Walter Lippman, 9/19/85, Minneapolis, MN	6.00
☐	1850	7¢ Abraham Baldwin, 1/25/85, Athens, GA	6.00
☐	1851	8¢ Henry Knox, 7/25/85, Thomaston, ME	6.00
☐	1852	9¢ Sylvanus Thayer, 6/7/85, Braintree, MA	6.00
☐	1853	10¢ Richard Russell, 5/31/84, Winder, GA	6.00
☐	1854	11¢ Alden Partridge, 2/12/85, Norwich Univ., VT	6.00
☐	1855	13¢ Crazy Horse, 1/15/82, Crazy Horse, SD	20.00
☐	1856	14¢ Sinclair Lewis, 3/21/85, Sauk Center, MN	6.00
☐	1857	17¢ Rachel Carson, 5/28/81, Springdale, PA	12.00
☐	1858	18¢ George Mason, 5/7/81, Gunston Hall, VA	6.00
☐	1859	19¢ Sequoyah, 12/27/80, Tahlequah, OK	12.00
☐	1860	20¢ Ralph Bunche, 1/12/82, New York, NY	8.00
☐	1861	20¢ Thomas Gallaudet, 6/10/83, West Hartford, CT	8.00
☐	1862	20¢ Harry S. Truman, 1/26/84, DC	8.00
☐	1863	22¢ John J. Audubon, 4/23/85, New York, NY	6.00
☐	1864	30¢ Frank Laubach, 9/2/84, Benton, PA	8.00
☐	1865	35¢ Charles Drew, 6/3/81, DC	10.00
☐	1866	37¢ Robert Millikan, 1/26/82, Pasadena, CA	10.00
☐	1867	39¢ Grenville Clark, 3/20/85, Hanover, NH	10.00
☐	1868	40¢ Lillian Gilbreth, 2/24/84, Montclair, NJ	10.00
☐	1869	50¢ Chester W. Nimitz, 2/22/85, Fredricksburg, TX	20.00

1981

☐	1874	15¢ Everett Dirksen, 1/4/81, Pekin, IL	18.00
☐	1875	15¢ Whitney Moore Young, 1/30/81, New York, NY	12.00
☐	1876-1879	18¢ Flowers, 4/23/81, Ft. Valley, GA	18.00
☐	1880-1889	15¢ Wildlife Booklet, 5/14/81, Boise, ID	18.00
☐	1890-1893	18¢ Flag Sheet, Coil, Booklet, 4/24/81, Portland, ME	15.00
☐	1896b	20¢ Flag, Booklet of 10, 11/17/83, Washington, DC	10.00

1981-84

☐ 1897	1¢ **Omnibus**, 8/19/83, Arlington, VA	12.00
☐ 1897A	2¢ **Locomotive**, 5/20/82, Chicago, IL	15.00
☐ 1898	3¢ **Handcar**, 3/25/83, Rochester, NY	15.00
☐ 1898A	4¢ **Stagecoach**, 8/19/82, Milwaukee, WI	15.00
☐ 1899	5¢ **Motorcycle**, 10/10/83, San Francisco, CA	15.00
☐ 1904	10.9¢ **Hansom Cab**, 3/26/82, Chattanooga, TN	12.00
☐ 1907	18¢ **Surrey**, 5/18/81, Notch, MO	15.00

1981

☐ 1910	18¢ **American Red Cross**, 5/1/81, DC	8.00
☐ 1911	18¢ **Savings Loans**, 5/8/81, Chicago, IL	8.00
☐ 11912-1919	18¢ **Space Achievement**, 5/21/81, Kennedy Space Center, FL	20.00
☐ 1920	18¢ **Professional Management**, 6/18/81, Philadelphia, PA	8.00
☐ 1921-1924	18¢ **Wildlife Habitats**, 6/26/81, Reno, NV	10.00
☐ 1925	18¢ **Int'l. Year of the Disabled Persons**, 6/29/81, Milford, MI	8.00
☐ 1926	18¢ **Edna St. Vincent Millay**, 7/10/81, Austerlitz, NY	10.00
☐ 1927	18¢ **Alcoholism**, 8/19/81, DC	8.00
☐ 1928-1931	18¢ **Am. Architecture**, 8/28/81, DC	8.00
☐ 1932-1933	18¢ **Babe Zaharias & Bobby Jones**, 9/22/81, Pinehurst, NC	8.00
☐ 1934	18¢ **Frederic Remington**, 10/9/81, Oklahoma City, OK	12.00
☐ 1937-1938	18¢ **Battle of Yorktown of the Virginia Capes**, 10/16/81, Yorktown, VA	12.00
☐ 1939	20¢ **Christman-Botticelli**, 10/28/81, Chicago, IL	10.00
☐ 1940	20¢ **Christmas - Bear & Sleigh**, 10/28/81,Christmas Valley, OR	14.00
☐ 1941	20¢ **John Hanson**, 11/5/81, Frederick, MD	10.00
☐ 1942-1945	20¢ **Desert Plants**, 12/11/81, Tucson, AZ	18.00

1982

☐ 1949a	20¢ **Bighorn Sheep**, 1/8/82, Bighorn, MT	18.00
☐ 1950	20¢ **Franklin D. Roosevelt**, 1/30/82, Hyde Park, NY	12.00
☐ 1951	20¢ **Love**, 2/1/82, Boston, MA	10.00
☐ 1952	20¢ **George Washington**, 2/22/82, MT. Vernon, VA	8.00
☐ 1953-2002	20¢ **50 State Birds & Flowers**, 4/14/82, DC (any Block of 4)	12.00
☐ 2003	20¢ **Netherlands Recognition**, 4/20/82, DC	15.00
☐ 2004	20¢ **Library of Congress**, 4/21/82, DC	8.00
☐ 2005	20¢ **Consumer Education**, 4/27/82, DC	8.00
☐ 2006-2009	20¢ **Knoxville World's Fair**, 4/29/82, Knoxville, TN	10.00
☐ 1010	20¢ **Horatio Alger**, 4/30/82, Willow Grove, PA	10.00
☐ 2011	20¢ **Aging Together**, 5/21/82, Sun City, AZ	10.00
☐ 2012	20¢ **The Barrymores**, 6/8/82, New York, NY	6.00
☐ 2013	20¢ **Dr. Mary Walker**, 6/10/82, Oswego, NY	8.00
☐ 2014	20¢ **International Peace Garden**, 6/30/82, Dunseith, ND	10.00
☐ 2015	20¢ **America's Libraries**, 7/13/82, Philadelphia, PA	8.00
☐ 2016	20¢ **Jackie Robinson**, 8/2/82, Cooperstown, NY	20.00
☐ 2017	20¢ **Touro Synagogue**, 8/22/82, Newport, RI	10.00
☐ 2018	20¢ **Wolf Trap**, 9/1/82, Vienna, VA	6.00
☐ 2019-2022	20¢ **Am. Architecture**, 9/30/82, DC	8.00
☐ 2023	20¢ **Francis of Assisi**, 10/7/82, San Francisco, CA	15.00
☐ 2024	20¢ **Ponce de Leon**, 10/12/82, San Juan, PR	10.00
☐ 2025	13¢ **Kitten & Puppy**, 11/3/82, Denvers, MA	15.00
☐ 2026	20¢ **Christmas (Religious)**, 10/28/82, DC	8.00
☐ 2027-2030	20¢ **Christmas-Secular**, 10/28/82, Snow, OK	15.00

1983

☐ 2031	20¢ **Science & Industry**, 1/19/83, Chicago, IL	10.00
☐ 2032-2035	20¢ **Ballooning**, 3/31/83, Albuquerque, NM	18.00
☐ 2032-2035	20¢ **Ballooning**, 3/31/83, DC	12.00
☐ 2036	20¢ **Swedish Trade Relations**, 3/24/83, Philadelphia, PA	8.00

☐ 2037	20¢ Civilian Conservation Corps, 4/5/83, Luray, VA	8.00
☐ 2038	20¢ Joseph Priestly, 4/13/83, Northumberland, PA	6.00
☐ 2039	20¢ Voluntarism, 4/20/83, DC	8.00
☐ 2040	20¢ German Immigration, 4/29/83, Germantown, PA	12.00
☐ 2041	20¢ Brooklyn Bridge, 5/17/83, Brooklyn, NY	6.00
☐ 2042	20¢ Tennessee Valley Authority, 5/18/83, Knoxville, TN	8.00
☐ 2043	20¢ Physical Fitness, 5/14/83, Houston, TX	8.00
☐ 2044	20¢ Scott Joplin, 6/9/83, Sedalia, MO	10.00
☐ 2045	20¢ Medal of Honor, 6/7/83, DC	12.00
☐ 2046	20¢ Babe Ruth, 7/6/83, Chicago, IL	20.00
☐ 2047	20¢ Nathaniel Hawthorne, 7/8/83, Salem, MA	8.00
☐ 2048-2051	13¢ Summer Olympics, 7/28/83, South Bend, IN	12.00
☐ 2052	20¢ Treaty of Paris, 9/2/83, DC	10.00
☐ 2053	20¢ Civil Service, 9/9/83, DC	8.00
☐ 2054	20¢ Metropolitan Opera, 9/14/83, New York, NY	6.00
☐ 2055-2058	20¢ Inventors, 9/21/83, DC	8.00
☐ 2059-2062	20¢ Streetcars, 10/8/83, Kennebunkport, ME	10.00
☐ 2063	20¢ Christmas (Religious), 10/28/83, DC	6.00
☐ 2064	20¢ Christmas (Secular), 10/28/83, Santa Claus, IN	6.00
☐ 2065	20¢ Martin Luther, 11/11/83, DC	10.00

1984

☐ 2066	20¢ Alaska Statehood, 1/3/84, Fairbanks, AK	6.00
☐ 2067-2070	20¢ Winter Olympics, 1/6/84, Lake Placid, NY	12.00
☐ 2071	20¢ Federal Deposit Ins. Corp., 1/12/84, DC	6.00
☐ 2072	20¢ Love, 1/31/84, DC	6.00
☐ 2073	20¢ Carter Woodson, 2/1/84, DC	6.00
☐ 2074	20¢ Soil & Water Conservation, 2/6/84, Denver, CO	8.00
☐ 2075	20¢ Credit Union Act, 2/10/84, Salem, MA	6.00
☐ 2076-2079	20¢ Orchids, 3/5/84, Miami, FL	12.00
☐ 2080	20¢ Hawaii Statehood, 3/12/84, Honolulu, HI	8.00
☐ 2081	20¢ National Archives, 4/16/84, DC	8.00
☐ 2082-2085	20¢ Olympics, 5/4/84, Los Angeles, CA	10.00
☐ 2086	20¢ Louisiana Exposition, 5/11/84, New Orleans, LA	8.00
☐ 2087	20¢ Health Research, 5/17/84, New York, NY	6.00
☐ 2088	20¢ Douglas Fairbanks, 5/23/84, Denver, CO	6.00
☐ 2089	20¢ Jim Thorpe, 5/24/84, Shawnee, OK	18.00
☐ 2089	20¢ Jim Thorpe (2nd Day), 5/25/84, Yale, OK	22.00
☐ 2090	20¢ John McCormack, 6/6/84, Boston, MA	8.00
☐ 2091	20¢ St. Lawrence Seaway, 6/26/84, Massena, NY	6.00
☐ 2092	20¢ Waterfowl Preservation Act, 7/2/84, Des Moines, IA	6.00
☐ 2093	20¢ Roanoke Voyages, 7/13/84, Manteo, NC	12.00
☐ 2094	20¢ Herman Melville, 8/1/84, New Bedford, MA	12.00
☐ 2095	20¢ Horace A. Moses, 8/6/84, Bloomington, IN	8.00
☐ 2096	20¢ Smokey The Bear, /8/13/84, Capitan, NM	10.00
☐ 2097	20¢ Roberto Clemente, 8/17/84, Carolina, PR	15.00
☐ 2098-2101	20¢ Dogs, 9/7/84, New York, NY	10.00
☐ 2102	20¢ Crime Prevention, 9/26/84, DC	6.00
☐ 2103	20¢ Hispanic Americans, 10/31/84, DC	6.00
☐ 2104	20¢ Family Unity, 10/1/84, Shaker Heights, OH	8.00
☐ 2105	20¢ Eleanor Roosevelt, 10/11/84, Hyde Park, NY	6.00
☐ 2106	20¢ Nation of Readers, 10/16/84, DC	8.00
☐ 2107	20¢ Christmas (Madonna), 10/30/84, DC	6.00
☐ 2108	20¢ Christmas (Santa), 10/30/84, Jamaica, NY	6.00
☐ 2109	20¢ Vietnam Vets Memorial, 11/10/84, DC	6.00

1985

☐ 2110	22¢ Jerome Kern, 1/23/85, New York, NY	6.00
☐ 2114-2115	22¢ Flag, (Sheet and Coil), 3/29/85, DC	10.00

☐ 2115b	22¢ Flag Over Capitol (Test Coil), 5/23/87, Secaucus, NJ	6.00
☐ 2116a	22¢ Flag (Booklet Stamp), 3/29/85, Waubeka, WI	6.00
☐ 2117-2121	22¢ Seashells, Booklet, 4/4/85, Boston, MA	15.00

1985-87

☐ 2123	3.4 School Bus, 6/8/85, Arlington, VA	12.00
☐ 2125 & 2128	4.9¢ Buckboard & 8.3¢ Ambulance, 6/21/85, Reno, NV	12.00
☐ 2126	5.5¢ Star Route Truck, 11/1/86, Fort Worth, TX	12.00
☐ 2127B	7.1¢ Tractor, 2/6/87, Sarasota, FL	12.00
☐ 2128B	8.5¢ Tow Truck, 1/24/87, Tucson, AZ	12.00
☐ 2130	11¢ Stutz Super Bearcat, 6/11/85, Baton Rouge, LA	12.00
☐ 2131	12¢ Stanley Steamer, 4/2/85, Kingfield, ME	12.00
☐ 2134	14¢ Iceboat, 3/23/85, Rochester, NY	12.00
☐ 2135	17¢ Dog Sled, 8/20/86, Anchorage, AK	12.00
☐ 2136	25¢ Bread Wagon, 11/22/86, Virginia Beach, VA	12.00

1985

☐ 2137	22¢ Mary McLeod Bethune, 3/5/85, DC	6.00
☐ 2138-2141	22¢ Duck Decoys, 3/22/85, Shelburne, VT	10.00
☐ 2142	22¢ Winter Special Olympics, 3/25/85, Park City, UT	10.00
☐ 2143	22¢ Love, 4/17/85, Hollywood, CA	8.00
☐ 2144	22¢ Rural Electrification Admin., 5/11/85, Madison, SD	6.00
☐ 2145	22¢ Ameripex '86, /5/25/85, Rosemont, IL	10.00
☐ 2146	22¢ Abigail Adams, 6/14/85, Quincy, MA	8.00
☐ 2147	22¢ Frederick Auguste Bartholdi, 7/18/85, New York, NY	12.00
☐ 2149	18¢ Washington Monument, 11/6/85, DC	12.00
☐ 2150	21.1¢ Sealed Envelopes, 10/22/85, DC	12.00
☐ 2152	22¢ Korean War Veterans, 7/26/85, DC	8.00
☐ 2153	22¢ Social Security Act, 8/14/85, Baltimore, MD	15.00
☐ 2154	22¢ World War I Vets, 8/26/85, Milwaukee, WI	8.00
☐ 2155-2158	22¢ Horses, 9/25/85, Lexington, KY	10.00
☐ 2159	22¢ Public Education in America, 10/1/85, Boston, MA	6.00
☐ 2160-2163	22¢ Int'l. Youth Year, 10/7/85, Chicago, IL	8.00
☐ 2164	22¢ Help End Hunger, 10/15/85, DC	6.00
☐ 2165	22¢ Christmas (Madonna & Child), 10/31/85, Detroit, MI	10.00
☐ 2166	22¢ Christmas (Poinsettia), 10/30/85, Nazareth, MI	6.00

1986-7

☐ 2167	22¢ Arkansas Statehood, 1/3/86, Little Rock, AR	6.00
☐ 2168	1¢ Margaret Mitchell, 6/30/86, Atlanta, GA	6.00
☐ 2169	2¢ Mary Lyon, 2/28/87, South Hadley, MA	12.00
☐ 2170	3¢ Dr. Paul Dudley White, 9/15/86, DC	6.00
☐ 2171	4¢ Father Flanagan, 7/14/86, Boys Town, NE	6.00
☐ 2172	5¢ Hugo Black, 2/27/86, DC	6.00
☐ 2176	10¢ Red Cloud, 8/15/87, Red Cloud, NE	8.00
☐ 2177	14¢ Julia Ward Howe, 2/12/87, Boston, MA	6.00
☐ 2179	17¢ Belva Ann Lockwood, 6/18/86, Middleport, NY	6.00
☐ 2183	25¢ Jack London, 1/11/86, Glen Ellen, CA	8.00
☐ 2191	56¢ John Harvard, 9/3/86, Boston, MA	8.00
☐ 2194	$1 Bernard Revel, 9/23/86, New York, NY	8.00
☐ 2195	$2 William Jennings Bryan, 3/19/86, Salem, IL	15.00
☐ 2196	$5 Francis Bret Harte, 8/25/87, Twain Harte, CA	18.00

1986

☐ 2198-2201	22¢ Stamp Collecting, 1/23/86, State College, PA	12.00
☐ 2202	22¢ Love, 1/30/86, New York, NY	6.00
☐ 2203	22¢ Sojourner Truth, 2/4/86, New Paltz, NY	6.00
☐ 2204	22¢ Republic of Texas, 3/2/86, San Antonio, TX	10.00
☐ 2204	22¢ Republic of Texas, 3/2/86, Washington on the Brazos, TX	10.00

☐ 2205-2209	22¢ Fish, 3/21/86, Seattle, WA	10.00
☐ 2210	22¢ Public Hospitals, 4/11/86, New York, NY	6.00
☐ 2211	22¢ Duke Ellington, 4/29/86, New York, NY	6.00
☐ 2216-2219	22¢ Presidents Souvenir Sheet, 5/22/86, Chicago, IL (first sheet only)	10.00
☐ 2220-2223	22¢ Polar Explorers, 5/28/86, North Pole, AK	6.00
☐ 2224	22¢ Statue of Liberty, 7/4/86, Liberty Island, NY/NJ	125.00
☐ 2226	2¢ Locomotive, Re-engraved, 3/6/87, Milwaukee, WI	12.00

1986

☐ 2235-2238	22¢ Navajo Art, 9/4/86, Window Rock, AZ	10.00
☐ 2239	22¢ T.S. Eliot, 9/26/86, St. Louis, MO	6.00
☐ 2240-2243	22¢ Woodcarved Figurines, 10/1/86, DC	6.00
☐ 2244	22¢ Christmas (Madonna), 10/24/86, DC	6.00
☐ 2245	22¢ Christmas (Winter Village), 10/24/86, Snow Hill, MD	6.00

1987

☐ 2246	22¢ Michigan, 1/26/87, Lansing, MI	6.00
☐ 2247	22¢ Pan Am. Games, 1/29/87, Indianapolis, IN	6.00
☐ 2248	22¢ Love, 1/30/87, San Francisco, CA	6.00
☐ 2249	22¢ Jean Baptiste Point Du Sable, 2/20/87, Chicago, IL	10.00
☐ 2250	22¢ Enrico Caruso, 2/27/87, New York, NY	6.00
☐ 2251	22¢ Girl Scouts of America, 3/12/87, DC	6.00
☐ 2255 & 2264	5¢ Milk Wagon & 17.5¢ Mormon Wasp, 9/25/87, Indianapolis, IN	10.00
☐ 2259	10¢ Canal Boat, 4/11/87, Buffalo, NY	10.00
☐ 2267-2274	22¢ Special Occasions Booklet, 4/20/87, Atlanta, GA	12.00
☐ 2275	22¢ United Way, 4/28/87, DC	6.00
☐ 2276	22¢ Flag & Fireworks, 5/9/87, Denver, CO	8.00
☐ 2286-35	22¢ American Wildlife, 6/13/87, Toronto, Canada	8.00
☐ 2336	22¢ Delaware Statehood Bicentennial, 7/4/87, Dover, DE	6.00
☐ 2337	22¢ Pennsylvania Statehood Bicentennial, 8/26/87, Harrisburg, PA	6.00
☐ 2338	22¢ New Jersey Statehood Bicentennial, 9/11/87, Trenton, NJ	6.00
☐ 2349	22¢ US - Morocco Diplomatic Relations, 7/17/87, DC	10.00
☐ 2350	22¢ William Faulkner, 8/3/87, Oxford, MS	8.00
☐ 2351-2254	22¢ Lacemaking, 8/14/87, Ypsilanti, MI	8.00
☐ 2355-2359	22¢ Drafting of the Constitution Bicentennial, 8/28/87, DC	10.00
☐ 2366a	22¢ Locomotive Booklet, 10/1/87, Baltimore, MD	12.00
☐ 2367	22¢ Christmas (Religious), 10/23/87, DC	6.00
☐ 2368	22¢ Christmas (Secular), 10/23/87, Holiday, CA	20.00

1988

☐ 2370	22¢ Australia Bicentennial, 1/26/88, DC	6.00
☐ 2372-2375	22¢ Cats., 2/5/88, New York, NY	10.00

AIR POST STAMPS

☐ C32	5¢ Skymaster, 9/25/46, DC	50.00
☐ C34	10¢ Pan Am. Bldg., 8/30/47, DC	30.00
☐ C35	15¢ N.Y. Skyline, 8/20/47, New York, NY	40.00
☐ C40	6¢ Alexandria, 5/11/49, Alexandria, VA	40.00
☐ C43	15¢ Globe & Doves, 10/7/49, Chicago, IL	40.00
☐ C44	25¢ Boeing, 11/30/49, Seattle, WA	40.00
☐ C46	80¢ Diamond Head, 3/6/52, Honolulu, HI	60.00
☐ C47	6¢ Powered Flight, 5/29/53, Dayton, OH	30.00
☐ C48	4¢ Eagle, 9/3/54, Philadelphia, PA	30.00
☐ C51	7¢ Blue Jet, 7/31/58, Philadelphia, PA	25.00
☐ C52	7¢ Blue Jet Coil, 7/31/58, Miami, FL	20.00
☐ C53	7¢ Alaska, 1/3/59, Philadelphia, PA	20.00
☐ C54	7¢ Balloon, 8/17/59, Lafayette, IN	20.00

☐ C55	7¢ **Hawaii**, 8/21/59, Honolulu, HI	20.00
☐ C56	10¢ **Pan Am. Games**, 8/27/59, Chicago, IL	20.00
☐ C57	10¢ **Liberty Bell**, 6/10/60, Miami, FL	20.00
☐ C58	15¢ **Statue of Liberty**, 11/20/59, New York, NY	25.00
☐ C59	25¢ **Lincoln**, 4/22/60, San Francisco, CA	30.00
☐ C60	7¢ **Red Jet**, 8/12/60, Arlington, VA	18.00
☐ C60a	7¢ **Red Jet, Booklet**, 8/19/60, St. Louis, MO	20.00
☐ C62	13¢ **Liberty Bell**, 6/28/61, New York, NY	15.00
☐ C63	15¢ **Statue of Liberty**, 1/13/61, Buffalo, NY	20.00
☐ C64	8¢ **Capitol**, 12/5/62, DC	20.00
☐ C66	15¢ **Blair**, 5/3/63, Silver Springs, MD	14.00
☐ C67	6¢ **Bald Eagle**, 7/12/63, Boston, MA	14.00
☐ C68	8¢ **Earhart**, 7/24/63, Atchison, KS	18.00
☐ C69	8¢ **Goddard**, 10/5/64, Roswell, NM	12.00
☐ C70	8¢ **Alaska**, 3/30/67, Sitka, AK	15.00
☐ C71	20¢ **Audubon**, 4/26/67, Audubon, NY	12.00
☐ C72	10¢ **50 Star Runway**, 1/5/68, San Francisco, CA	14.00
☐ C74	10¢ **Jenny**, 5/15/68, DC	12.00
☐ C75	20¢ **"USA,"** 11/22/68, New York, NY	14.00
☐ C76	10¢ **Moon Landing**, 9/9/69, DC	15.00
☐ C76	10¢ **Moon Landing, 2nd Day**, 9/10/69, Apollo, PA	40.00
☐ C77 & UXC10	9¢ **Delta Plane**, 5/15/71, Kitty Hawk, NC	15.00
☐ C78	11¢ **Jet**, 5/7/71, Spokane, WA	15.00
☐ C79	13¢ **Winged Envelope**, 11/16/73, New York, NY	12.00
☐ C79a & C83	13¢ **Winged Envelope, Booklet, Coil**, 12/27/73, Chicago, IL	20.00
☐ C80	17¢ **Statue of Liberty**, 7/13/71, Lakehurst, NJ	18.00
☐ C81	21¢ **USA**, 5/21/71, DC	15.00
☐ C82	11¢ **Jet, Coil**, 5/7/71, Spokane, WA	20.00
☐ C83 & 79a	13¢ **Winged Air Envelope Coil**, 12/27/73, Chicago, IL	25.00
☐ C84	11¢ **City of Refuge**, 5/3/72, Honaunau, HI	25.00
☐ C85	11¢ **Olympics**, 8/17/72, DC	8.00
☐ C86	11¢ **Electronics**, 7/10/73, New York, NY	25.00
☐ C87	18¢ **Statue of Liberty**, 1/11/74, Hempstead, NY	20.00
☐ C89-C90	25¢ & 31¢ **Plane & Globe**, 1/2/76, Honolulu, HI	25.00
☐ C91-C92	31¢ **Wright Bros.**, 9/23/78, Dayton, OH	14.00
☐ C93-C94	21¢ **Octave Chanute**, 3/29/79, Chanute, KS	14.00
☐ C95-C96	25¢ **Wiley Post**, 11/20/79, Oklahoma City, OK	14.00
☐ C97	31¢ **Olympic Games**, 11/1/79, Colorado Springs, CO	14.00
☐ C98	40¢ **Philip Mazzei**, 10/13/80, DC	8.00
☐ C99-C100	28¢ **Blanche Stuart Scott & 35¢ Glenn Curtiss**, 12/30/80, Hammondsport, NY	14.00
☐ C101-C104	28¢ **Olympics**, 6/17/83, San Antonio, TX	14.00
☐ C105-C108	40¢ **Olympics**, 4/8/83, Los Angeles, CA	14.00
☐ C109-C12	35¢ **Olympics**, 11/4/83, Colorado Springs, CO	14.00
☐ C113-C114	33¢ **Alfred Verville & 39¢ Lawrence & Elmer Sperry**, 2/13/85, Garden City, NY	8.00
☐ C115/UXC22	44¢ **Transpacific Air Mail**, 2/15/85, San Francisco, CA	8.00
☐ C116	44¢ **Junipero Serra**, 8/22/85, San Diego, CA	8.00

SPECIAL DELIVERY STAMPS

☐ E21	30¢ **Letter**, 9/3/57, Indianapolis, IN	30.00
☐ E22	45¢ **Arrows**, 11/21/69, New York, NY	20.00
☐ E23	60¢ **Arrows**, 5/10/71, Phoenix, AZ	20.00

POSTAGE DUE STAMPS

☐ J89 - 101	½¢-$5 **Postage Due (no stamps)**, 6/19/59, NY, NY	100.00

STAMPED ENVELOPES

☐ U541	1¼¢ **Franklin**, 6/25/60, Birmingham, AL	20.00
☐ U542	2½¢ **Washington**, 5/28/60, Chicago, IL	20.00
☐ U543	4¢ **Pony Express**, 7/19/60, St. Joseph, MO	25.00
☐ U544 & UX48	5¢ **Lincoln**, 11/19/62, Springfield, IL	15.00
☐ U546 & 1244	5¢ **World's Fair**, 4/22/64, World's Fair, NY	18.00
☐ U547 & U549	1¼¢ **Liberty Bell & 4¢ Old Ironsides**, 1/6/65, DC	18.00
☐ U548	1.4¢ **Liberty Bell**, 3/26/68, Springfield, MA	18.00
☐ U549 & U547	4¢ **Old Ironsides & 1¼¢ Liberty Bell**, 1/6/65, DC	18.00
☐ U550	5¢ **Eagle Envelope**, /1/5/65, Williamsburg, PA	15.00
☐ U551	6¢ **Liberty**, 1/4/68, New York, NY	15.00
☐ U554	6¢ **Moby Dick**, 3/7/70, New Bedford, MA	12.00
☐ U555	6¢ **Youth Conf.**, 2/24/71, DC	20.00
☐ U557 & UC43	8¢ **Eagle**, 5/6/71, Williamsburg, PA	20.00
☐ U563	8¢ **Bowling**, 8/21/71, Milwaukee, WI	15.00
☐ U564	8¢ **Aging Conference**, 11/15/71, DC	20.00
☐ U565	8¢ **Transpo**, 5/2/72, DC	18.00
☐ U567	10¢ **Liberty Bell**, 12/5/73, Philadelphia, PA	18.00
☐ U568	1.8¢ **Volunteer Non-Profit**, 8/23/74, Cincinnati, OH	12.00
☐ U571	10¢ **Seafaring**, 10/13/75, Minneapolis, MN	12.00
☐ U572	13¢ **Homemaker**, 2/2/76, Biloxi, MS	12.00
☐ U573	13¢ **Farmer**, 3/15/76, New Orleans, LA	12.00
☐ U574	13¢ **Doctor**, 6/30/76, Dallas, TX	12.00
☐ U575	13¢ **Craftsman**, 8/6/76, Hancock, MA	12.00
☐ U576	13¢ **Liberty Tree**, 11/8/75, Memphis, TN	12.00
☐ U577	2¢ **Star and Pinwheel**, 9/10/76, Hempstead, NY	10.00
☐ U578	2.1¢ **Non-Profit**, 6/3/77, Houston, TX	10.00
☐ U582	13¢ **Centennial Design**, 10/15/76, Los Angeles, CA	12.00
☐ U587	15¢ **Racing Car**, 9/2/78, Ontario, CA	12.00
☐ U589	3.1¢ **Non-Profit**, 5/18/79, Denver, CO	10.00
☐ U595	15¢ **Veterinary Medicine**, 7/24/79, Seattle, WA	10.00
☐ U597	15¢ **Bicycling**, 5/16/80, Baltimore, MD	10.00
☐ U598	15¢ **America's Cup Yacht Races**, 9/15/80, Newport, RI	15.00
☐ U599	15¢ **Honey Bee**, 10/10/80, Paris, IL	15.00
☐ U600	18¢ **Remember The Blinded**, 8/13/81, Arlington, VA	8.00
☐ U602	20¢ **Great Seal**, 6/15/82, DC	10.00
☐ U603	20¢ **Purple Heart**, 8/6/82, DC	10.00
☐ U605	20¢ **Paralyzed Veterans**, 8/3/83, Portland, OR	6.00
☐ U606	20¢ **Business**, 5/7/84, DC	8.00
☐ U609	6¢ **Old Ironsides**, 5/3/85, Boston, MA	8.00

AIR POST STAMPED ENVELOPES

☐ UC18	6¢ **Skymaster**, 9/22/50, Philadelphia, PA	30.00
☐ UC33	7¢ **Blue Jet**, 11/21/58, New York, NY	35.00
☐ UC34	7¢ **Jet, Red**, 8/18/60, Portland, OR	30.00
☐ UC35	11¢ **Air Letter Sheet**, 6/16/61, Johnstown, PA	20.00
☐ UC37	8¢ **Jet Triangle**, 1/7/65, Chicago, IL	20.00
☐ UC38	11¢ **Kennedy Air Letter Sheet**, 5/29/65, Boston, MA	15.00
☐ UC39	13¢ **Kennedy, Air Letter Sheet**, 5/29/67, Chicago, IL	20.00
☐ UC40	10¢ **Jet Triangle**, 1/8/68, Chicago, IL	15.00
☐ UC42	13¢ **Human Rights Air Letter Sheet**, 12/3/68, DC	18.00
☐ UC43 & U557	11¢ **Jet**, 5/6/71, Williamsburg, PA	18.00
☐ UC44	15¢ **Birds Air Letter Sheet**, 5/28/71, Chicago, IL	18.00
☐ UC46	15¢ **Ballooning Air Letter Sheet**, 2/10/73, Albuquerque, NM	10.00
☐ UC47	13¢ **Bird in Flight**, 12/1/73, Memphis, TN	12.00
☐ UC50	22¢ **USA Air Letter Sheet**, 1/16/76, Tempe, AZ	10.00
☐ UC51	22¢ **USA Air Letter Sheet**, 11/3/78, St. Petersburg, FL	10.00

☐ UC53	30¢ Tourism Air Letter Sheet, 12/29/80, San Francisco, CA	10.00
☐ UC54	30¢ USA Air Letter Sheet, 9/21/81, Honolulu, HI	10.00
☐ UC55	30¢ USA & Globe Air Letter Sheet, 9/16/82, Seattle, WA	10.00
☐ UC56	30¢ Communications Air Letter Sheet, 1/7/83, Anaheim, CA	12.00
☐ UC57	30¢ Olympic Sports Air Letter Sheet, 10/14/83, Los Angeles, CA	12.00
☐ UC58	36¢ Landstat Air Letter Sheet, 2/14/85, Goddard Fl. Ctr., MD	8.00
☐ UC60	36¢ Comet Tail Air Letter Sheet, 12/4/85, Hannibal, MO	8.00

POSTAL CARDS

☐ UX48 & U544	4¢ Lincoln, 11/19/62, Springfield, IL	15.00
☐ UX49	7¢ Vacationland, 8/30/63, New York, NY	18.00
☐ UX50	4¢ Customs, 2/22/64, DC	18.00
☐ UX51	4¢ Social Security, 9/26/64, DC	18.00
☐ UX52	4¢ Coast Guard, 8/4/65, Newburyport, MA	18.00
☐ UX53	4¢ Census Bureau, 10/21/65, Philadelphia, PA	18.00
☐ UX54	8¢ Vacationland, 12/4/67, DC	15.00
☐ UX55	5¢ Lincoln, 1/4/68, Hodgenville, KY	20.00
☐ UX56	5¢ Women Marines, 7/26/68, San Francisco, CA	15.00
☐ UX57	5¢ Weathervane, 9/1/70, Fort Myer, VA	15.00
☐ UX58	6¢ Paul Revere, 5/15/71, Boston, MA	12.00
☐ UX59 & UXC11	10¢ Vacationland, 6/10/71, New York, NY	15.00
☐ UX64	6¢ John Hanson, 9/1/72, Baltimore, MD	12.00
☐ UX65	6¢ Centenary of Postal Card, 9/14/73, DC	12.00
☐ UX66	8¢ Samuel Adams, 12/16/73, Boston, MA	12.00
☐ UX67 & UXC15	12¢ Ship's Figurehead, 1/4/74, Miami, FL	15.00
☐ UX68	7¢ C. Thomson, 9/14/75, Bryn Mawr, PA	10.00
☐ UX69	9¢ J. Witherspoon, 11/10/75, Princeton, NJ	10.00
☐ UX70	9¢ Ceasar Rodney, 7/1/76, Dover, DE	10.00
☐ UX71	9¢ Federal Court House, 7/20/77, Galveston, TX	20.00
☐ UX72	9¢ Nathan Hale, 10/14/77, Coventry, CT	10.00
☐ UX73	10¢ Cincinnati Music Hall, 5/12/78, Cincinnati, OH	15.00
☐ UX74	10¢ Domestic Rate, J. Hancock, 5/19/78, Quincy, MA	12.00
☐ UX75	10¢ John Hancock, 6/20/78, Quincy, MA	12.00
☐ UX76	14¢ Coast Guard Eagle, 8/4/78, Seattle, WA	10.00
☐ UX77	10¢ Molly Pitcher, 9/8/78, Freehold, NJ	12.00
☐ UX78	10¢ George R. Clark, 2/23/79, Vincennes, IN	12.00
☐ UX79	10¢ Casimir Pulaski, 10/11/79, Savannah, GA	18.00
☐ UX80	10¢ Olympic Games, 9/17/79, Eugene, OR	12.00
☐ UX81	10¢ Iolani Palace, 10/1/79, Honolulu, HI	15.00
☐ UX82	14¢ Olympic Games - Skater, 1/15/80, Atlanta, GA	12.00
☐ UX83	10¢ Salt Lake Temple, 4/5/80, Salt Lake City, UT	10.00
☐ UX84	10¢ Count Rochambeau, 7/11/80, Newport, RI	15.00
☐ UX85	10¢ Battle of Kings Mountain, 10/7/80, Kings Mountain, NC	10.00
☐ UX86	19¢ Drake's Golden Hinde, 11/21/80, San Rafael, CA	10.00
☐ UX87	10¢ Battle of Cowpens, 1/17/81, Cowpens, SC	12.00
☐ UX89	12¢ Isaiah Thomas, 5/5/81, Worchester, MA	8.00
☐ UX90	12¢ Nat. Green, 9/8/81, Eutaw Springs, SC	10.00
☐ UX91	12¢ Lewis & Clark Expedition, 9/23/81, St. Louis, MO	8.00
☐ UX93	13¢ Robert Morris, 11/10/81, Philadelphia, PA	8.00
☐ UX94	13¢ Francis Marion, 4/3/82, Marion, SC	10.00
☐ UX95	13¢ LaSalle Claims Louisiana, 4/7/82, New Orleans, LA	10.00
☐ UX96	13¢ Phila. Academy of Music, 6/18/82, Philadelphia, PA	10.00
☐ UX97	13¢ Old Post Office, St. Louis, MO, 10/14/82, St. Louis, MO	10.00
☐ UX98	13¢ Oglethorpe, 2/12/83, Savannah, GA	10.00
☐ UX99	13¢ Old Washington Post Office, 4/19/83, DC	8.00
☐ UX100	13¢ Olympics-Yachting, 8/5/83, Long Beach, CA	10.00
☐ UX101	13¢ Maryland 350th Aniv., 3/25/84, St. Clements Is., MD	8.00
☐ UX102	13¢ Olympic Torch, 4/30/84, Los Angeles, CA	8.00

☐ UX103 13¢ **Baraga,** 6/29/84, Marquette, MI   8.00
☐ UX104 13¢ **Historic Preservation,** 9/16/84, Compton, CA   6.00
☐ UX106 14¢ **Charles Carroll,** 3/6/85, Annapolis, MD   6.00
☐ UX107 25¢ **Clipper Flying Cloud,** 2/27/85, Salem, MA   6.00
☐ UX108 14¢ **George Wythe,** 6/20/85, Williamsburg, VA   6.00
☐ UX109 14¢ **Connecticut,** 4/18/86, Hartford, CT   6.00
☐ UX110 14¢ **Stamps,** 5/23/86, Chicago, IL   8.00
☐ UX111 14¢ **Francis Vigo,** 5/24/86, Vincennes, IN   6.00
☐ UX112 14¢ **Rhode Island,** 6/26/86, Providence, RI   6.00
☐ UX113 14¢ **Wisconsin,** 7/3/86, Mineral Point, WI   6.00
☐ UX114 14¢ **National Guard Heritage,** 12/12/86, Boston, MA   6.00
☐ UX116 14¢ **Convening of the Constitutional Convention,** 5/25/87, Philadelphia, PA   6.00
☐ UX117 14¢ **Flag,** 6/14/87, Baltimore, MD   6.00
☐ UX118 14¢ **Take Pride in America,** 9/22/87, Jackson, WY   6.00
☐ UX119 14¢ **Timberline Lodge,** 9/28/87, Timberline Lodge, OR   6.00

AIR POST POSTAL CARDS

☐ UXC3 5¢ **Eagle,** 6/18/60, Minneapolis, MN   25.00
☐ UXC4 6¢ **Bald Eagle,** 2/15/63, Maitland, FL   20.00
☐ UXC5 11¢ **Visit USA,** 5/27/66, DC   20.00
☐ UXC6 6¢ **Virgin Islands,** 3/31/67, Charlotte Amalie, VI   20.00
☐ UXC7 6¢ **Boy Scouts,** 8/4/67, Farragut State Park, ID   18.00
☐ UXC8 13¢ **Visit the USA,** 9/8/67, Detroit, MI   15.00
☐ UXC9 8¢ **Eagle,** 3/1/68, New York, NY   15.00
☐ UXC10 & C77 9¢ **Eagle,** 5/15/71, Kitty Hawk, NC   12.00
☐ UXC11 & UX59 15¢ **Visit the USA,** 6/10/71, New York, NY   15.00
☐ UXC14 11¢ **Modern Eagle,** 1/4/74, State College, PA   10.00
☐ UXC15 & UX67 18¢ **Eagle Weathervane,** 1/4/74, Miami, FL   15.00
☐ UXC16 21¢ **Angel Weathervane,** 12/17/75, Kitty Hawk, NC   15.00
☐ UXC17 21¢ **Jenny,** 9/16/78, San Diego, CA   10.00
☐ UXC18 21¢ **Olympics-Gymnast,** 12/1/79, Fort Worth, TX   10.00
☐ UXC19 28¢ **First Transpacific Flight,** 1/2/81, Wenatchee, WA   10.00
☐ UXC20 28¢ **Soaring,** 3/5/82, Houston, TX   8.00
☐ UXC21 28¢ **Olympics-Speedskating,** 12/29/83, Milwaukee, WI   6.00
☐ UXC23 33¢ **Chicago Skyline,** 2/1/86, Chicago, IL   6.00

☐☐ _____
☐☐ _____
☐☐ _____
☐☐ _____
☐☐ _____
☐☐ _____
☐☐ _____
☐☐ _____
☐☐ _____
☐☐ _____
☐☐ _____
☐☐ _____
☐☐ _____
☐☐ _____
☐☐ _____
☐☐ _____
☐☐ _____
☐☐ _____
☐☐ _____
☐☐ _____
☐☐ _____
☐☐ _____
☐☐ _____
☐☐ _____
☐☐ _____
☐☐ _____
☐☐ _____
☐☐ _____
☐☐ _____
☐☐ _____
☐☐ _____
☐☐ _____
☐☐ _____
☐☐ _____
☐☐ _____
☐☐ _____
☐☐ _____
☐☐ _____
☐☐ _____

☐☐ _____
☐☐ _____
☐☐ _____
☐☐ _____
☐☐ _____
☐☐ _____
☐☐ _____
☐☐ _____
☐☐ _____
☐☐ _____
☐☐ _____
☐☐ _____
☐☐ _____
☐☐ _____
☐☐ _____
☐☐ _____
☐☐ _____
☐☐ _____
☐☐ _____
☐☐ _____
☐☐ _____
☐☐ _____
☐☐ _____
☐☐ _____
☐☐ _____
☐☐ _____
☐☐ _____
☐☐ _____
☐☐ _____
☐☐ _____
☐☐ _____
☐☐ _____
☐☐ _____
☐☐ _____
☐☐ _____
☐☐ _____
☐☐ _____
☐☐ _____
☐☐ _____

PLATE NUMBER COIL FDC
Compiled by Ken Lawrence

Since early 1981, nearly all coil stamps issued by the United States have plate numbers printed on the stamps at regular intervals. The tiny digits printed in the stamps' bottom margins have given rise to the fastest growing area of modern United States stamp collecting — plate number coils (PNC).

Much of the enthusiasm has been sparked by the booming popularity of the Transportation coil series, which includes the majority of PNC's. Not surprisingly, interest in PNC's has spread to first-day cover collecting.

Not all plate numbers exist on FDC's, only the ones that are printed before the stamp is issued or very shortly after the first day, during the grace period for submitting covers to be canceled.

Traditional FDC collectors have to adapt somewhat when they get interested in PNC's. The first thing they learned is that many PNC's can only be found on certain cachets, which may not be their favorites. The usual cachet multiplier would apply to recent issues, where a substantial choice is available, but not to many of the coils issued in 1981 and 1982, nor any of the precancels issued before 1986.

While it often isn't possible to be choosy about cachets, some collectors have strong feelings about the format they prefer. Thus, because some of the earlier PNC's are usually found in line pairs or even single stamps on FDC's, those who insist on strips of three or longer, with the number or joint line at the center, should expect to pay a premium, or, in some cases, to do without the particular plate. Prices in this list are for the most typical format for each stamp on FDC's.

On the other hand, since the principal factor in this type of collecting is the plate number itself, FDC's are worth considerably less than the prices shown here if the plate numbers are obscured in any way by the cancel, or if they are cut. Each plate number should be whole, clear of the edge of the stamp. Otherwise, usual philatelic criteria apply.

Because some PNC first-day covers are scarce and expensive, and some forgeries have already appeared on the philatelic market, collectors are advised to have costly FDCs expertized.

Scott	Description	Plate No.	Value
☐ 1891	18¢ Flag, 4/24/81	1	75.00
☐		2	500.00
☐		3	*600.00*
☐		4	200.00
☐		5	150.00
☐ 1895	20¢ Flag, 12/17/81	1	18.00
☐		2	150.00
☐		3	350.00
☐ 1897	1¢ Omnibus, 8/19/83	1	11.00
☐		2	11.00
☐ 1897A	2¢ Locomotive, 5/20/82	3	11.00
☐		4	11.00
☐ 1898	3¢ Handcar, 3/25/83	1	12.00
☐		2	12.00
☐		3	15.00
☐		4	15.00
☐ 1898A	4¢ Stagecoach, 8/19/82	1	11.00
☐		2	11.00
☐		3	11.00
☐		4	11.00
☐ 1899	5¢ Motorcycle, 10/10/83	1	12.50
☐		2	12.50
☐		3	75.00
☐		4	75.00

Cacheted covers are unknown for Plates 3 and 4 of the 5-cent Motorcycle stamp, but they exist on USPS Souvenir Pages with FDOI cancels.

☐ 1900	5.2¢ Sleigh, 3/21/83	1	30.00
☐		2	30.00
☐ 1900a	5.2¢ Sleigh, precanceled, 3/21/83	1	*750.00*
☐		2	*750.00*
☐ 1901	5.9¢ Bicycle, 2/17/82	3	30.00
☐		4	30.00
☐ 1901a	5.9¢ Bicycle, precanceled, 2/17/82	3	*1500.00*
☐		4	*1500.00*
☐ 1902	7.4¢ Baby Buggy, 4/7/84	2	20.00

Scott	Description	Plate No.	Value
☐ 1903	9.3¢ Mail Wagon, 12/15/81.............................	1	30.00
☐		2	30.00
☐		3	*2000.00*
☐		4	*2000.00*
☐ 1904	10.9¢ Hansom Cab, 3/26/82.............................	1	30.00
☐		2	30.00
☐ 1904a	10.9¢ Hansom Cab, precanceled, 3/26/82................	1	*2000.00*
☐		2	*2000.00*
☐ 1905	11¢ Caboose, 2/3/84.................................	1	20.00
☐ 1906	17¢ Electric Auto, 6/25/81..........................	1	15.00
☐		2	15.00
☐ 1907	18¢ Surrey, 5/18/8..................................	1	30.00
☐		2	25.00
☐		3	*1000.00*
☐		4	*1000.00*
☐		5	250.00
☐		6	250.00
☐		7	300.00
☐		8	100.00
☐		9	350.00
☐		10	350.00
☐ 1908	20¢ Fire Pumper, 12/10/81...........................	1	200.00
☐		2	600.00
☐		3	35.00
☐		4	35.00
☐		5	85.00
☐		6	85.00
☐		7	*1500.00*
☐		8	*1500.00*
☐ 2005	20¢ Consumer Education, 4/27/82	1	20.00
☐		2	20.00
☐		3	20.00
☐		4	20.00
☐ 2112	(22¢) "D," 2/1/85...................................	1	12.00
☐		2	12.00
☐ 2115	22¢ Flag, 3/29/85..................................	1	30.00
☐		2	15.00
☐ 2115b	22¢ Flag, pre-phosphored paper, 5/23/87..............	T1	11.00
☐ 2123	3.4¢ School Bus, 6/8/85.............................	1	11.00
☐		2	11.00
☐ 2124	4.9¢ Buckboard, 6/21/85.............................	3	12.50
☐		4	12.50
☐ 2124a	4.9¢ Buckboard, precanceled, 6/21/85.................	3	*2000.00*
☐		4	*2000.00*
☐ 2125	5.5¢ Star Route Truck, 11/1/86......................	1	12.00
☐ 2125a	5.5¢ Star Route Truck, precanceled, 11/1/86	1	25.00
☐ 2126	6¢ Tricycle, 5/6/85	1	11.00
☐ 2126a	6¢ Tricycle, precanceled, 5/6/85	1	*850.00*
☐ 2127	7.1¢ Tractor, 2/6/87...............................	1	11.00
☐ 2127a	7.1¢ Tractor, precanceled, 2/6/87....................	1	25.00
☐ 2128	8.3¢ Ambulance, 6/21/85.............................	1	11.00
☐		2	11.00
☐ 2128a	8.3¢ Ambulance, precanceled, 6/21/85	1	*2000.00*
☐		2	*2000.00*

Scott	Description	Plate No.	Value
☐ 2129	8.5¢ Tow Truck, 1/24/87............................	1	11.00
☐ 2129a	8.5¢ Tow Truck, precanceled, 1/24/87..................	1	20.00
☐ 2130	10.1¢ Oil Wagon, 4/18/85	1	11.00
☐ 2131	11¢ Stutz Super Bearcat, 6/11/85.....................	3	11.00
☐		4	11.00
☐ 2132	12¢ Stanley Steamer, 4/2/85.........................	1	11.00
☐		2	11.00
☐	12¢ Stanley Steamer, B. Press, precanceled	1	—
☐ 2132a	12¢ Stanley Steamer, Precanceled, 4/2/85	1	*2,000.00*

There was no official first day of issue for the B Press version of this stamp. Cacheted covers exist canceled September 3, 1987, the date the stamp was placed on sale at the Philatelic Sales Unit in Washington, DC, currently the earliest known postmark. The stamp actually was placed on sale prior to that date at other locations, so there is a possibility of even earlier covers.

☐ 2133	12.5¢ Pushcart, 4/18/85	1	11.00
☐ 2134	14¢ Iceboat, 3/23/85	1	11.00
☐		2	11.00
☐	14¢ Iceboat, B Press, 9/30/86........................	2	—

There was no official first day of issue for the B Press version of this stamp. The earliest known use was September 30, 1986, but no cacheted covers are known, and no earliest use covers have been offered for sale.

☐ 2135	17¢ Dog Sled, 8/20/86.............................	2	12.50
☐ 2136	25¢ Bread Wagon, 11/22/86	1	11.00
☐ 2149	18¢ George Washington, 11/6/85	1112	25.00
☐		3333	25.00
☐ 2149a	18¢ George Washington, precanceled, 11/6/85	11121	75.00
☐		33333	50.00
☐ 2150	21.1¢ Letters, 10/22/85	111111	20.00
☐ 2150a	21.1¢ Letters, precanceled, 10/22/85................	111111	35.00
☐ 2225	1¢ Omnibus, re-engraved, 11/26/86	1	11.00
☐ 2226	2¢ Locomotive, re-engraved, 3/6/87..................	1	11.00
☐ 2228	4¢ Stagecoach, re-engraved, 8/15/86.................	1	*750.00*

There was no official first day of issue for Scott 2228, but cacheted covers exist canceled August 15, 1986, the earliest known use.

☐ 2231	8.3¢ Ambulance, B Press, precanceled 8/9/86............	1	*1500.00*

There was no official first day of issue for the B Press version of this stamp, but cacheted covers exist canceled August 29, 1986, the earliest known use.

☐ 2253	3¢ Congestoga Wagon, 2/29/88	1	7.50
☐ 2255	5¢ Milk Wagon, 9/25/87.............................	1	7.50
☐ 2259	10¢ Canal Boat, 4/11/87..............................	1	8.50
☐ 2264	17.5¢ Racing Car, 9/25/87............................	1	7.50
☐ 2264a	17.5¢ Racing Car, precanceled, 9/25/87	1	15.00

OFFICIAL STAMPS

☐ O135	20¢ Seal, 1/12/83..................................	1	30.00
☐ O139	(22¢) Seal, 2/4/85.....................................	1	30.00

U.S. PRESIDENTIAL INAUGURATION, RESIGNATION AND DEATH-IN-OFFICE COVERS

All prices given are for cacheted covers postmarked on date of the presidents' inauguration, resignation or death-in-office. Uncacheted covers sell for about one half of the catalog price. Prices for covers after 1945 are for unaddressed cacheted covers. Addressed covers after 1949 sell for about one half of the catalog price.

President	Description	Cacheted Single
☐ McKinley	Sept. 14, 1901, Assassination cover - Death in Office	1500.00
☐ H. Hoover	March 4, 1929	100.00
☐ FDR	**1st Term,** March 4, 1933	40.00
☐ FDR	**2nd Term,** Jan. 20, 1937	100.00
☐ FDR	**3rd Term,** Jan. 20, 1941	75.00
☐ FDR	**4th Term,** Jan. 20, 1945	75.00
☐ FDR	**Date of Death,** Apr. 12, 1945, canceled at Roosevelt, NY	50.00
☐ H. Truman	**1st Term,** Apr. 12, 1945	60.00
☐ H. Truman	**2nd Term,** Jan. 20, 1949	35.00
☐ IKE	**1st Term,** Jan. 20, 1953	15.00
☐ IKE	**2nd Term,** Jan. 21, 1957	10.00

Note: 1/20/57 was a Sunday. However, some Artcraft cacheted covers do have the 1/20/57 cancel, $25.00.

President	Description	Cacheted Single
☐ JFK	January 20, 1961	15.00
☐ JFK	**Assassination cover,** Nov. 23, 1963	15.00
☐ JFK	**Assassination cover,** Nov. 23, 1963, canceled on FDC of JFK Scott #1246 on May 29, 1964	20.00
☐ LBJ	Jan. 20, 1965	5.00
☐ R. Nixon	**1st Term,** Jan. 20, 1969	5.00
☐ R. Nixon	**2nd Term,** Jan. 20, 1973	5.00
☐ R. Nixon	**Announces resignation,** canceled Aug. 8, 1974 on same cover canceled Jan. 20, 1973	20.00
☐ R. Nixon	**Resigns to Congress,** canceled Aug. 9, 1974 on same cover canceled Jan. 20, 1973	10.00
☐ R. Nixon	**Resigns to Congress,** Aug. 9, 1974	2.00
☐ G. Ford	Aug. 9, 1974	3.00
☐ J. Carter	Jan. 20, 1977	3.00
☐ R. Reagan	Jan. 20, 1981	3.00
☐ R. Reagan	Jan. 20, 1985	3.00

PATRIOTIC COVERS OF WWII

Listed below are significant WWII patriotic dates. Prices are for related, printed-cacheted covers, canceled on the appropriate date. The listed prices reflect the work of the following cachetmakers: Crosby, Fidelity, Fleetwood/Knapp, Fleetwood/Staehle, Fluegel, Richardson/Knapp, Smartcraft, and Teixeria.

In addition, Minkus and several other cachetmakers made a group of general purpose patriotic covers such as "Win the War", and "Sink the Japs". These covers catalog for $2.00 each, while uncanceled covers catalog at 75¢ each.

WWII Covers	Description	Cacheted Single
☐ Pearl Harbor, 12/7/41		75.00
☐ U.S. Declares War on Japan, 12/8/41		15.00
☐ Germany and Italy Declare War on U.S., 12/11/41		15.00
☐ Churchill Arrives at the White House, 12/22/41		15.00
☐ Manila and Cavite Fall, 1/2/42		25.00
☐ MacArthur Post Office, 4/15/42		10.00
☐ Singapore Surrenders, 2/15/42		15.00
☐ Japan takes Java, 3/10/42		15.00
☐ Marshall Arrives in London, 4/8/42		15.00
☐ Air Raid on Tokyo by Dolittle, 4/18/42		25.00
☐ Fort Mills Corregidor Island Surrenders, 5/6/42		15.00
☐ Madagascar Occupied by U.S., 5/9/42		15.00
☐ Bombing of Cologne, 6/6/42		15.00
☐ Japan Bombs Dutch Harbor, 6/6/42		15.00
☐ Six German Spies Sentenced to Death, 8/7/42		15.00
☐ Brazil at War, 8/22/42		15.00
☐ Battle of El Alemain, 10/23/42		30.00
☐ Invasion of North Africa (Operation Torch), 11/8/42		25.00
☐ Gas Rationing is Nationwide, 12/1/42		15.00
☐ The Casablanca Conference, 1/22/43		30.00
☐ The Quebec Conference, 8/43		30.00
☐ Battle of the Bismarck Sea, 3/13/43		30.00
☐ Invasion of Attu, 5/11/43		30.00
☐ Italy Surrenders, 9/8/43		15.00
☐ Mussolini Escapes, 9/18/43		15.00
☐ U.S. Drives Germans out of Naples, 10/2/43		15.00
☐ Italy Declares War on Germany, 10/13/43		15.00
☐ Hull Eden Stalin Conference, 10/25/43		15.00
☐ U.S. Government Takes over Coal Mines, 11/3/43		15.00
☐ The Cairo Meeting, 11/25/43		30.00
☐ The Teheran Meeting, 11/28/43		30.00
☐ Soviets Reach Polish Border, 1/4/44		15.00
☐ U.S. Captures Cassino, 3/15/44		15.00
☐ D-Day Single Face Eisenhower, 6/6/44		90.00
☐ Invasion of Normandy-D Day, 6/6/44		15.00

WWII Covers	Description	Cacheted Single
☐ U.S. Bombs Philippines, 8/10/44		15.00
☐ Liberation of Paris, 8/23/44		30.00
☐ Liberation of Brussels, 9/4/44		25.00
☐ Liberation of Luxembourg, 9/10/44		25.00
☐ Liberation of Athens, 10/14/44		25.00
☐ Liberation of Belgrade, 10/16/44		25.00
☐ Invasion of the Philippines, 10/20/44		25.00
☐ The Pied Piper of Leyte-Philippine Invasion, 10/21/44		35.00
☐ Liberation of Tirana, 11/18/44		25.00
☐ 100,000 Yanks Land on Luzon, 1/10/45		25.00
☐ Liberation of Warsaw, 1/17/45		30.00
☐ Liberation of Manila, 2/4/45		25.00
☐ Budapest Liberated, 2/13/45		25.00
☐ Corregidor is Ours, 2/17/45		25.00
☐ Cologne is Taken, 3/6/45		15.00
☐ Bombing of Tokyo, 3/10/45		15.00
☐ Capture of Iowa Jima, 3/14/45		15.00
☐ Battle of the Inland Sea, 3/20/45		15.00
☐ Crossing of the Rhine, 3/24/45		15.00
☐ Okinawa Invaded, 4/1/45		15.00
☐ Japanese Cabinet Resigns, 4/7/45		15.00
☐ Liberation of Vienna, 4/10/45		15.00
☐ Death of Roosevelt-Truman becomes President, 4/12/45		50.00
☐ Patton Invades Czechoslovakia, 4/18/45		15.00
☐ Berlin Invaded, 4/21/45		15.00
☐ Berlin is Encircled, 4/25/45		15.00
☐ GI Joe and Ivan Meet at Torgau-Germany, 4/26/45		15.00
☐ Liberation of Italy, 5/2/45		15.00
☐ Berlin Falls, 5/2/45		15.00
☐ Liberation of Rangoon, 5/3/45		15.00
☐ 5th and 7th Armies Meet at the Brenner Pass, 5/4/45		15.00
☐ Liberation of Copenhagen, 5/5/45		15.00
☐ Liberation of Amsterdam, 5/5/45		15.00
☐ Liberation of Oslo, 5/8/45		15.00
☐ Liberation of Prague, 5/8/45		15.00
☐ V-E Day, 5/8/45		20.00
☐ Invasion of Borneo, 6/11/45		15.00
☐ Okinawa Captured, 6/21/45		15.00
☐ United Nations Conference, 6/25/45		25.00
☐ American Flag Raised Over Berlin, 7/4/45		25.00
☐ Big Three Meet at Potsdam, 8/1/45		25.00
☐ Atomic Bomb, 8/6/45		55.00
☐ Russia Declares War on Japan, 8/8/45		15.00
☐ Japan Capitulates, 8/14/45		15.00
☐ Liberation of China, 9/2/45		15.00
☐ V-J Day, 9/2/45		20.00
☐ Liberation of Korea, 9/2/45		15.00
☐ Flag Raising over Tokyo-MacArthur takes over, 9/8/45		15.00
☐ 'Skinny' Wainwright Rescued from the Japanese, 9/10/45		15.00
☐ Nimitz Post Office, 9/10/45		15.00
☐ Operation Crossroads, 6/3/46		100.00
☐ Bikini Atomic Bomb Test, 7/1/46		75.00
☐ Independence of the Philippines, 7/4/46		100.00
☐ Moscow Peace Conference, 3/10/47		15.00

- [ ] _____
- [ ] _____
- [ ] _____
- [ ] _____
- [ ] _____
- [ ] _____
- [ ] _____
- [ ] _____
- [ ] _____
- [ ] _____
- [ ] _____
- [ ] _____
- [ ] _____
- [ ] _____
- [ ] _____
- [ ] _____
- [ ] _____
- [ ] _____
- [ ] _____
- [ ] _____
- [ ] _____
- [ ] _____
- [ ] _____
- [ ] _____
- [ ] _____
- [ ] _____
- [ ] _____
- [ ] _____
- [ ] _____
- [ ] _____
- [ ] _____
- [ ] _____
- [ ] _____
- [ ] _____
- [ ] _____
- [ ] _____
- [ ] _____
- [ ] _____

☐☐ _____
☐☐ _____
☐☐ _____
☐☐ _____
☐☐ _____
☐☐ _____
☐☐ _____
☐☐ _____
☐☐ _____
☐☐ _____
☐☐ _____
☐☐ _____
☐☐ _____
☐☐ _____
☐☐ _____
☐☐ _____
☐☐ _____
☐☐ _____
☐☐ _____
☐☐ _____
☐☐ _____
☐☐ _____
☐☐ _____
☐☐ _____
☐☐ _____
☐☐ _____
☐☐ _____
☐☐ _____
☐☐ _____
☐☐ _____
☐☐ _____
☐☐ _____
☐☐ _____
☐☐ _____
☐☐ _____
☐☐ _____
☐☐ _____
☐☐ _____
☐☐ _____